READING THE BIBLE

READING THE BIBLE

A Study Guide

Timothy R. Carmody

Paulist Press
New York/Mahwah, N.J.

Book design by Lynn Else
Cover design by Cindy Dunne

Library of Congress Cataloging-in-Publication Data

Carmody, Timothy R.
   Reading the Bible : a study guide / Timothy R. Carmody.
      p.   cm.
   ISBN 0-8091-4189-2 (alk paper)
   1. Bible—Criticism, interpretation, etc. I. Title.

BS511.3C37 2004
220.6′1—dc22

2004004497

Published by Paulist Press
997 Macarthur Boulevard
Mahwah, New Jersey 07430

www.paulistpress.com

Printed and bound in the
United States of America

CONTENTS

Contents

Contents

Dedication

For Larry

Χάριν ἔχω τῷ ἐνδυναμώσαντί με
"I am grateful to the one who has strengthened me"
1 Timothy 1:12
(Author's Translation)

PREFACE

THE BOOK

The book is about the "art of reading" because I am convinced that both intensive training in methods and techniques and training in using imagination and creativity are required for reading the Bible. In my fifteen years of teaching the Bible I have found that a certain amount of survey material is useful and interesting to students of the Bible. They need to know what books are in the Bible, when they were written, and what they are about. However, there are very few students who care to be walking encyclopedias of Bible information—memorizing a complete list of names, dates, and events. Most students are interested in knowing what the Bible means, and they especially want to learn how to discover this on their own. Students of the Bible need to be trained in methodology. I have found that students are eager to learn how to ask the right questions of a text, to learn to recognize different genres and forms, to recognize sources and traditions, and to be able to use cross-references to appreciate intertextuality and concordances to do word studies. Once students learn these methodologies they are not only able to read the Bible with much more understanding but also able to read commentaries and scholarly articles and make their own judgments about interpretation. In the course of teaching methodology, I have found that an inductive approach works best. Mythological language is best explained by looking at Genesis 1 and 2, and the differences in the sources of the Pentateuch are best explained by comparing examples of the law from each of the different sources. It is one thing to describe the nature of Hebrew poetry, but it is much more productive to examine a prophetic oracle, a psalm, or a proverb. Students don't understand the concept of redaction criticism of the gospels until they are able to compare a story of Matthew with its source in Mark and begin to draw their own conclusions from the changes Matthew has made.

As a result of my experience in teaching, this textbook is a hybrid. It has three different learning goals. First, the book provides a survey of the entire Bible, its sections, its books, and its social, religious, and historical contexts. Second, it also serves as a primer in the methodologies of biblical interpretation. Finally, it is a workbook, giving examples of how to use the background knowledge from the survey and the methodological training to examine in some depth a few selected texts. The texts that are selected for in-depth analysis are ones that I have found interesting and successful teaching tools. They are not necessarily the most important texts of the Bible. The books and texts of different genres and from different times were chosen to give variety and breadth to the reader's knowledge of the Bible.

THE AUTHOR

In teaching I have found that students are more interested in what you find interesting and exciting than in what is most important. This book then contains a lot of my interests, a lot of me. Training readers of the Bible is a process of engaging both their minds and their hearts. In my own training I learned the most from those who shared their enthusiasm and drew me into the process of interpreting the Bible. Learning to interpret the Bible is a matter of discipleship—learning from a trusted and loved teacher. For this reason I have not attempted to remain invisible in the book. My own opinions, preferences, interests, and strengths come through. I was trained in the best of historical critical method under Joseph Fitzmyer, S.J., at The Catholic University of America, although typical of many students of my time, I became interested in many of the other methodologies that were coming into vogue—social science criticism, reader response criticism, and structuralism. My special area of interest at the present is narrative criticism. I usually get more excited about a concentric parallelism, a narrative gap, or a character study than I do about a historical fact. So unlike most textbooks that try to be as neutral and universal as possible, this textbook is deliberately my book. However, I do envision that other teachers will be able to use the book effectively. Other teachers will be able to engage with their students in a dialogue with my interpretations in the book, giving their students the opportunity to hear two sides of the story. I often found in teaching that the students became more engaged in a discussion when I disagreed with the author of our textbook.

THE READER

The intended readers of this book are Christians who have had little or no exposure to academic biblical studies and whose acquaintance with the Bible is limited mostly to the readings at church on Sunday. This is meant to be the first and most basic introduction to biblical studies. However, because the book is not a simple survey of the Bible but contains many examples of interpretation, readers who are more familiar with the Bible and who have had a general survey of the Bible already may still find much that is new and interesting in this book. The reader will need to have his or her own Bible because the discussions and analyses in the textbook presuppose that the biblical text has been read and is at the reader's side for reference. I have used the New Revised Standard Version of the Bible throughout.

ACKNOWLEDGMENTS

This book was written during a sabbatical from Spring Hill College. I am most grateful to the college and especially to the theology department for allowing me this opportunity. While I was on sabbatical in Atlanta, I made frequent use of Pitts Theological Library at the Chandler School of Theology, Emory University. I am indebted to Pitts Theological Library's director, Patrick Graham, who graciously allowed me access to this superb library. I am grateful to all my students over the last fifteen years, but especially those students who used the book in its draft form and offered very helpful comments. Finally, I am grateful to Fr. Christopher Viscardi, S.J., who used a draft of this book as a text book and gave many helpful suggestions and to my sister, Lois Fahey, my graduate student, John McGregor, past graduate students Dori Berahya and Deborah Madonia, and my colleague, Fr. William Harmless, S.J., who served as editors and proofreaders as the book came into its final form. Any mistakes that remain in the book are mine alone.

Chapter 1
BIBLE BASICS:
READING THE BIBLE IN FAITH

Creating Readers of the Bible

There are a number of ways that an introduction to the Bible can be approached. Most often an introduction to the Bible is a survey of the Bible, in which each book is summarized for the reader and placed within its context in the history of Israel or early Christianity. There are also biblical introductions that explain and give examples of the methodologies used in studying the Bible. These books seek to train the reader in the different scholarly approaches to the texts of the Bible. Finally, there are introductions that focus more on the Bible as a text for spiritual reading. These books, often by focusing on the great themes in scripture, offer the reader an experience of the transforming power of the Bible as the word of God. It seemed to me that there was a need for an introduction to the Bible that combined all three of these approaches. The purpose of this book is to create competent readers of the Bible. This requires a combination of breadth and depth. For readers to be adequately introduced to the art of reading the Bible, they should know what is in the Bible, when the books were written, and what were the major historical contexts out of which the Bible grew. Competent readers should also be familiar with and be able to use some of the major methodologies for studying the Bible. In other words, a competent reader should know what kinds of questions to ask the text. Finally, competent readers or—better—readers who will be inspired to grow in competence will be ones who have experienced the power of the Bible as it touches them personally and as it engages the world in which they live.

As a survey of the Bible, this text will introduce readers to all of the major sections of the Bible and explain the kinds of texts found in each section. Several books from each section will be chosen for deeper investigation. (There will not be a summary of every book.) There will be a study of the selected book in general and then a more thorough investigation of individual texts from that book. Each text will be examined according to its historical background (world behind the text), according to its literary genre, structure, rhetoric, and themes (world of the text), and according to its possibilities for engaging its contemporary readers (world in front of the text). As we study each text in these three ways, we will be training readers in the methodologies appropriate to each kind of investigation. In all of our study, however, the intention of this introduction is to open up the Bible for readers to experience the text as the word of God with power to engage their lives. So, although this text is meant to be used in the classroom and claims to be an academic text, I do not believe that an academic study of the Bible should remain detached from the experience and involvement of its readers.

The Bible as the Word of God

Word of God in Context

How a person understands the nature of the Bible determines how that person will read it. Is the Bible a great piece of literature? Is it an enlightened and holy book of a religious group? Is it the word of God? For Catholics it is all three. Christians and Jews generally believe that the Bible is the word of God. However, if you pay attention to what different groups or persons say about the Bible as God's word, you will soon realize that they are not all making the same claim. Although there is no absolute definition of what "word of God" means for Catholics, the following is an attempt to delineate some of the ways Catholics have tended to define what it does and does not mean. First, there is not one correct meaning for any given text. The fathers of the church spoke of the literal meaning, the allegorical meaning, and the spiritual meaning. There are different ways of reading the text and different meanings possible for it. Catholics have never maintained that a literal reading of the text is the one and only way, or even the best way, to read the Bible. Second, the church has traditionally recognized, but recently stated much more clearly, that the text should be understood first in its original historical context. Again, we often find the church fathers discussing the original situation of a given text. Today our tools for understanding and retrieving the original context of a text are greatly improved, and our appreciation of historicity and social situation is heightened, but the principle remains the same. Third, Catholics have never held the position of *"sola scriptura"* (scripture alone as determinative of faith). The Bible is one of three sources of teaching in the church. It may be the first among equals, but it is never to be used and interpreted alone, outside the context of the traditions of the church (the history of interpretation) and outside the context of the believing community following the Spirit in its own day and time.

Word of God, Inspiration, and Inerrancy

The expression **word of God** can be used in three ways. Jesus Christ is described as the Word of God incarnate. He is the fullest expression of what God has to say to humans. Second, God spoke to Moses and the prophets. The words that they received from God can be called the word of God. Finally, though, the Bible as a written text in its final form is called the word of God. This does not have exactly the same meaning as the other two uses. Not everything in the Bible is directly about Jesus Christ. Not everything in the Bible was given to its authors as a word of God like the law to Moses or the prophecies to Isaiah or Jeremiah. Rather, to say that the Bible is the word of God says that in its entirety the book expresses the relationship God has with humans and the plan God has for their salvation.

Related to this issue are several other expressions that are used to describe the word of God. Christians claim that the Bible is inspired. This does not mean that every word in the Bible was dictated to the authors or that every word is a word of God directed to humans for their salvation. There are many words in the Bible that reflect human wisdom and are human opinion. Rather, the claim of **inspiration** says that the entire book expresses God's desire for humans. Even the human wisdom and opinions, the historical facts that might be inaccurate, the prescientific understanding of how the world works and how human biology and psychology function, all of this is inspired by God. The writers were being led by the Spirit of God in such a way that the book, even when it is human opinion, will further the divine–human relationship.

Christians will also claim that the Bible is inerrant. Some Christians mean by this that no line, story, law, or expression in the Bible contains any error whatsoever. Catholics do not hold such a literal understanding of inerrancy. For Catholics, **inerrancy** means that as a whole the Bible does not lead to error but will lead to a deeper and truer understanding of and relationship with God. In *Dei Verbum* 11, the Vatican Council notes that "we must acknowledge that the books of Scripture firmly, faithfully and without error teach that truth which God, for the sake of our salvation, wished to see confided to the sacred Scriptures." The Bible teaches without error a truth that is for our salvation. There is no claim of total inerrancy, where every historical or scientific fact is regarded as true. The truth claim of the Bible is restricted to God's plan for human salvation.

Even understood only in the context of truths for human salvation, however, an individual reader can misunderstand the Bible, can take a text out of context, and can enter into error. Many of the great heresies of the church have come from the Bible, and their proponents have believed that they were accurately reading the Bible. There is nothing about the Bible that guarantees that a reader will not ever be led into error by something that he or she reads in the Bible. That is why for Catholics the reading and interpreting of the Bible must take into account the Bible as a unified whole, must be aware of the tradition of interpretation in the church, and must be done in the context of the authoritative teaching of the *magisterium*. These three elements guarantee the reader that he or she will not be led into error.

"Mistakes" or Healthy Dialogue?

It is very easy to find in the Bible contradictions, inaccuracies, misunderstandings, and even some rather poor and inadequate theological reflections. There are two stories of creation, three stories of patriarchs pretending that their beautiful wife is only their sister, two versions of David's introduction to the court of Saul, and two complete histories of the monarchy. Different authors took up the same event or topic and developed it in their own way. There are critics of Christianity and Judaism who eagerly pore over the Bible finding all these "mistakes." The Bible is not a static, homogeneous, and consistent document. It is a document that developed over the course of at least one thousand years. It is a document that was written in numerous historical, social, and even religious situations. Although its final compilers sometimes did some editing to join the books together as a whole and give them some framework and similar form, for the most part there was no final editor who went through to eliminate all contradictions and inconsistencies. The document we have has various authors from various times with various points of view.

Even beyond that, though, this document is self-reflective and self-criticizing. The different books of the Bible will often reflect on earlier books and expand on their ideas, change their ideas, refute their ideas, and even mock their ideas. As some of the early stories and texts take on a "canonical" status (the story of the Exodus and the giving of the Law), later writers used these texts to develop their own themes. The prophets took up the stories and laws from Genesis and Exodus and reworked them, reapplied them, and even transformed them. The wisdom writings took up the traditions of the law and the prophets and mocked them, contested them, invoked them, or celebrated them. The earlier texts were presumed to express God's word, but were never thought to be so sacrosanct that they could not be engaged in dialogue. The Book of Job, for example, expanded images in Jeremiah (cursing the day of his birth), called into question the theology embedded in the Book of Deuteronomy (the Deuteronomistic principle states that the good will be blessed and the wicked cursed), and turned Psalm 8 on its head (Psalm 8 marvels that God pays so

5

much positive attention to lowly man; Job marvels that God pays so much attention to torment lowly man). To read the Bible is to engage in a dialectic, an ongoing wrestling match with God's revelation. The Bible is not a static expression of God's will for us or a finished historical account of how people in the past wrestled with the word of God. The Bible is a living arena for an ongoing engagement with God's word. The reader of the Bible must be willing to enter the fray to come to know the word of God revealed for our salvation. The Bible enshrines the process of God's word finding voice—sometimes faint, sometimes strong, sometimes building on previous words, sometimes tearing them down. To lift one story or saying out of the Bible and assign it the status of God's definitive command to us is to misunderstand the origins of the Bible and to shortchange the dynamic nature of God's word.

The Canon of the Bible

A second important issue confronting readers of the Bible is the "canon": which books are accepted as belonging in the authoritative collection of the Bible? The canon signifies those books that are measured (with a reed, *qaneh*) and found to belong to the self-definition of the community. They are normative and so form the measure of the community's identity. In the course of the life of the people of Israel, certain stories, poems, sayings, laws, and rituals, by their use and reuse, came to be fixed as central and normative for the life of the community. As these were written down, their written forms also became fixed and normative. Over time the collection of these writings became fixed and normative. By about 400 B.C.E. there was a fixed collection that was the Law (what we know as the first five books of the Bible, the Pentateuch). By 300 B.C.E. the historical books took form, and by 200 B.C.E. the collection of prophets was final. In a similar way, but over much less time, the gospels and letters of the New Testament were used, collected, and finally fixed. The process of canonization took time, was dependent on use, and was the consensus of the community.

One of the major issues of the canon for the early Christian community was whether to include the Old Testament (the Jewish scriptures) as part of the books that the community considered to be inspired by God and normative for the life of the Christian community. Some in the early Christian community felt that the revelation that had taken place in Jesus surpassed and made unnecessary the revelation that had previously come to the Jews. Others went so far as to claim that the God of the Hebrew scriptures (Yahweh) was an inferior or even evil god, and that the Old Testament revelation was opposed to the revelation of Jesus Christ. The great majority of the community, however, realized that the revelation of God in the Old Testament was essential for understanding the revelation in Jesus Christ. They understood that, although the revelation in Jesus Christ surpassed the previous revelation, it was firmly based on that revelation and was a fulfillment of that revelation. They realized that the God and Father of Jesus Christ was the same God who was the God of Abraham, Isaac, and Jacob and who revealed himself to Moses and who spoke through the prophets. They saw clearly that this understanding was central to the message of Jesus, to the letters of Paul, and to the gospels.

A second issue in accepting the Old Testament as part of the canon was which books to accept. In the first centuries of the early church there was not one accepted version of the Jewish scriptures. For the most part, the Jewish communities of Palestine and the East tended to accept a smaller number of books as part of their canon than the Jewish communities in Egypt and the West. The Jews in the East tended not to use the books that were, or were supposed to have been, written in Greek. The Hellentistic Jewish communities (those in Asia Minor, Egypt, and the West) tended to use the books that were in the Septuagint (the Greek translation of the Jewish scriptures) and these included some later books written in Greek. The Christian communities, especially those in the West, used the Greek Septuagint as the Old Testament in their scriptures. Over time the Jewish community as a whole rejected the books that were written in Greek, and so there came to be a Jewish canon that was different from the Christian canon for the Old Testament. Originally, however, the Christians merely chose to use the books of the Jewish scriptures that other Hellenistic Jews were using. Later, during the time of the Reformation, Luther and the reformers chose to accept as canonical only those books in the Hebrew scriptures of the Jews of his day, those books that were originally written in Hebrew. Therefore, at the time of the Reformation and the Counter-Reformation, two different Christian canons became fixed. The Protestant canon of the Old Testament included thirty-nine books. The other books that were in the Roman Catholic and Orthodox canon, the books thought to have been written in Greek, were referred to as the Apocrypha ("hidden") by the Protestants. The Roman and Orthodox canon of the Old Testament included forty-six books, but called the books that the Protestants referred to as the Apocrypha, Deuterocanonical (secondarily canonical).

The Process of Creating the Bible

Even before the process of creating a canon, there is the process of creating individual books of the Bible. This process involves using and reworking earlier material, collecting related texts, and finally editing the book as a whole. The first stage in the process of the Bible is the stage of action and speech. An event happens and a word is spoken. The next stage is the stage of retelling and interpretation. The event is interpreted and described; the speech is repeated orally. The third stage would be the collecting of various stories or sayings together. We find in the Bible collections of stories about Joseph, Jacob, and Abraham. We find collections of sayings by Isaiah, Jeremiah, and Ezekiel. We find collections of laws about marriage, property, and ritual. At some point in time after the events and persons involved, later generations would gather the related stories into a collection. Stories about the patriarchs would have been joined together. The sayings of the prophets would have been collected by their disciples and put into a collection of sayings. Stories about the lives of the prophets would have been similarly collected. There is evidence that before the gospels there were collections of the sayings of Jesus (Q is one notable example) and collections of miracle stories. When the books of the Bible were being finalized, some editors were responsible for gathering the collections together and creating the books. Thus the collections of sayings of a prophet, sayings of his disciples, stories about the prophet, and even historical accounts taken from the historical books were all collected to be put into one scroll. This final collection often has a very noticeable structure. In the book of the prophet Isaiah, the words and stories about Isaiah son of Amoz come in chapters 1—39, whereas the sayings of his later disciples (Second and Third Isaiah) come in chapters 40—66. In the chapters devoted to Isaiah son of Amoz, the editors have placed the sayings about judgment first (1—12), followed by oracles against the nations (13—23), and then the words of consolation (28—35). These are followed by the stories about the life of Isaiah, the battle with Assyria, and the death of Hezekiah taken from 2 Kings (36—39). Although not all books have such a clear order, they were all put into some final structured form. The Gospel of Mark contains the sayings and deeds of Jesus, which were gathered together in earlier collections and used by Mark (the name we give to the final author of this gospel) to create his gospel. The overarching structure of the gospel is Mark's creation. The Bible enshrines a process that can be called "living text." There is no one point in the process that can be identified as inspired, or God's word, as opposed to the other points. However, the final canonical form is the form that is normative and declared by the church to be the inspired word of God. This does not take away from the fact that the text remains alive and constantly engages new readers in new situations.

Even after the Hebrew Bible became fixed and there were no changes allowed to the text, the process of the living text continued in commentaries, interpretations, and translations. The Septuagint, although a fairly literal translation into Greek of the Hebrew Bible, still interprets what is not understandable, changes what is deemed problematic, and in general updates the text for a new situation. The Aramaic translations of the Hebrew Bible, known as the Targums, are even more freewheeling with their translations as interpretations. The living text goes even further in the traditions of exposition, explanation, and commentary found in the Midrash and Talmud. For the Christian New Testament, Jerome's Vulgate (an early Latin translation of both the New and

Old Testaments) was an interpretation as well as translation and was for a time considered the inspired version of the Bible for Catholics in the West. The early church fathers commented on the texts in such a way that continued to give them new life and vitality. The councils of the church made the move away from merely restating the biblical text, to interpreting its meaning in a new context for a new time and yet never replacing the canonical version of the text.

Two forces are at work in the process of the "living Bible." Both are important and both may reflect the use and the respect given to the sacred writings. The first force is the force of variation, repetition, updating, and new creation. The scriptures were constantly being used for new reflection or being placed in a new context. They inspired new creations on the same model or genre, or inspired the desire to fill in the gaps in the older stories or laws. The second force is the force of canonization. This is the desire to save the great heritage as it is, the desire to make sure that the first force does not destroy or subvert the ancient tradition, the desire to use the texts over and over in their original form in all the places that God's people gather to pray and worship. We see this force in the placement of two stories of the same event side by side. Although it might not make logical sense in terms of the narrative to do this, it makes canonical sense in preserving the whole of the tradition.

The Meaning of the Bible

Every reading of the Bible is an engagement between the reader and the text that results in an effect on the reader that we call *meaning*. The question is how and where does the reader get the meaning of a text in this process of reading. It is possible to separate out three loci of meaning, or to find in the discourse three different players who contribute to the meaning of a text. These are the author, the text, and the reader. (This separation is artificial and overly simplistic, but does allow us to see the process of finding meaning in a text.) The three players, or three loci of meaning, are: the world behind the text, the world of the text, and the world in front of the text. It is important to point out that, although different readers with different concerns and abilities tend to focus on one or the other of the loci of meaning, all three loci are important for any reading of the text. It is not possible to focus exclusively on the world behind the text without taking into account the text and the reader.

World behind the Text

The world behind the text refers to the world that generated the text. Primarily this means the author, who had a reason and purpose for writing the text. The author is male or female, Jew or Gentile, slave or free, peasant or retainer class, priest or lay. These characteristics affect the way the author produces the text and can sometimes be determined with a fair amount of accuracy. For the most part, though, there is very little in the biblical texts that reveals to us who the author was.

The social, historical, religious world in which the author lived is also an important feature of the world behind the text. Usually we know more about the world at the time of a text than we do about the author. Although we know very little if anything about the author of chapters 40–55 of the Book of Isaiah, we can reasonably place the writing to about 540 B.C.E. We know from other biblical books that are dated to the same period something about the religious life at the time and the religious innovations and developments that have taken place. We know from other ancient Near Eastern writings something of the history of that period, especially the decline and fall of the Babylonian Empire and the rise to power of Cyrus of Persia. The world behind the text involves the study of the persons or events that are the subject of the writing. If the text tells us about the life of David, we will want to find out if the text paints an accurate picture of David or even generally of the life of a royal family at that time.

Another aspect of the world behind the text is the language of the time. If we are interested in finding the meaning of the text, we need to know what the words, images, and expressions meant at that particular time in history. We need to understand how grammar worked and what idioms meant. Here, other writings from that period are indispensable for our study.

Finally, we want to know something about the original intended audience. Was the text written for all Jews, for a certain group of Jews, or for Gentiles? What was the audience's particular situation? The search for meaning in the world behind the text seeks to find out as much as possible about the persons and society that went into the making of and accepting the text in its original context. As modern readers, we want to know this so that we do not impose our own meanings onto the text. A word, action, or relationship can have quite a different meaning in a world so different from our own. It is important to remember that the world of the Bible is a foreign world. Context is everything in reading a text, and the original context is privileged in helping us to find meaning. If we do not understand the original context of a text, we might miss or misinterpret the humor, sarcasm, pathos, or tragedy of a story. What might seem like a very funny image to us could have very tragic overtones given a different historical context. Similarly what might seem like a rather bland statement of fact to us might be a hilarious mockery of an ancient situation or belief. A modern reader can never dispense with the work of placing the text as carefully as possible within the context of its genesis. However, the meaning of a biblical text is not restricted to what the original author intended for an original audience (especially because that is impossible to completely reconstruct without having the author present to interrogate).

World of the Text

The second locus of meaning is the text itself. The text is not the slave of the author, doing and saying only what was intended. Once the text is written, it takes on a life of its own, with power to continue to engage readers in meaning long after the author and the original purpose of the text have passed. The study of the world of the text focuses on the characteristics of the text that help the reader find meaning. Biblical texts can be studied in this way just like any other text. To understand what the text is saying to us, we want to know first the genre of the text. Is the text a narrative, a poem, a list, or an essay? If the text is a narrative, we will want to know who the protagonist is and who the antagonist. How is each of the characters portrayed? What are the textual clues that tell us how to evaluate each character? We will also want to know about the narrator in the text. Is the narrator omniscient and reliable? When is the narrator narrating the story, and when is the narrator speaking directly to the reader? What is the plot of the story: the ascending action, the denouement, the descending action? Are there any plot twists in the story? If the text is poetry, we will examine the structure of the poem. What kinds of poetic devices are used and what images are employed? If the text is a list, we will want to know if it a list of laws, of offspring, or of articles for the Temple. How is this material arranged and what is left out? If the text is an essay, we will ask whether it is a sermon, a philosophical discourse, or a letter. What is the form that the essay takes? What rhetorical techniques are used to make the argument? All of these questions help us to understand the text itself. The meaning we will find here is the meaning we might be more accustomed to finding in a contemporary text. Any careful reader is aware of the ways that an author manipulates the feelings, expectations, and ideas of the reader to create an effect or make a point.

World in front of the Text

The third locus of meaning is the reader. When I described the second locus, I made it sound as if the text by itself creates a meaning, but of course that is an overstatement. The text can do nothing without a reader reading it. However, for the sake of clarity, it is helpful to separate the two. The reader as a locus of meaning comes to the text and must respond to the text. Clearly, the modern reader will respond to the biblical text differently than the ancient Jewish or Christian reader. What the reader brings to the text is an important part of the meaning of the text. In this way a modern Christian who reads the biblical prophets brings to the text two thousand years of Christian reflection on the prophetic message as fulfilled in Jesus. This is inevitable and not undesirable. It is legitimate as long as it is recognized to be what the reader is bringing and not what the author intended. Problems have arisen in biblical interpretation when readers believe that what they bring to the text (Christian beliefs, modern sensibilities, modern science) are really in the text and were the intention of the author. That is to confuse the world in front of the text with the world behind the text.

The effort to find meaning in the world in front of the text starts with the experience and worldview of the reader. Usually some issue in the experience of the reader provides a lens to read the text. Feminist readers of the Bible have the experience of discrimination because of gender. Their experience is that the Bible is linked to the system of patriarchy that devalues women and their unique worldview. This experience is brought to the reading of the text. The text is engaged with this issue in the forefront. The text is questioned, challenged, reevaluated, and even rewritten. The danger for this method of finding meaning is when the experience of the reader is canonized as more important than the text or the author's intention. If this is the case, no real dialogue takes place. The reader becomes a bully, demanding that the text live up to the standards that the reader sets for it. The ideal situation occurs when readers come to the text honestly, bringing their concerns and experiences, engage the text openly, and allow the text to respond. This kind of engagement is a creative process of meaning giving that allows the text to mean much more than what was intended by the author. At the same time it allows the text to remain authentic and true without becoming the puppet of the reader.

Traditionally, academic biblical studies have focused primarily on the world behind the text, and only secondarily on the world of the text. For the most part, the world in front of the text was left for homilies, sermons, and spiritual reading. Recently, scholars have begun to recognize the importance of all three loci of meaning, even in academic study. Further they have realized that the reader's worldview, presuppositions, social location, and ideology influence any reading, even ones that claim to focus exclusively on the world behind the text. Scholars now realize that it is imperative that they acknowledge the world in front of the text to keep every reading honest.

The Bible as History

An important issue in biblical studies and in Christian faith communities is the "historicity" of the Bible. To understand the Bible as history we need to make a distinction between historical fact and historical discourse. If we are concerned with historical fact in the Bible and we judge it by modern standards, it is easy to find "untruths" in the Bible. There are sometimes two contrasting or even contradictory accounts of the same event. Recent archaeological discoveries or discoveries of ancient writings have shown us that certain "facts" are false. A simple example is Daniel's references to the kings of Babylonia and Persia, which are incorrect. It is not correct to reduce the possibilities for reading the Bible to two. It is myth, story, or theology, which are not concerned with historical facts, or it is history by modern standards and does relate accurate historical facts throughout. There is a third and more accurate way to approach the Bible as history. First, the Bible is an ancient document. Therefore, the Enlightenment concern for science, historical fact, and rigorous objectivity is not part of the biblical worldview. Second, the Bible emphasizes that the stories being told are not fiction or myths like the myths of surrounding cultures. The concern for linear history is what makes the Bible original and unique as a literary document of its time. One of the great insights of the Bible is that the relationship of God and God's chosen people is found in history and not in some mythical, cyclical reality.

It is important to remember that the Bible is a discourse between the text and the reader. It is not productive to step outside the discourse and make judgments concerning claims that the discourse is not making. To go looking for Noah's ark is really a refusal to engage the discourse that is the word of God. Looking for Noah's ark is focusing on only one element in the discourse. The discourse is not saying to the reader to go and find the ark and you will know this is all true. Rather, the discourse is asking the reader to enter this world, this story, and see how God works and how humans fail and what are the possibilities for human–divine relationship. These possibilities are unique in that they are not mythic but historical, but that is quite different from

15

attributing to the discourse the claim to be telling the reader about historical facts. Looking for the facts in a story is to become distracted from the real meaning of the discourse and so to miss what the biblical text is asking of us.

To make the argument that God is at work in history is very different from making the argument that historical facts prove the existence and power of God. Fundamentalists try to go the second road and are not faithful to the discourse of the Bible. To argue over facts, try to prove them, hold on to them, and claim them as divine revelation is not the point and intention of the narrative.

Genres of the Bible

The word *Bible*, as most people know, means books (or library). The Bible is a collection of books. The books are also collections. In short, the Bible is a collection of collections. This gives us a great deal of variety in the Bible. There are many different kinds of writing in the Bible, and sometimes even similar genres are from very different periods of history and so must be read in very different ways. It is always a matter of how you listen to the words in the Bible. The books of the Bible make a claim to be the word of God and to be able to be trusted, but different genres do this differently. As a reader of the Bible, we must take these different claims seriously. To lump the Bible all together as the word of God homogeneously presented and homogeneously making the same claims is to misunderstand the Bible and the word of God. The genres of the Bible range from poetry to narrative prose, to lists of laws and genealogies, to sermons and letters. The types of poetry range from love poetry, to funeral laments, to hymns of praise used in worship. The types of narratives range between archetypal (or mythical) narratives of primeval history, to folk legends, to legends explaining how things got their names, to court histories of kings, to historical novels, to apocalyptic visions. We have lists of laws that are apodictic (general prohibitions) and laws that are casuistic (accompanied by the specific punishment that corresponds to the crime). We have discourses that are philosophical essays, sermons, and letters. The great range of genres in the Bible requires the reader to make a distinction between the kinds of claims each kind of writing is making. It would be a mistake to read the historical novel of Esther in the same way you read the court history of David or the apocalyptic vision of Daniel.

The Text of the Bible

The Bible that you are reading is a modern English translation—but a translation of what? Do we have the original Bible somewhere? No! As noted earlier, the text of the Hebrew Bible was fixed about 100 B.C.E. The text of the New Testament was fixed by a council of the church in about 400 C.E. The earliest "Bibles" were manuscripts of individual books. During the time of Jesus, there would have been a scroll of Isaiah, a scroll of Genesis, and so on. Until 1947 the oldest copies of any books of the Bible that we had access to were from the fourth century C.E. This is perhaps nine hundred years after much of the Hebrew Bible was written in its final form and two to three hundred years after the books of the New Testament were written. In 1947 scrolls that dated to the last century B.C.E. were discovered in caves next to the Dead Sea (the Dead Sea Scrolls). These copies of books of the Hebrew Bible increased our knowledge of the text immensely. However, we do not have anything close to the original autograph copy of any of the books of the Bible. The copies that we have are hand-copied copies of copies of copies....

In the process of hand-copying a text, a number of problems could occur. One frequent problem is known as haplography—the copyist's eye jumped ahead to the same or similar word later in the text and so a section of the text was skipped in the copied manuscript. Another mistake is known as dittography—the copyist's eye went back to the same or similar word earlier in the text and so a section of the text was repeated. Sometimes the copyist would simply miswrite a word as a different word. Sometimes the copyist would try to clean up a text that the copyist thought was incorrect or too difficult to understand. Also some copyists would make notes in the margins of the text and later copyists would include these notes in the text. These are called *glosses*. In the hundreds of years of copying the texts before any copies survived for us, many changes and mistakes were made. Now when we study the Book of Isaiah, for example, and examine the hundred oldest and best manuscripts of that text, they are not the same at all. Some of the differences between manuscripts are minor and easily figured out, but some are major and impossible to decide which is the original or best reading. For the New Testament, because the amount of time elapsed in copying before the surviving texts is much smaller, the textual differences are minor compared to those found in the Hebrew Bible. The point of this discussion is to make it clear that we do not have the original text of any of the books. The Bible text you are reading is a translation of a text, which is a composite, based on decisions of scholars about which reading is the best in each particular case. So in verse 5 the compilers of the Greek or Hebrew text may have chosen the reading from the text found in Alexandria; for verse 8 they have chosen the reading found in the text housed in the Vatican; and on and on. Thus there are major decisions being made about what the text says long before the student of the Bible ever gets to read it.

There are scholarly versions of the Hebrew Bible (the MT) the Greek Old Testament (LXX) and the New Testament (NT) that are generally accepted and used as the starting point for modern translations. Even when all the translations begin with the same reconstructed text, however, the translations can be quite different. Translations tend to be either literal or interpretive. A *literal translation* will be faithful to the exact wording of the text and often even to the word order of the text. These translations will often be difficult to read and understand for the modern reader. The value of such a translation is that it allows the reader to experience more accurately the Hebrew or Greek mind. An *interpretive translation* seeks to put ideas, expressions, and experiences into language that is faithful to the meaning of the original but understandable for the modern reader. The decision to interpret can be made at many different levels. A first level has to do with the difference in grammar between Hebrew and English. In a strictly literal rendering, Genesis 3:1 says that "the serpent was crafty from all the animals." Hebrew has no superlative form (i.e., "best" or "most"). Instead, Hebrew uses the word "from" to create a superlative. This is known as the "partitive." So whereas the Hebrew literally says "crafty from all animals," this really means "most crafty"

18

or "more crafty than any other." Although not a major change, it is still an interpretation to translate this into English as: "the serpent was more crafty than any other wild animal."

At another level, the translator must contend with images and idioms in Hebrew that have no counterpart in English. The Hebrew of Amos 4:6 quotes God as saying, "I gave you cleanness of teeth." In the context, it is clear that the author uses this image as a figurative expression for saying that God caused a famine. Should the translator help the reader to understand the meaning of the text by translating the figurative expression as "I afflicted you with a famine"? Or should the translator translate it literally and hope that the reader realizes that God is not claiming to be a dental hygienist? The translator must decide what images and figures of speech need to be translated in a way that the reader will be able to understand. (Many of the more scholarly translations tend to translate the image literally and use footnotes to explain the meaning.)

A third level, at which translations can interpret or be literal, is the level of theology. Translating a Hebrew or Greek word into English always involves a number of possibilities. It will make a difference which word a translator chooses, when one or more of the possibilities carry theological implications. To choose to translate the Hebrew *berit* as "covenant" instead of "pact" or "agreement" makes a difference. The word *covenant* carries many theological connotations. Translators have to make the decision whether they want the word to carry these connotations. The reader must also be aware that all the meaning we modern Christians associate with the word *covenant* may not be intended at this point in the text. Another good example is the word *ruach*, in Hebrew. Because it can mean "wind," "breath," and "spirit," when is it appropriate to translate *ruach elohim* as the "wind of God" (mighty wind), as the "breath of God," or as the "Spirit of God"?

In all of this, readers should be aware that the translation of the Bible that they are reading is based on a best guess about the original text and is an interpretation influenced by many factors. A particular translation (such as the Vulgate or the King James Version) should never be canonized as the word of God.

Order of Study

It is possible to study the Bible in three different orders—chronologically, thematically, or canonically. Many introductions to the Bible study the Bible in the chronological order in which scholars believe that it was written. Among the prophets, a student would read Amos and Hosea before Jeremiah and Ezekiel. It is possible to separate out texts in Genesis and Exodus and study the oldest sections (the parts known as the Yahwist source) first. A thematic study of the Bible looks at themes that run throughout the entire Bible—themes of justice, mercy, sin, redemption, covenant, and so forth. This kind of study is not concerned with when a book was written or where it is placed in the canon. Theologies of the Old Testament and the New Testament often take this form. Finally, a study of the Bible can follow the order of the books as they appear in the canon. Although the Bible is clearly a collection of different books, it is also a fixed collection with a definite story line. In the Old Testament, from Genesis 1 to the end of 2 Maccabees there is a loose and repetitive, but chronological, narrative of God's dealings with God's chosen people. The wisdom literature and then the sayings of the prophets follow this history. In the New Testament the gospels precede the earlier letters of Paul, and these are followed by other letters and the Book of Revelation. It is my decision in this textbook to study the Bible in the order in which the books are placed in the Christian canon. I do this because I believe that the overarching canonical narrative is central to the theology of the Bible. The Bible is telling a story of God relating to God's people in history. This story has a beginning, middle, and end. We should take the story seriously in the order in which it is told and in the logic that it creates.

Using Your Bible

Citations

The text of the Bible used in this book is the New Revised Standard Version (NRSV). Every translation of the Bible will have different titles, notes, cross-references, and related materials. It is worth the readers' time to acquaint themselves with the aids to study that their Bible offers. First, to use the aids properly or to read any discussion of biblical texts, it is essential to understand the method for citing biblical texts. This is not uniform from translation to translation. What is recommended by the Modern Language Association is not what is normally used in translations of the Bible or even in most scholarly articles. The method of citation used in this book follows that used in the *Catholic Biblical Quarterly*. Simply put, a citation of a text begins with the abbreviation of the book (usually in three or four letters) followed by a space then the chapter number of the book, then a colon, then the verse or verses—for example: Gen 3:10. (You will find forms of citing the text that use either a comma or a period instead of the colon between chapter and verse, and you will find some forms that use Roman instead of Arabic numerals. Also, the accepted abbreviations for books can vary.) If a citation includes more than one verse, there is a dash between the first and last verse of the citation. For example: Exod 12:29–36. If a citation lists more than one verse and the verses are not continuous, a comma is placed between the verses. For example: Lev 23:4, 23, 26. If the citation includes more than one book or more than one chapter of the same book, a semicolon separates these. For example: Num 3:45; 8:14. If the citation runs not just for several verses but for several chapters of a book, a dash is placed between the chapter and verse that open the citation and the chapter and verse that close the citation. For example: Deut 12:1—26:19. In reading citations in your Bible, you will also notice that sometimes there will be letters after the verse number. These represent two different things. The letters "a," "b," and "c" refer to the parts of a verse. Often a verse will be made up of different sentences, clauses, or sections that need to be distinguished. A good example of this is Gen 2:4b, which is the beginning of the second story of creation. The first story of creation ends with Gen 2:4a. The letters "f" or "ff," after a verse number, indicate that the following verse or verses are to be included in the citation. Matt 4:15f means that verses 15 and 16 are included in the citation.

Cross-References and Footnotes

Cross-references, which often appear to the side of or beneath the text, are helpful aids provided by most translations of the Bible. Because so many texts of the Bible quote or allude to other texts of the Bible, it is imperative that a careful reader know what text is being quoted or alluded to. The Old Testament background for the New Testament is essential for understanding the New Testament.

The translators of the Bible will often give footnotes to explain the meanings of places, events, or concepts that might be foreign to the reader. The notes can also explain the reasons for a certain translation (giving either the literal rendering or the interpretive meaning), can alert the reader to puns or plays on words, and can inform the reader of changes that have been made to the text (often by rearranging the order of verses or leaving some verses out altogether).

Learning Achievements

After studying this chapter, the student should be able to:

- Define what Catholics mean by the word of God, inerrancy, and inspiration.

- Define the canon and describe the process of creating it.

- Describe the process of "writing" the books of the Bible and the "living Bible."

- Describe the three loci of meaning: World behind the Text; World of the Text; and World in front of the Text.

- Differentiate between historical fact and historical discourse.

- Discuss textual criticism and the difference in translations.

- Read citations and use cross-references and footnotes in their Bible.

Recommended Reading

Bowley, James E., ed. *Living Traditions of the Bible: Scripture in Jewish, Christian, and Muslim Practice.* St. Louis: Chalice Press, 1999. Especially see Joseph Fitzmyer, "Scripture in the Catholic Tradition," 145–161.

Brown, Raymond E. *Biblical Exegesis and Church Doctrine.* Ramsey, N.J.: Paulist, 1985.

Gillingham, Susan E. *One Bible, Many Voices: Different Approaches to Biblical Studies.* Grand Rapids: Eerdmans, 1998.

Grant, Robert M., and David Tracy. *A Short History of the Interpretation of the Bible.* 2d ed. Minneapolis: Fortess, 1984.

Schneiders, Sandra. *The Revelatory Text: Interpreting the New Testament as Sacred Scripture.* 2d ed. Collegeville, Minn.: Liturgical Press, 1999.

Chapter 2
OLD TESTAMENT INTRODUCTION

World behind the Text

Entering a Strange World

When modern Americans read the Old Testament they are entering a world that is as strange to their own as any in science fiction or fantasy. These readers must put aside contemporary worldviews and presuppositions and learn from historical, sociological, and anthropological criticism what the world was like in Palestine in the last millennium B.C.E. Just as J.R.R. Tolkein provided a map of Middle Earth, a synopsis of its history, and a description of the different types of characters who inhabited it, so this chapter will offer the reader a brief introduction to the world of the Old Testament.

Historical Context of Israel

The most important empire at the beginning of the story of Israel is Egypt. The Empire of Egypt is divided into three kingdoms: the old, middle, and new. It is during the Old Kingdom (2575–2134 B.C.E.) that the three great pyramids of Giza were built. This kingdom predates any of the biblical history and so is not of concern for us. The Middle Kingdom (2040–1650 B.C.E.) encompasses the time of the Patriarchs. It may be during this period that the sons of Jacob migrated to Egypt. During the period 1650–1550 B.C.E., Semitic foreigners, called the Hyksos, ruled Egypt for about one hundred years. Scholars have suggested that this foreign rule of Egypt is reflected in the story of Joseph's rule in Egypt. After the Hyksos are driven out of Egypt, the New

Figure 1. Ancient Near East

Kingdom (1550–1070) brings Egypt to the height of its power. It is during this period that the Exodus occurs. Most believe that the Exodus took place during the reign of Rameses II (1290–1224). During this period, Egypt had control of all of Palestine and even some of Syria. To the north of Palestine in Anatolia was the Hittite Empire. After about 1200 the Hittite Empire collapsed, and after 1150 Egypt became weak and lost control of Palestine. This opened the door for the creation of an independent nation in Palestine.

History of Israel

The Biblical story begins with the creation of the universe and moves through the lives of the patriarchs to the Exodus from Egypt and on to the confederacy of twelve tribes living in Canaan. However, the people of the Bible, the Hebrews/Israelites/Jews, became a distinct and unified group only at the time of the confederacy. In about 1200 B.C.E. several tribes and groups of Semitic peoples formed a political confederacy in the highland areas of Palestine and thus formed the Hebrew people who will be the nation of Israel. There are many possible reconstructions of who they were and where they came from. It is widely agreed that the biblical account of the premonarchical history is artificially unified, oversimplified, and exaggerated. The peoples that eventually became the nation of Israel were not all descendents of one ancestor, Jacob, nor had they all been held in slavery in Egypt or spent the last forty years wandering in the desert. Most likely the tribes of Israel were groups of nomads from the desert who decided to settle in the highlands of Canaan, groups from the Philistine city states who wanted to start their own lives outside of that strict class system, and groups of ex-slaves from Egypt and other lands who settled down between the great highways from Egypt to Mesopotamia. These groups were separate tribes, with their own histories, ancestors, folk legends, rituals, and beliefs; but eventually they formed a confederation to protect themselves against the Philistines and other surrounding peoples and tribes. In the process of forming a political confederacy, cultural and religious assimilation also took place. In this way, the ancestors of each of the tribes were joined to form a unified family tree. This confederacy was characterized by a shared God, a shared Ark of the Covenant, a shared legal code, shared rituals, and a shared story. The event in this story that served to form them into a people was the saving act of the **Exodus.** Their existence as a unified group living in Canaan was attributed to a miraculous intervention of God. God delivered them from slavery in Egypt and led them to this Promised Land. In the process of delivering and leading them, God formed them into a people who owed their allegiance to God and gave them a law by which to express their allegiance. The Exodus event thus became the founding event for all the tribes, even for those who may not have been enslaved in Egypt.

At the end of the second millennium B.C.E., the Philistine nation states came to see these tribes as a threat and engaged in war against them. It was during this period that the military leader, Saul, was proclaimed king and the **kingship** established. Later in Saul's career, one of his generals, David, made a claim for the throne (he had been anointed by the last of the judges, Samuel) and upon the death of Saul in battle asserted his control over all the tribes of the confederacy. This was the beginning of the Davidic dynasty. The reigns of David and his son Solomon lasted for nearly eighty years, but at the death of Solomon, the twelve tribes were split. The northern tribes chose not to support Solomon's son, Rehoboam, as king and formed their own nation, the nation of Israel. The tribes of Judah and Benjamin formed the nation of Judah under the Davidic ruler.

The northern kingdom of Israel was the larger and wealthier nation and was ruled by a succession of dynasties. It was also geographically much nearer to the world power of that time, Assyria. There was a succession of failed rebellions against the power of Assyria, and in 722 Samaria, the capital of Israel, was destroyed and the people of Israel taken into exile. This marked the end of the northern kingdom and the disappearance of the ten northern tribes. The southern kingdom of Judah remained under the leadership of the Davidic dynasty (except for several years when the wife of a Davidic king ruled) and survived a number of narrow escapes at the hands of the Assyrians. Then in 630 the Babylonians replaced the Assyrians as the ruling empire in the Near East. In 598 the Babylonian king, Nebuchadnezzar, captured Jerusalem, took the young king and many of the ruling class of Judah into exile in Babylon, and placed the king's uncle on the throne; but in 587 he too rebelled against Babylonia, and in 586 Jerusalem was again captured, the Temple destroyed, and most of its inhabitants taken into **exile,** thus bringing to an end the kingdom of Judah and the Davidic dynasty.

In 539 Cyrus of Persia conquered Babylon and in 538 issued the Edict of Cyrus allowing the people of Judah to return home and rebuild Jerusalem and the Temple. Most of the exiles, however, chose not to return, and the rebuilding of Jerusalem was slow and marred by conflict. Finally in 519 the Temple was rededicated by Zerubbabel. For the two hundred years of the Persian period, Judah was insignificant and not prosperous. It was during this time, however, that much of what we have today as the Old Testament was compiled and codified. Early in the Persian period, Ezra and Nehemiah led a reform of Judaism in Judah. Under their leadership Judaism developed into the form it had at the time of Jesus.

In 330 B.C.E. Alexander the Great conquered the Persian Empire, and Palestine came under Hellenistic rule. At his death Alexander's kingdom was divided among his four generals, with Syria going to Seleucus and Egypt going to Ptolemy. Situated between these two areas, Palestine was continuously fought over, belonging now to one and now to the other. In the middle of the second century B.C.E., Judea was under the control of the Seleucids, whose ruler, Antiochus IV, sought to repress traditional Jewish custom, and went so far as to erect an altar to Zeus in the Temple. The Jews of Palestine revolted and, under the leadership of Judas Maccabeus and his brothers, waged a successful guerilla war against the Seleucid forces. In 164 B.C.E. the Temple was cleansed and rededicated. For the next one hundred years the Maccabees, known as the Hasmonean dynasty, ruled in Judea.

In 60 B.C.E. Pompey conquered Jerusalem, and the Hasmoneans became vassals to the Roman Empire. Herod, an Idumean (Judea's neighbors to the south), married a Hasmonean princess, supported the successful contender to the leadership of Rome, and paid a large bribe to become the ruler of Judea in 44 B.C.E. He ruled for the next forty years as a strong, ruthless, and productive king, earning the title of "great." He built many cities, palaces, and public works and expanded and upgraded the Temple. After the death of Herod the Great, his kingdom was divided among three of his sons. Archelaus was the ruler of Jerusalem and Judea proper, Herod Antipas was the ruler of Galilee, and Philip was the ruler of the Decapolis (an area of ten cities east of the Jordan). After only a few years, the Romans deposed Archelaus and placed a governor over Jerusalem and Judea. From this point on, the Romans had direct rule of Judea.

Old Testament Chronology

2000–1500	Patriarchal period
1700–1300	Time in Egypt
1300–1200	**Exodus** and forty years wandering in the desert
1200–1020	Conquest of Canaan and Confederacy of twelve Tribes
1020–586	**Kingship**
1020–1000	Saul as king
1000–961	David
961–922	Solomon
922–586	Divided Monarchy
722	Fall of Israel to the Assyrians
598	Judah conquered by Babylonians, king and elite taken into exile
586	**Exile:** Judah conquered by Babylonians, Temple destroyed, most inhabitants of Jerusalem taken into exile
539	Beginning of return of exiles
520	Dedication of rebuilt Temple
333	Alexander the Great
167	Maccabees gain independence and rededicate the Temple
60	Pompey and Rome gain control over Palestine

Geography of Palestine

Canaan is the word used in the Old Testament to refer to this area as the political region formerly inhabited by the Canaanites. The word *Palestine* is not used until 400 B.C.E. or so. Although Palestine and Canaan are essentially interchangeable, we will use the name Palestine here because it is a neutral term that refers to the whole geographical region. Palestine is divided into four climatic and geographical areas. The **Mediterranean coast** is the western boundary of Palestine. It includes beaches, coastal plains, and foothills. Although the coast receives a fair amount of rain and the weather is temperate, the area of the coast that was under the control of Israel was heavily forested and with no natural harbors, so Israelites never settled there. The Phoenicians lived along the coast to the north (Lebanon) in the cities of Tyre and Sidon, and the Philistines lived along the coast to the south (Gaza strip) in the cities of Gaza, Ashdod, Ashkelon, and Ekron.

The main middle section of Palestine is the **central hill country** and consists of a range of hills that extends from Lebanon in the north to the desert in the south. In Israel the highest point in the hill country is about 3,300 feet. The range of hills is broken in only one place, the valley of Jezreel, which separates the hill country of Galilee from the hill country of Samaria. The valley of Jezreel offers the most fertile land and best farming in all of Israel. In the middle section of the hill country is Samaria, which has an abundance of arable land. In the south are the more rugged hills of Judah. One of the attractions of this southern region is that it is easily defended. At the eastern edge of the hill country of Judah steep cliffs fall to the Jordan and the Dead Sea. To the west are rocky hills. The best farming in Judah is the lowland hills to the west of the higher plateau, but Judah is not known for arable land. This area gets much less rain and experiences much cooler temperatures than the coast. Much of the hill country reaches elevations of 3,000 feet. Whereas today much of this region consists of barren and rocky hills, in ancient times much of it would have been covered with forests, which were cleared for farming and used for building.

To the east of the hill country is the **rift valley.** The rift is the major geological feature of the region. It begins in Lebanon with the Leontes River and continues south with the Jordan River and into the Sea of Galilee. At this point the valley is 700 feet below sea level. From the Sea of Galilee it continues with the Jordan River down to the Dead Sea, which is 1,290 feet below sea level, the lowest place on earth. Below the Dead Sea, the rift continues in the dry riverbed known as the Arabah then into the Gulf of Aqebah and the Red Sea. Around the Sea of Galilee, a fresh water lake surrounded by sloping hills, and along the Jordan River there is plentiful water and good farming, but most of the rift valley is hot and dry. The Dead Sea is literally dead, with a salt content of 25 percent.

East of the Jordan there are more hills that level off into the **Transjordan plateau.** This area is a high plateau that receives adequate rainfall, has more arable land than the hill country, and is the location of the king's highway that runs from Mesopotamia to Egypt. Rivers divide this plateau into five regions. In the north is Bashan, a fertile area known for its cattle. Moving to the south, the next area is Gilead, which was the area of Transjordan most often considered part of Israel. Continuing south, one comes to Ammon, which was sometimes controlled by Israel, and then Moab, which was rarely controlled by Israel. The area furthest to the south is Edom. The Edomites were considered the offspring of Jacob's brother Esau and were frequently under the control of Israel.

Climate of Palestine

The four different regions have relatively different climates, but one thing all of the regions share in common is a wet season in the fall, winter, and spring and a dry season during the summer. The rains begin in mid-October and run through mid-April, with the heaviest rains coming in December and January. The summer drought lasts about five months from May to September. The winters are cooler than the summers but temperatures below freezing are not common except in the highest mountains. The coastal plains average a daytime temperature of about 84° F in the summer and 63° F in the winter. The central hill country averages 86° F in the summer and 55° F in the winter, with a winter average at night being 41° F. It is not uncommon in the hill country for there to be snow, and even heavy snow because it is the rainy season. Jerusalem receives 50 inches of rain a year, but most of that is concentrated in December, January, and February. The rift valley gets less rain and sees much hotter temperatures. The average daytime temperature in the Jordan Valley is 102° F in the summer and 68° F in the winter. The average annual rainfall at the Dead Sea is two inches.

Political and Religious Situation

There are three social and political situations of Israel during the time of the Old Testament: the confederacy, the monarchy, and the rule of governors and priests. During the time of the confederacy, each of the tribes was autonomous. What they shared was a covenant allegiance to the one God, Yahweh. This shared allegiance to Yahweh meant that they also shared the worship of Yahweh at his primary sanctuaries, Shechem and Shiloh. They shared a festival of covenant renewal when they would all gather each year to reconfirm their allegiance to Yahweh and to each other. Finally, they shared a commitment to protect and defend each other when attacked by an enemy. The judge (a charismatic position and not a hereditary title) was the most important leader in the confederacy. He or she had the role of calling together all the tribes to perform their duty as vassals of Yahweh their king, whether that was to renew the covenant, to punish an offending tribe, or to fight against an external enemy. During this period, the most frequent external enemies were the Philistines who lived along the southern Mediterranean coast and the Ammonites and Moabites who lived on the Transjordan plateau to the east.

The religious life of the tribes centered on the Ark of the Covenant in its mobile tent, several important shrines, and numerous smaller shrines. The feasts of Passover, Weeks, and Booths were celebrated as the main feasts celebrating the acts of Yahweh. The feast of Booths was the most important of these because it included the covenant renewal ceremony. These festivals would have been chances for the tribes to gather at one of the important shrines, Shechem, Shiloh, or Gilgal. The festivals were all associated with agricultural events. Passover was the beginning of the spring barley harvest, Weeks (known to us as Pentecost) was the end of the spring barley and wheat harvests, and Booths was the end of the fruit (grapes and olives) harvest. These harvest feasts were also associated with the saving events of Israel's history. Passover was associated with the escape from Egypt; Weeks, with the giving of the law on Mount Sinai; and Booths, with the wandering in the desert for forty years. This tendency to change agricultural feasts into historical feasts reflects the ongoing conflict with the religions of Canaan.

The Hebrews, who formed the twelve tribes of Israel, replaced the Canaanites in the central hill country of Israel. The religion of the Canaanites was a continuous thorn in the side of the religion of Yahweh through the time of the monarchy. In Canaanite religion, the primary God was El, the creator and father God who was not directly involved in the running of the world. His consort was Asherah, the goddess of life and fertility. Baal, one of the sons of El, was the ruler and king of creation. He was the god of thunder and rain and was most often depicted as a bull. As the god of rain, he was a god of fertility. In Palestine it rains during the fall, winter, and spring, and is dry during the summer months. The story of Baal included his death and rebirth every year, as the rains ceased and returned. The worship of Baal, the fertility god, included sexual couplings that celebrated the rebirth of Baal and were meant, by sympathetic magic, to induce Baal to return to fertilize the earth with his sperm (rain). The Hebrews had no difficulty in equating Yahweh with El, the father god, but the religion of Yahweh constantly struggled against any association with the cult of Baal. It must be remembered that the Hebrews were for the most part nomadic peoples who radically changed their way of life when they settled in the hill country of Palestine and became farmers. We moderns have no problem in separating farming techniques from religious beliefs and practices, but that would not have been the case in the ancient world. Farming techniques included religious practice. To move into Canaan and learn how to farm would almost necessarily have involved learning the religious practices of the Canaanites who farmed this region. This struggle to become farmers in Canaan without becoming devotees of the cult of Baal took the Hebrews many centuries. It will be one of the main issues addressed by the prophets.

The main change brought about by the monarchy was greater centralization in all areas of life. First, power and authority were centralized in one person. No longer did a judge symbolize the unity of the tribes; now the king was the unity of the tribes. Jerusalem became the center of power and worship. Under Solomon, the worship of Yahweh was centralized in the Temple, and the cultic centers of Shechem and Shiloh were destroyed. No longer did the tribes muster when needed, but under the monarchy there was a standing army, supported by taxation. The value of the monarchy was that a more unified front could be formed against an opposing enemy. One of the problems with the monarchy was that during the confederacy Yahweh had been their only king. Now the human king was assuming the power and privilege that had been reserved for Yahweh alone. The priesthood also became centralized with a special group of priests replacing the ordinary Levites as the leaders of Temple worship. The feasts of Passover, Weeks, and Booths were now feasts celebrated only in Jerusalem. All male Jews were expected to travel to Jerusalem three times a year. This too contributed to a sense of one nation.

The Temple was the central aspect of the worship of Israel. The Temple of Solomon was divided into three basic areas. The courtyard contained the altar of burnt offerings and the large bowl of water. The large room inside the Temple building itself contained the altar of incense, the ten lampstands, and the table for the showbread. The inner room of the Temple (the holy of holies) contained the Ark of the Covenant with statues of cherubim (winged lions) on either side. The Temple served as the only recognized place for the offering of sacrifices to Yahweh, and sacrifices were the primary means for the people to relate to their God. There were three basic kinds of sacrifices. Some sacrifices were meant simply as gifts offered to God. These would be animals slaughtered and then burned whole on the altar of burnt offerings. Some sacrifices were meant to unite the community around God. These animals would be divided up so that the fat was burned as an offering to God, some prize portions set aside for the priests, and the rest of the animal eaten by the people. Finally, some sacrifices were meant to bring about a reconciliation between God and the people. These sin or guilt offerings involved the sprinkling of blood into the holy of holies, the daubing of blood on the horns of the altar of incense, and the pouring of blood at the base of the altar of burnt offerings. Thus, blood was applied in all three areas of the Temple. The blood brought about a cleansing from sin.

When the nation split into two, the northern kingdom established two new cult centers at Bethel and Dan. These were intended to represent a return to the time of the confederacy when there was not one centralized place of worship. For the southern kingdom, Jerusalem (Mount Zion) took on an even greater religious significance as the place where Yahweh dwelt. The Davidic dynasty also took on a religious significance as the recipient of a special covenant with God, an everlasting covenant that for a time surpassed the Sinai covenant in importance.

With the loss of the land, the Temple, and the king during the time of the exile, religious beliefs and practices again had to be redefined. In Exile, the Sinai covenant took on renewed importance. Many rituals that could be performed without the Temple became the center of Jewish life. Observance of the Sabbath (abstaining from work on the seventh day of the week); purification of food, utensils, and bodies; choice of the correct food; and observance of marriage laws all gained importance during the time of the Exile. Synagogues as places of prayer and worship, but not of sacrifice, also were established during the time of the Exile. With the return to the land after the Exile and the building of a second Temple, there was a return to sacrifices in the Temple and to the celebration of the pilgrim feasts, but there was no return of the king. The secular ruler of the land would have been a governor appointed by the Persians. The Sinai covenant continued as the most important definition of the people's identity.

World of the Text

The Jewish Scriptures and the Christian Old Testament

Most Christians are aware that the Old Testament is taken from the Jewish scriptures but do not understand the differences between these two documents. The Jewish scriptures are composed of three groups of books—the *Torah* (law), the *Nebiim* (prophets [former and latter]), and the *Ketubim* (writings)—together called the *TaNaK*. First, to call this Jewish collection the Old Testament is not correct, and second it is insulting to Jews. The collection known to Christians as the Old Testament has some different books in it (for Catholics at least), is arranged in a different order, and is understood as sacred scripture and normative word of God for a different community in a different context. Seven books that are included in the Catholic Old Testament are not in the Jewish TaNaK: Judith, Tobit, Wisdom, Sirach, Baruch, and 1 and 2 Maccabees. These books were part of the Greek translation of the Jewish scriptures (made by Jews in about 200 B.C.E.) known as the Septuagint (commonly abbreviated as LXX). This was the Bible that the early Christians (mainly Greek-speaking Jews and Gentiles) used as their scriptures.

The order of the TaNaK as we said is Law, then Prophets, and finally Writings. For Jews the Prophets include the former prophets (what we would call the historical books: Joshua, Judges, 1 and 2 Samuel, 1 and 2 Kings, etc.) and the latter prophets (the biblical prophets: Isaiah, Jeremiah, Ezekiel, etc.). The Christian Old Testament is ordered differently. The Law is still first, but it is followed by the Historical Books (Jewish former prophets), then by the Wisdom Books (Jewish Writings), and concludes with the Prophetic Books (Jewish latter prophets). This order allows the Prophetic Books to be read as an introduction to the story of Jesus found in the gospels, the beginning of the New Testament. This leads us to the third point we noted earlier: that the Old Testament must be understood in a different context than the TaNaK. The Old Testament is arranged in such a way that it is meant to serve as a prelude to and prophecy for the fulfillment that comes in the story of Jesus. In that sense, the Old Testament is the testament of prophecy (old) that points to the testament of fulfillment (new). For Christians to refer to this section of their scriptures in this way is not to denigrate the Jewish scriptures but to receive them and make them their own. To call the scriptures of the Jews the Old Testament is both chauvinistic and incorrect.

Old Testament as Narrative

A remarkable feature of the Old Testament that is often overlooked by contemporary readers is that it is compiled as a story, and much of its contents are narratives. The overall text of the Old Testament begins with creation and then tells the story of God's people from Abraham to the time of the Maccabees. It then includes the prayers and wisdom of God's people and concludes with the words of the prophets. The prophets point ahead to the coming of the LORD. History, God working in time to form a people and accomplish salvation, is central to the Old Testament account. The Old Testament is not primarily laws or prophecies, but story/narrative/history. Narrative may be the best word to use. To say "story" implies fiction for many, and to say "history" implies modern scientific history. The Old Testament narrative is neither fiction nor history by modern standards. It is historical narrative. The implication then is that we should read the Bible with this in mind—not only the texts that are themselves narratives, but also the texts that are laws, hymns, oracles, or proverbs, which are set within the overarching context of the narrative of God's people.

World in front of the Text

How to Read the Old Testament

The Old Testament has its own context in the history of Israel and needs to be read within that context. To be good readers of the Old Testament we must know and understand as much about Judaism as possible. As Christians our Bible not only contains the scriptures of Judaism, but the Christian scriptures themselves are almost thoroughly Jewish in their origins and thought world. To Christianize the Old Testament and isolate it from its Jewish context is to do both the text and ourselves a great disservice.

The Old Testament also has a context within Christianity. It is the scriptures of Christians because it is understood to point to the saving mission of Jesus Christ. Therefore, the Old Testament should not be treated as if it is only a text of Judaism. It is correctly read as coming from Judaism but also as pointing to Christ. This is a delicate balancing act. All too often, the average Christian reader will read the Old Testament only within the context of its Christian fulfillment. And all too often scholars will read the Old Testament only within the context of it Jewish origins. To be faithful to both of its contexts the Old Testament must be read dynamically and historically. It has a history both in Judaism and in Christianity. It comes from one context and opens another context. It has a past, a present, and a future.

Learning Achievements

After studying this chapter students should be able to:

- Outline the history of Israel centered on the three pivotal events of Exodus, Kingship, and Exile.

- Describe the geography and climate of Israel, especially the four areas west to east: coast, central highland, rift valley, and Transjordan plateau.

- Discuss the Temple, its sacrifices, and the three major agricultural/historical feasts.

- Differentiate the order of the books in the Jewish Bible (TaNaK) from the order in the Christian Old Testament.

- Describe the Jewish heritage of Christianity.

Recommended Reading

Bimson, John. *The Compact Handbook of Old Testament Life.* Minneapolis: Bethany House, 1988.

Boadt, Lawrence. *Reading the Old Testament: An Introduction.* New York: Paulist, 1984.

Flanders, Henry Jackson, Robert Wilson Crapps, and David Anthony Smith. *People of the Covenant: An Introduction to the Hebrew Bible*, 4th ed. New York: Oxford University Press, 1996.

Chapter 3
PENTATEUCH

Introduction

World behind the Text

Sources of the Pentateuch

The first five books of the Bible are known as the Pentateuch, meaning five books, the name given those books by the Septuagint. These are the books referred to in the Hebrew Bible as the *Torah* (Law). One of the most important theories about the Bible was developed concerning these books. When scholars began to look at the Bible scientifically, they noticed, especially in the Pentateuch, contradictions, repetitions, and differing styles, which led them to question whether these books constituted a unified work written in its entirety by Moses, as was supposed. The theory, known as the Documentary Hypothesis of the Pentateuch, was put into its definitive form by Julius Wellhausen in 1885. (The hypothesis has been around for over one hundred years and with some adjustments is still generally considered to be a helpful explanation of the data.) Wellhausen theorized that the differences in style and content of the various stories resulted from the use of different documents or sources, which came from different places and times. One of the first clues that there were different sources for the Pentateuch was the name of God. In the book of Genesis, God is called "Yahweh" in some stories and "Elohim" in others. This led scholars to posit two sources: the Yahwist and the Elohist. The Yahwist source calls God "Yahweh" (the personal name of God from the four letters YHWH). The Elohist calls God "Elohim," the ordinary Hebrew word for any god. Two other sources were added based on characteristics of the text—names, grammar, style, themes, and worldview. These sources were the Deuteronomist and the Priestly writer.

In the past twenty years there has been increasing disillusionment with this hypothesis. At first scholars simply questioned whether the sources were actually written documents. The Elohist source especially came under attack. Out of these questions developed the Traditions Hypothesis, which held that there were numerous oral and written traditions that went into the making of the Pentateuch but not four separate written documents. The Traditions Hypothesis sees a long and organic process for the development of the Pentateuch. Although no serious scholar seeks to return to an understanding of Moses as the single author of the Pentateuch, more and more scholars are suggesting that the final form of the Pentateuch may have been put together by a single author who used both oral and written sources/traditions. This single author would have written this document late in the history of Israel, probably after the Exile.

What follows is a generally accepted summary of each of the traditions according to the Documentary Hypothesis. Even though there is not universal agreement on all the details, it is still worthwhile to learn the Documentary Hypothesis and the characteristics of its traditions as a starting point for further study. Because of this state of uncertainty in scholarship, recent introductions to the Old Testament often do not present the Documentary Hypothesis as four sources but as four traditions, keeping open the question of whether they were oral or written, fixed or developing. We will use the traditional designation of each as a source, keeping in mind that they may not have been written or fixed documents. Each of the sources is named for a hypothetical author (or authors). The name describes an identifying characteristic of that author. The Yahwist uses the name Yahweh for God from the beginning of the story; the Elohist uses the generic name for God, "Elohim," until the time of the Exodus; the Deuteronomist wrote the Book of Deuteronomy; and the Priestly writer is concerned about the ritual, laws, and cult of the priestly class.

Yahwist. Written in Jerusalem around 950 B.C.E., the Yahwist, or "J" source, contains the best-known stories of the Pentateuch—Adam and Eve, Cain and Abel, Noah, the Tower of

Babel. In this source God is called "Yahweh" right from the beginning of the Bible. In German "Yahweh" is written with a "J" (*Javeh*) and hence the use of "J" to symbolize the source. The NRSV (and many other English Bible translations) use the word LORD (in small caps) instead of writing out the name "Yahweh." This is done out of respect for Jewish readers whose veneration of the sacred name of God does not allow them to even write out these letters. The stories of the Yahwist source are psychologically insightful, often telling a story of sinfulness and human failing with little or no moral comment but rather presenting reality as it is. In contrast to this sinful human reality, the Yahwist describes a God who is constantly choosing persons to draw them into relationship—Abraham, Jacob, and Moses. Stylistically, the source is folkloric and anthropomorphic (God acts very much like a human person). Given that the source has its origins in the southern kingdom, it makes sense that a majority of its stories are about southern locations and persons. The source is concerned with the Davidic kingship, the Temple of Jerusalem, and the holy city of Jerusalem itself. Thus, the "J" can also be remembered as referring to Judah, the name of the southern kingdom.

Elohist. The Elohist, or "E" source, uses "Elohim" as the name by which the narrator and characters refer to God until the point in Exodus 3 when Elohim reveals the sacred name of "Yahweh" to Moses. Written in the northern kingdom of Israel in about 850 B.C.E., this source is northern in its outlook and theology. The main tribe of the northern kingdom was Ephraim, a name frequently used by the prophets to refer to the northern kingdom. So, although "E" refers to the Elohist, it can also refer to Ephraim and remind us of its northern connections. The tone and concerns of the source are reminiscent of the early prophets. It is moralistic, concerned with social justice, and puts emphasis on the time in the desert as the high point in Israel's relationship with God. It tends to be critical of the kingship. Again in contrast to the Yahwist's anthropomorphic portrayal of God, the Elohist is reluctant to portray God as in direct contact with humans. God will send angels or appear in dreams or visions. An important theme in the Elohist source is the "fear of God," which is the awe humans should feel before the terrible glory of God. The Elohist stories in the Pentateuch do not form a complete narrative, and there is question whether it ever was a complete northern narrative parallel to, and in competition with, the Yahwist source. More recently scholars have suggested that it may never have been a document on its own but was only a collection of northern stories that were added to the Yahwist source after the fall of the northern kingdom in 722 B.C.E.

To get a feel for the differences between the Yahwist and the Elohist sources one can simply compare the two stories of Abraham pretending that Sarah is his sister so that he is not killed. The Yahwist version of the story is found in Genesis 12:10–20 and tells of Abram and Sarai going to Egypt. Abram asks Sarai to lie and say that she is his sister. The Pharaoh is told about the beautiful Sarai and takes her into his palace as part of his harem. The story seems to presume that Sarai becomes part of Pharaoh's harem, presumably having sexual relations with him. The story tells us that on her account Abram received great wealth—flocks and herds, and slaves. So in the Yahwist version, Abram is portrayed as telling his wife to lie and getting rich from her becoming a part of the Pharaoh's harem. Abram is a liar and a pimp, and his wife is an adulteress. In the Elohist version, found in Genesis 20:1–18, Abimelech, the king of Gerar, takes Sarah. In a dream (notice this feature of the Elohist) God tells Abimelech that he is going to die for taking another man's wife. Abimelech replies that he took her thinking she was unmarried and has not yet slept with her. God replies that he has kept them from committing adultery. The Elohist version makes sure the reader does not think that the original matriarch of the chosen people had ever been involved in adultery. Abimelech then confronts Abraham about lying to him, and Abraham defends himself by saying that in fact Sarah is his half-sister. Here too the Elohist makes sure that we do not think that Abraham is a liar. Finally, Abimelech sends Abraham and Sarah on their way and only then gives the gifts of flocks and herds and slaves to him. The Elohist does not want the reader to think that Abraham received money for giving his wife to another man. These stories show one of the major differences between these two sources. The Yahwist presents human reality in all its failing and frailty. The Elohist presents a picture of Israel's ancestors as above reproach and gives the readers a clear moral commentary.

Deuteronomist. The "D" source, unlike the other three, is primarily confined to just one document (the Book of Deuteronomy), and as the last of the five books of the Pentateuch is not really part of the story line that goes from Genesis through Numbers. The only thing that Deuteronomy adds to the narrative is the story of the death of Moses and the succession of Joshua as leader of the people. The suggestion is that the Book of Deuteronomy (or at least its core chapters) was written by priests/prophets from the north who fled to the south at the time of the overthrow of the northern kingdom by Assyria in 722 B.C.E. These writers rewrote the laws found in Exodus as Moses' parting exhortation to his fellow Hebrews, a sort of last will and testament. The point of Deuteronomy is to have Moses remind the people of the covenant and all its requirements (the laws of Exodus) and exhort the people to obey these laws carefully lest God throw them out of the land that he is now giving to them. In the text, the sermons of Moses are given just before his death, as the people are about to enter Canaan under the leadership of Joshua. The actual message of Deuteronomy is meant for the people of the southern kingdom of Judah who are not obeying the covenant laws very diligently. The authors of Deuteronomy are convinced that the northern kingdom of Israel has been destroyed and its people taken into exile as a result of their disobedience of the laws of the covenant. To prevent this from happening to the southern kingdom, they exhort the people (through the mouth of Moses) to follow the law or lose the land. In 620 B.C.E. a book of the law is "discovered" in the Temple, and King Josiah begins a reform of Judah based on the reading and acceptance of this law. Most scholars consider this "book of the law" to be the core chapters of the Book of Deuteronomy.

Priestly Writer. The source known as the Priestly, or "P" source, is the last written (though much of it consists of older material), and its author is thought to be the editor of the whole of the Pentateuch. The source was probably written during the time of the Exile (about 550 B.C.E.). Some question whether the Priestly source was a separate written source that existed as an independent document before the editing of the four sources into one unit. The Priestly writer puts his story of creation first and makes it the introduction to the whole book. Many see the whole of the Pentateuch as organized around the idea of covenants— first with Adam, then Noah, then Abraham, and finally Moses— which is the work of the Priestly writer. The Priestly source is characterized by a stiff, orderly, and repetitive style. This writer is concerned with measurements, genealogies, numbers, and years. The writer is also concerned with purity, laws, and rituals. The source is written during the Exile when everything valued by the people of Judah has collapsed: the Temple is destroyed, the king is in prison, and the people are exiled from their land. The Priestly writer has several important messages for the people in this situation. First, the author describes a world that is orderly, good, and under the complete control of Yahweh. Given that the world has spun out of control and the people of Judah are now under the power of the Babylonians and the Babylonian god, Marduk, this message is timely. Second, the writer describes a way of life that emphasizes the rituals and purity of ordinary, daily life. The writer describes a holiness that can be performed in exile: marriage laws, food laws, personal hygiene laws, and Sabbath observance. The writer gives a law that is not dependent on the nation, the king, the Temple, or being in the land. The Priestly source is a reinterpretation of the law for the time of the Exile. Third, there is a message of hope that the people will return to the land. The Exile is seen as punishment for sin; and if the people return to observance of the law, they will be able to return to the land. The Priestly writer spends a good bit of time describing the characteristics of the perfect Temple and worship for the day when the people will return, with the hope that this time they will be careful to observe all of the law.

From this brief overview, we can see that the style, message, theology, and images of each of the different sources are related to the time, place, and circumstances in which it was written. The biblical text is historically conditioned. This is the great insight of the historical critical method. It helps us to understand the meaning of a text in the context of its original historical situation. So when we read a narrative in Genesis or a law in Exodus, we need

Documentary Hypothesis		
Source	**Date**	**Place**
Yahwist	950 B.C.E.	Southern kingdom, Jerusalem
Elohist	850 B.C.E.	Northern kingdom
Deuteronomist	650 B.C.E.	Northern traditions, finished in south
Priestly Writer	550 B.C.E.	Babylonia

to look at which source it comes from to help us interpret its meaning and understand its significance. A law about purity that comes from the Priestly writer should be read keeping in mind the importance of purity regulations for the Jewish community living in exile. A law about the treatment of slaves that comes from the Elohist source should be read against the background of the successful, rich, and oppressive culture of the northern kingdom, which is being criticized by the prophetic, moralistic writers of the Elohist source. To read the text apart from any of these considerations is to do a disservice to the text as the word of God originally given for a particular historical situation.

World of the Text

The Story of the Pentateuch

The Pentateuch contains material from different sources and in different genres, but it is unified by an overall narrative structure. It is helpful for the reader to know the basics of this narrative when reading any of the sections of the Pentateuch. The story of the Pentateuch begins with God creating the world and then the first human couple. This first couple disobeys a command of God and is exiled from paradise, although—in keeping with the blessing of God—they propagate. Evil also multiplies on the earth, and God decides to wipe out humankind. Noah, having found favor with God, is rescued from the flood that destroys the rest of life and begins to repopulate the earth. Again, the earth is filled with sin as the people of the earth seek to build a tower to heaven. At this point God again chooses an individual couple, Abraham and

Sarah, and makes a special covenant with them promising to make them a great nation and give them the land of Canaan as their home. The narrative now focuses on this family. The blessing of fertility becomes a major concern because many of the stories about this family have to do with difficulties in bearing offspring to carry on the covenant. The narrative tells the stories of Abraham and Sarah, Isaac and Rebekah, Jacob and Rachel and Leah, and then Joseph and his brothers. Although the stories of Jacob and his wives begin with issues of barrenness, by the end the family has become quite large (Jacob has twelve sons). The stories of Joseph (Jacob's second-to-youngest son) end with all of Jacob's sons joining Joseph (who has become vizier to the pharaoh) in Egypt. The Book of Genesis ends with the death of Jacob.

The Book of Exodus takes up the story many years later when the descendants of Jacob have multiplied greatly and have encountered problems in Egypt. The present pharaoh, who does not remember Joseph, oppresses the Hebrews and orders the murder of Hebrew boys. The first chapters of Exodus tell the story of the birth of Moses, his killing an Egyptian, and his fleeing to the desert where he is married. While in the desert he receives a call from God and returns to Egypt to lead his people to freedom. A struggle of wills ensues, with the plagues being God's punishment on Egypt for pharaoh's unwillingness to let the Hebrews leave. Finally the Hebrews are allowed to leave, but the pharaoh soon changes his mind and chases after. The Hebrews' escape is accomplished by their crossing of the Red Sea on dry land and pharaoh's army being destroyed by the sea's return. In Exodus 19 the Hebrews arrive at Mount Sinai, where Moses receives the law. The rest of Exodus consists of the laws given on Mount Sinai. The narrative introduction to the Book of Leviticus indicates that the collection of laws that makes up that book are being given to the Hebrews while they are still at Mount Sinai. The first ten chapters of Numbers, which deal with rules for the priesthood, continue the laws and instruction that the Hebrews receive at Mount Sinai.

In chapter 10 of Numbers, the Hebrews leave Mount Sinai and begin a forty-year journey in the desert. The story of this journey is a story of rebellions against Moses' authority, complaining on the part of the people, and attempts by those they encounter to destroy them or impede their progress. The Book of Numbers ends with the Hebrews in Moab across the Jordan River from Jericho. Each of the twelve tribes and each of the clans of those tribes is assigned an inheritance in the land. The Book of Deuteronomy takes place in this same location. It is introduced as the last speech of Moses before he dies. He reminds the people that the land they are about to enter is a gift from God and that if they are not faithful to the covenant they have made with God, God will drive them out of the land. The final chapter of the Book of Deuteronomy recounts the death and burial of Moses.

We can see that the macro narrative of the Pentateuch is the story of a journey beginning with Abraham being called out of Haran and ending with his descendants poised to cross the Jordan into the land that God had promised to Abraham long ago. It is a journey from Canaan to Egypt and back again.

The Three Kinds of Literature in the Pentateuch

The theory of the four sources of the Pentateuch is a theory that has to do with the historical background of the text. Now we will examine the text itself and see that there are three divisions in the Pentateuch that are based first on narrative type as well as chronology.

Mythical Prehistory. The first eleven chapters of Genesis are considered a literary unit. This narrative begins with the creation and continues up to the time of the call of Abraham (which is the beginning of the "history"). These chapters are in the genre of *myth.* For many Americans, the word *myth* has come to mean a fictional story that contains elements of the supernatural or the unreal. It is essentially a fairy tale. The way the word is used in biblical scholarship and world religions is quite different and so requires some discussion before we continue. A myth is a story developed by a group over a long period of time that tells a universal truth in a symbolic way. The word *myth*, as used of the Bible and of other religious literature, points not to its untruth but to its universal significance. Because a myth is meant to be universal, it will not have the same kind of one-on-one historical referent as a news story in the Sunday paper. The Sunday paper will tell us that Bill Smith murdered David Jones. The Bible will tell us that Cain killed his brother Abel. The first story is meant to inform us of an actual historical fact with each of the details correct and corresponding to a particular historical person, place, and time. The time of the murder was 10:43 P.M. EST, the weapon was a 32-caliber pistol, the place was the kitchen in the home of the victim located at 925 Maple Street. The second story is meant to inform us of the character of human rivalry, jealously, and the consequences of the rejection of God. To be concerned with the details of this story (What weapon did Cain use? What time of day was it? Did Abel die quickly or did he linger? How did Eve feel when she found out that her younger son was murdered by her elder son?) is to miss the point of the story. The questions that we should ask of the second story are about its universal meaning. What does this story tell us about human rivalry, jealously, and anger? What does this story tell us about ways to avoid these?

Myths are archetypal. They are about everyman, and not about a particular person. For instance, the first character (after God) we meet in the Bible is a human called Adam. Because this is a common personal name in the United States, we might think of an individual named Adam. However, in Hebrew the word *adam* means human. It would be as if you were to read a modern story whose main character was named "Human." You would probably recognize right away that this story is not meant to be about an individual (fictional or factual) but is about an archetypal person. (One of the great works of medieval theater is a play whose title character has the name "Everyman.") A universal person is not meant to have unique and personal characteristics. So it is with the stories of Adam and Eve, Cain and Abel, and Noah. These stories are mythical and archetypal. They are not untrue; rather, their truth is of a different kind than the truth we find in the stories about David in 1 and 2 Samuel, or the stories about Paul in the Acts of the Apostles. The stories about David or Paul are meant to help us come to understand the important contributions a particular individual has made and how God has led this particular individual. The myths of Genesis are not interested in our appreciation of the unique and individual contributions of a particular person. They are interested in making us aware of the nature of all humanity and the way God has chosen to deal with humanity. The defining character of this narrative is Adam who represents all of humanity. Even Noah is presented as a new Adam, beginning God's relationship with humanity again. The focus of the text is on the general relationship of God to humans, which is being destroyed by human sinfulness.

Ancestral History. Beginning with the call of Abraham in chapter 12 and running through the end of Genesis is a literary unit referred to as the *ancestral history*. This section tells the stories of the patriarchs and matriarchs of Israel, the ancestors of the tribes that eventually become the nation of Israel. The narrative tells of Abraham, his son Isaac, and Isaac's two sons Esau and Jacob. Jacob is the one chosen by God to carry on the role of the ancestor. Jacob has twelve sons, each of whom is the father of one of the twelve tribes that become the nation of Israel. One of the twelve is Joseph, who becomes the focus of the end of the story. He is sold into slavery in Egypt, rises to power under the pharaoh, and brings all his brothers and his father to live in Egypt. This last story describes how all of Israel ends up in Egypt, where they will still be years later when the story of Exodus begins. The defining character of this section could be identified as Abraham (but includes all his heirs), and the focus of the text is the special relationship God has with Abraham and the promise God gives to him to make his offspring a great nation. As the promise is passed down from generation to generation, each of the heirs shares in the promise of God. The ancestral narratives also have their own unique type of literature. The stories are probably amalgamations of many stories about many different ancestors reduced to paradigmatic stories about these four generations of ancestors. Often the stories explain how place names, relationships with other nations, and tribal characteristics/roles came to be.

Exodus and the Law. The story resumes many years after the death of Joseph in the land of Egypt with the Hebrews (the descendants of Jacob whose other name is Israel) greatly multiplied and bound in slavery for forced labor in Egypt. (It is customary to call this people the Hebrews. Once they form the nation of Israel, they will be known as Israelites. Later, when the nation is destroyed and the people are in exile, some to return to Judea and some to remain scattered throughout the Near East, the name Jews is used to identify them as having come from the territory of Judea.) This part of the story, consisting of Exodus through Deuteronomy, also has a narrative framework, which begins with the birth of Moses and continues until Moses' death east of the Jordan as the Hebrews are about to enter into and conquer Canaan, the Promised Land. The story tells of Moses' call, his negotiations with pharaoh for the release of the Hebrews from slavery, the Exodus itself (the miraculous crossing of the Red Sea and the destruction of the Egyptian army), the giving of the law on Mount Sinai, the wandering in the desert, and the scouting of Canaan. Although the narrative framework encompasses all of the material from the birth of Moses in Egypt to his death at the Jordan River (Exodus to Deuteronomy), the bulk of the material describes the giving of the law (first at Mount Sinai and then at the edge of the Jordan). Nearly one half of this material is, therefore, not narrative but law. The defining character in this material is Moses, and the focus of the text is on the law that God gave his people through Moses.

Narrative Criticism

One of the biggest advances in Old Testament study in the last twenty years has been in the use of narrative criticism. It was traditional to approach the narratives in the Pentateuch or in the Historical Books with the lens of history and ask what in the story matched known historical data, or with the lens of theology and ask what theological message the story was intended to convey. It is now much more common for scholars to approach the text looking at the rhetorical techniques of narrative. Scholars examine how the narrative uses foreshadowing, summary, gaps, irony, misdirection, and humor to lead the hearer/reader to an experience of the text. The previous methods were one-dimensional. The narrative contained facts or fictions. It made this or that theological point. Narrative criticism allows the student of the Bible to appreciate the dynamic interaction between the text and the hearer/reader, an interaction that is rich and multidimensional. The hearer/reader may learn about history or theology but will also be engaged in a process of questioning, evaluating, guessing, deciding, objecting, and accepting as the narrative progresses. It is this process that is much more to the heart of the "meaning" of the Old Testament than a mere knowledge of history or theology.

World in front of the Text

The Law as the Expression of Hebrew Faith

Because of the way that Christians have interpreted the words and life of Jesus and the writings of Paul, it has been typical to characterize Judaism as a religion based on law and therefore meticulous, narrow, and judgmental. It is important for Christian readers to appreciate that the Law is not just a dry collection of legal prescriptions but is primarily a story of God's love for creation. God constantly seeks to overcome the sinfulness of the world by greater and greater love. God focuses attention on Abraham, not to the exclusion of the world, but as a way to bring blessing and knowledge of God to the world. The Law is summarized in the Book of Deuteronomy, which most eloquently expresses the Jewish understanding of Law as covenant commitment. It is God's love for God's people that motivates the covenant, and what God wants in return is love, not just slavish obedience to law. The *Shema*, which is said twice a day by observant Jews, is taken from Deuteronomy 6:4: "Hear, O Israel: The LORD is our God, the LORD alone." This profound statement is less a declaration of monotheism than a statement that Israel is committing itself to letting nothing else be God for them. The conclusion that follows from this in verse 5 is that "You shall love the LORD your God with all your heart, and with all your soul, and with all your might." Jesus used this as the summary of the law. The insight that the law is essentially about love was not an invention of Jesus or of John the Evangelist but is at the heart of the story of the Pentateuch.

Mythical Prehistory

GENESIS 2—3

World behind the Text

Yahwist Source

Genesis 2—3 is from the Yahwist source. (Remember that many translations use LORD instead of the Hebrew, Yahweh, out of respect for Jewish readers.) Many scholars see in the story of Adam and Eve a reflection of issues from the time of the united monarchy. The conflict with the serpent would reflect the conflict with the Canaanite fertility religions. The naming of the animals presents Adam as a kinglike figure on the earth. Acquiring knowledge of good and evil reflects the power and authority of the monarchy, especially in the areas of law and worship. Finally, the wisdom that comes from the trees reflects the wisdom tradition attributed to Solomon.

Women, Creation, and the Ancient World

Although Genesis 1 seems to present a fairly modern view of creation that does not distinguish men and women, Genesis 2–3 has often been the weapon of misogynists and the target of feminists. To appreciate what is being said in the world behind the text, we must understand the place of women in the ancient world. A common view in the ancient world was that the first humans created were men; and later, the gods created women to weaken the power of men. They were created as seductresses who could lead men astray. In that cultural context, this story's calling the woman a helper and the use of the full human material (Adam's rib) to create the woman is a major step forward.

The tree of the knowledge of good and evil and the tree of life were important images in the ancient world. Trees were frequent symbols for a royal dynasty and could represent the cyclical regeneration of nature. Often a special tree held a gift of life, wealth, knowledge, or fertility. If a person could find the tree and pick its fruit, that person (or all humanity) would obtain this possession.

The snake is also an important symbol in this story, and its background must be properly understood. First, most Christians read the snake as the devil, although the idea of the devil as it came to be understood later in Christianity, was not in existence at that time. When Genesis 2—3 was written (about 950 B.C.E.) there was no personification of evil that was nearly the equal to God and opposed to God in every way. Other gods existed (full monotheism did not develop until the time of the Exile), and some of them may have tried to work against Yahweh. There was also a character known as the Satan. The word means adversary. The Satan was a heavenly being in the court of God whose job it was to play "devil's advocate" in the heavenly court. In the story of Genesis, however, the snake is just a snake and not the Satan, nor another god, nor the devil in disguise, although the snake does symbolize some of the concerns of the ancient Israelites. The snake is identified as more crafty than any other animal. The craftiness of the snake seems to consist in how he manipulates the woman with lies and shows the woman how humans can gain wisdom to become gods themselves. In the ancient Near East, especially in Canaan, there was a proliferation of fertility deities. Knowing how to manipulate the gods through fertility rites was a great wisdom that gave humans power. The snake has traditionally been seen as a symbol of fertility and eternity. The snake biting its tail is a symbol of eternity. The snake sheds its skin, is seemingly reborn, and never seems to die, making it a symbol of fertility and regeneration. Because of this, the snake probably symbolized aspects of the fertility religions for the first audiences of this text.

World of the Text

Two's Company

There is no structure to the story of creation and fall in Genesis 2—3 that is comparable to that in chapter 1; yet if we pay close attention to certain literary characteristics in the text, we can see a rhetorical style that offers us a means to approach the text. Notice how the text describes everything in pairs. Although this could just be characteristic of oral literature (as it is characteristic of Hebrew poetry), it creates a harmony of twos. Everything is balanced and dual. "In the day that the LORD God made the *earth* and the *heavens,* when no *plant* of the field was yet in the earth and no *herb* of the field had yet sprung up—for the LORD God had not *caused it to rain* upon the earth, and there was no *one to till* the ground; but a stream would rise from the earth, and water the whole face of the ground—then the LORD God formed man from *the dust of the ground,* and breathed into his nostrils *the breath of life*" (italics added) [Gen 2:4–7]. "Out of the ground the LORD God made to grow every tree that is *pleasant to the sight* and *good for food,* the *tree of life* also in the midst of the garden, and the *tree of the knowledge of good and evil*" (italics added) [2:9]. The four rivers converging on this place create in a sense the diagram for this story (2:10–14). The Human being is defined by the convergence of two axes.

God's Breath

(gift and restriction)

|

Man — Human — Woman

|

Dust of Ground

(beauty and food)

In the vertical axis, the Human is made out of the ground and of God's breath of life. There is a word play between the human *(adam)* and the ground *(adama).* The trees of the garden represent the human relationship to the ground. They are pleasant to the sight and good for food. The human relationship to the ground is one of sustenance (food) and estheticism (beauty). Then God gives the human a command that establishes a relationship between God and Human. "You may freely eat of every tree of the garden; but of the tree of the knowledge of good and evil you shall not eat" (2:16–17). Again, we find a harmonious balance of twos. God gives all the trees of the garden as a gift to the human for food, but the tree of knowledge God restricts to humans. The human relationship to God is characterized by the gift of God balanced with the restrictions placed on that gift. When God says that it is not good for the human to be alone (one), the narrative moves to the horizontal axis. Human must be a pair. God creates woman, and then human is man and woman. So, we can clearly see the two axes. The human is the center of the vertical axis as made up of ground and God's breath. The human is also the center of the horizontal axis as not single but a couple. So, chapter 2 is a structured diagram of what it means to be human. Humans are created to be in harmony with the ground and with God. The relationship to the ground is a balance of enjoyment of beauty and practical sustenance. The relationship with God is a balance of grateful acceptance of the gift of the earth and faithful obedience to the restrictions put on that gift. On the horizontal axis, humans are seen as belonging in community. It is not good that the human should be alone. The importance of this horizontal axis is emphasized by a change in style. When the man and the woman are joined and two become one, the text breaks into poetry. The harmonious union of two humans, man and wife, is the object of such delight and amazement that the only possible way to describe it is in poetry.

This analysis shows how the structural and rhetorical features of a text can lead us to discover possible meanings and interpretations. This kind of close reading of the text reveals the poverty of a literal reading of the text that sees the story simply as a literal account of what God did at creation. In contrast, our reading is able to discover a richer, more profound, and insightful meaning in the text.

Three's a Crowd

Chapter 2 ends with the statement that the man and woman were naked but were not ashamed. We will see how this is an introduction to the next chapter, which not only has the same setting and characters but also describes a human choice that brings shame as a consequence. The first verse of chapter 3 introduces the trouble: "Now the serpent was more crafty than any other wild animal that the LORD God had made." Once we have seen the perfect harmony that exists between the two humans bound together as one, we might be able to infer that the introduction of a third actor will cause disharmony—and so it does. Notice what the serpent says to the woman. (It should be noted that in a rhetorical reading such as this, the woman is not chosen because she is weak and gullible, but because of what she represents in the story. Before the creation of the woman, Human was alone. The woman does not represent the female gender as much as she represents human nature as bipolar [male and female] and human nature as needing to be in community, especially the community of two [male and female] becoming one and giving birth to more humans.) The serpent asks the woman whether God said that they could not eat from any of the trees of the garden. Reading from our structural rhetoric, we can see what the serpent is actually suggesting. The command of God was a harmonious balance of gift and restriction. By suggesting that God's command was only restriction, the serpent makes the command oppressive and God an ogre. The whole point of the relationship with God is one of balance. The whole reason for the restriction is the gift. Without the gift, the restriction is arbitrary and cruel. The serpent, just by being a third party, ruins the harmony; but his words seek even more to destroy the harmonious balance in the human relationship to God as portrayed in chapter 2.

The woman's answer, although correcting the serpent, still does not accurately repeat God's words. (It is not appropriate to wonder how the woman would know what God had said given that she was not created yet. The words of God were spoken to Human, and the woman is just as much Human as is the man.) The woman adds the words, "nor shall you touch it," to God's command (see Gen 3:3). Although this may seem like a small and irrelevant addition on the part of the woman, in a rhetorical reading such as this it is very significant. When someone's words are repeated verbatim, any change (no matter how small) is a clue to meaning. The woman has started on the path of expanding the restrictions of God so that they seem oppressive and harmful.

The serpent takes up the words of God that if you eat of the tree you will die, and suggests that not only will the couple not die but, instead, become as gods who know good and evil. The implication is that God is restricting the human diet to keep them from having knowledge that would make them godlike. The serpent is clearly developing the theme of his first question (God is a restrictive and oppressive ogre) and playing off the woman's own expansion of the restriction of God. With this new information, the woman now begins to see things differently, and the harmony of chapter 2 begins to unravel. The woman sees that the tree is good for food, pleasing to the eyes, and desirable for gaining wisdom. The dual and harmonious purpose of the trees in chapter 2 now has become threefold and destructive of harmony with the introduction of the tree as the object of desire for the gaining of wisdom. Desire is the opposite of the acceptance of gift and the obedience of restriction. Desire demands for itself. Wisdom in this story seems to be equivalent to the knowledge of good and evil. The woman wants the power of wisdom to become like God.

Over the course of history, the woman has been blamed for the fall of humanity because of this story. However, if we look at the story closely as narrative, we can see that the woman is the one addressed by the serpent and the one who responds simply because she represents humanity as community. From the rest of the stories in Genesis 1—11, it is clear that sin and revolt against God happen in community. Part of the curse of human society is its desire to become its own god. Human community creates wisdom, knowledge, power, violence, and so forth. Also, when the woman takes the fruit, the text says, "she took of its fruit and ate; and she also gave some to her husband, who was with her, and he ate" (3:6). This could simply mean that he was in the garden with her (which is obvious), although it is more likely that the author wants us to understand that the man was at the side of the woman through the whole dialogue with the serpent. Human, as man and woman, makes the decision to eat the forbidden fruit. The woman is not being portrayed as a temptress.

The humans' eyes are opened, and they realize they are naked. Now that they have chosen the way of desire, they experience shame. The sexual imagery here is used as a metaphor for all desire and shame. Humans now desire knowledge, wisdom, possessions, power, and pleasure. Because of desire, they also know shame. They recognize the inordinate and destructive nature of their desire, which separates them from each other and from God and causes them to hide. Perfect examples of their shame are their separation from each other by sewing fig leaves to cover their loins and their separation from God by hiding in the garden.

The result of this move to desire is the destruction of the harmony that was created in chapter 2. When God questions the man about eating the fruit, the man blames both God and the woman: "The woman whom you gave to be with me, she gave me fruit from the tree, and I ate" (3:12). It is clear that the harmonious relationships between human and God and among humans in community have been destroyed. (Again I want to emphasize that God speaks to the man, not because he is in charge and more important than the woman, but because the man represents the human relationship with God in this story, whereas the woman represents the human relationship in community. Both man and woman are in relationship with God and able to be in conversation with God, and both man and woman are in human community and able to be led astray by the serpent.)

When God announces the consequences of the humans' action, the destruction of the harmony in chapter 2 becomes even more apparent. The woman, who represents human community, will suffer two consequences. She will suffer pain in childbirth (creating more human community) and her husband will be her master. Both of these consequences destroy the perfect horizontal harmony established for human community in chapter 2. The beautiful poetry of two becoming one flesh in chapter 2 has been marred and distorted. Now one person is master over the other, and terrible pain is involved in giving birth to the life that the two create together. The consequences for the man are related to the vertical human relationship to the earth. (Remember that the name Adam contains a word play in Hebrew with the ground from which human is created.) The ground (*adama*) is now cursed because of the man (*adam*), and the man must die and return to the ground from which he was taken. By striving to become more than what they are (trying to become gods), the humans end up losing the fragile harmony that comes from their origins (ground and God) and must return to the physical element from which they are composed (ground). Genesis 2—3 is a well-organized narrative that leads the reader to understand the perfect harmony of God's creation and the terrible destruction of that harmony that comes about by human choice.

> The narrative structure of the text is a means by which we as readers can come to understand the meaning of the text.

World in front of the Text

Sin or Growth?

Contemporary interpretations of this text are most often concerned with two issues: the gender implications of the role of the woman in the story or the theological implications of the role of sin and guilt. The interpretation based on myth that we have given here shows that the woman is not secondary to the man nor is she responsible for the original sin. My reading of the text does not have negative implications for women.

However, the reading I have given still interprets the actions of the humans as disobedience, a sin, and a "fall." Some scholars view this kind of interpretation as contributing to a harmful view of human nature. They interpret the action of the humans as a necessary step in the process of growing up. God does not punish the humans but only articulates what, as adults, they have learned—that the world is filled with good and evil, birth and pain, food and weeds, life and death. They are sent out of the garden, not because they have sinned, but because they have become adults and no longer need the nurturing protection of the garden. The value of this reading is that it promotes a positive view of human nature instead of a guilt-ridden and destructive view. However, I am not convinced that the story itself supports this interpretation. The story contains a negative evaluation of the choice that the humans make. The results of the action of the humans are described as curses. The serpent, instead of being a helper in the process of human maturation, is cursed as an enemy of humankind. Finally, the structure of the text as we described it points to the third element (the serpent and wisdom) as ruining the harmony of the garden situation.

Humans in Relationship

Instead of focusing on the themes of sin and guilt, I propose that modern readers focus on the relationships that describe what it means to be human. To be human is to be in relationship to God, to the earth, and to other humans. It is especially significant that all three of these relationships are interdependent. When one's relationship with God is damaged so is one's relationship to the earth and to other humans. A modern reading of this text might suggest that our relationship to the earth is damaged and is related to our marred and distorted view of God and relationship with God. Similarly, our damaged (and damaging) relationship with other humans affects and is affected by our relationships with God and with the earth. An emphasis on maintaining my personal relationship with God without regard to my relationship to the earth and to the human community is fruitless and destructive.

Ancestral Narratives

INTRODUCTION

World behind the Text

Historical Ancestors

The dating that is obtained from the Bible for the move of Jacob's family to Egypt is 1870 B.C.E. Generally, scholars are willing to accept the dating that is found in the Bible unless there is reason to reject it. The migration of Abraham from Haran in Mesopotamia to Canaan corresponds with migrations from the beginning of the second millennium B.C.E. The migration of Jacob and his family into Egypt corresponds with migrations of that time and corresponds to the time when the Hyksos (a Semitic people) were in control of Egypt. The description of Abraham and his descendants as being nomadic peoples corresponds with what we know of many of the peoples at this time, although the dating cannot be at all exact because there were migrations of nomadic peoples in earlier and later times. It is generally accepted that the stories in Genesis do not represent any kind of accurate history. If they were written down in about 1000, as scholars suppose, these stories would have gone through an eight hundred–year oral gestation process. Although oral stories fared far better in ancient cultures than any modern person could imagine, it is still beyond credibility to believe that an eight hundred–year-old story could be historically accurate by modern standards. What scholars do attribute to these stories is historical verisimilitude. They are not history in the strictest sense, but the stories do reflect the general nature of the times in which they are set.

World of the Text

Folktales and Novellas

The ancestral narratives have many characteristics of folktales or hero legends. They are self-contained stories that can be read separately. The ancestor hero of the story is usually symbolic of national or tribal fortunes. They use many standard formulas and literary motifs that are common to folktales, most notably etiologies (stories that tell the origins of place names, or traditions).

The Joseph stories are different from the rest of the ancestral narratives. As a unified group of stories with a sustained plot, they are more like a short story. There are a number of stories like the Joseph story in the Old Testament (Tobit and Esther are of this type). They are often called novellas. They have a sustained plot, which usually involves a reversal of fortune. God is not usually central to the plot of these stories.

World in Front of the Text

Matriarchs as Well as Patriarchs

One of the areas for study of the ancestral narratives in recent years has been feminist analysis of the matriarchs. The role of the matriarchs in Genesis is much greater than has traditionally been understood. Their stories offer much in the areas of family rearing, marriage, suffering, and power for modern readers to reflect on.

JACOB AND ESAU (GENESIS 27)

World behind the Text

Nomadic Shepherds versus Hunter Gatherers; Israelites versus Edomites

Defining the source of this story is more difficult than with the stories of creation. Although this story has often been attributed to the Yahwist source, that is no longer certain. We can speak of at least three levels for the genesis of this story. At the first level, the story is a folktale that pits the trickster shepherd against the dull hunter. The hunter is described as ruddy, hairy, smelling of the earth, and not too bright; but as the eldest son, he is his father's favorite. The shepherd is pictured as staying at home, fed and pampered by his mother. The shepherd extorts the hunter's birthright from him in exchange for some food. Later, with the help of his mother, the shepherd deceives his father into giving him the hunter's blessing as the eldest and the heir. In its most ancient roots, this story was a wonderfully comic tale of how the seemingly weaker and less masculine shepherd outwitted the powerful and masculine hunter by intelligence and craftiness. This kind of story may have had it roots in a time when there were tensions between the older hunter-gatherer societies and the newer shepherding societies.

At a second level, this stock folktale about a clever shepherd was taken over as a story of Israel's eponymous ancestor, Jacob.

Often the Jacob stories are associated with the northern tribes and northern locations. At a third level the story shows characteristics of being from the Yahwist source, and so we can find in it resonances of issues from the time of David and Solomon. At the time of the Yahwist source, tensions between hunters and shepherds no longer exist. Now the focus of the story is on the nations of Edom and Israel. The hunter and elder son, Esau, is described in Genesis 25:25 as reddish and hairy. In Hebrew, the word *Edom* comes from the word for red and the word *Seir* is similar to the word for being hairy. Seir and Edom were both names for the nation of Edom, which lay just to the east of Israel. The name Esau is also a word for hairy. The Yahwist writer is clearly taking a story about Jacob and Esau and making it fit a new issue by using a play on words. Because Esau and Seir both mean hairy, there must be a connection between the person Esau and the nation called Seir. To make the connection even more explicit Esau is described as "red man," playing on the word Edom. The Yahwist leaves no doubt that we should read Esau as representing the nation of Edom. Jacob is known as the father of the twelve tribes of Israel, but he is explicitly given the name "Israel" in a later story (Gen 32:28). It is clear that at this level the story is about a conflict between the nations of Edom and Israel, with Israel gaining power over Edom.

Younger Sons and God's Favor

Another aspect of the story that may reflect the context of the Yahwist writer is the theme of the younger brother. The story of David in 1 Samuel 16 makes much of the fact that David is the youngest of Jesse's sons. In fact, he has seven older brothers, none of which God chooses for Samuel to anoint as king over Israel. God chooses to favor whomever he wants, and that is often the younger or weaker. Similarly, Solomon is not the eldest of David's surviving sons, but is the one who is chosen (by David and by God) to succeed. Although we can see in this a great theological insight about God's freedom and power as opposed to human vanity, there is also a contemporary political benefit to such a story. Jacob, the clever younger son chosen by God, is the type for

David, the clever usurper of the throne of Saul and the youngest of many brothers. However, it should be noted that scholars are not eager to place this story in the context of the Yahwist writer because of the uncertainty of its being part of that source.

Blessings

This story revolves around a blessing that Isaac plans to give to his oldest son, Esau. Blessings are important in the theology of the Old Testament. First, they reflect an understanding of the power of the spoken word that is foreign to us. The spoken word is a real and effective thing. When Isaac blesses Jacob instead of Esau, he gives to him a real thing of power that establishes Jacob's role in the family. When one speaks a blessing (or a curse) it takes on an existence of its own and will do its own work, despite the fact that the speaker may have been mistaken or may change his/her mind. Esau asks whether Isaac has saved some blessing for him, but Isaac replies that it has gone to Jacob and cannot be reversed (27:37). There is no undoing a blessing that has been spoken. Second, blessings in the Old Testament reflect an understanding of a relationship with God. God's relationship with Israel is always one of particular choice. Blessings are not earned but given. God has chosen the nation and individuals and given them blessings to accomplish their tasks. When God blesses Abraham, God's power works to bring about the blessings on his descendants. The blessing that Isaac passes on to Jacob is the blessing that God gave to Abraham: abundant offspring, agricultural success, and political power. However, we will also see that the blessing as a choice made by God for the nation and the individual is what we might also call "a mixed blessing." Being chosen by God brings with it uprooting, conflict, and insecurity.

World of the Text

The Jacob Cycle

The story that we are studying here is the first of a series of stories about Jacob that continues through chapter 35. These stories are arranged in a concentric structure as follows:

A Jacob and Esau—Jacob cheats Esau out of birthright and blessing

  B Jacob and God—Dream of Jacob's ladder at Bethel

    C Jacob and Laban—Jacob is tricked by Laban into marrying Leah before Rachel

      D Births of Jacob's offspring

    C' Jacob and Laban—Jacob tricks Laban by getting all the black and spotted sheep

  B' Jacob and God—Jacob wrestles with the angel of God at Peniel

A' Jacob and Esau—Jacob meets Esau, gives him gifts, and reconciles

The cycle of stories focuses primarily on God's choice of Jacob to be the one to receive the blessing, although receiving the blessing for Jacob brings with it conflict—with his brother and with his uncle. Finally, the whole point of the blessing is fertility and the right to pass on God's promise to the next generation. The story at the center of this series concerns barrenness and offspring, and culminates with the birth of the chosen son by the chosen spouse—the birth of Joseph to Rachel (Gen 30:22–24).

Who Will Inherit the Blessing of Abraham?

The story we have chosen for study is the first in this series of stories and focuses on Jacob's obtaining the blessing of his father that will put into effect God's choice of Jacob that has already been made (25:23). The theme of this chapter is the blessing of Isaac to be bestowed on the son who will carry on the family name and inherit the promise. The stories of the ancestral narratives are about the lineage of Abraham and the promise God made to that lineage. The first story about Abraham in Genesis 12 is God's call to Abraham to leave his father's house and travel to Canaan. God promises Abraham that he will make him a great nation and will bless him. The narrative then becomes concerned with offspring and the passing on of the blessing. Will Abraham have a son? Will the son be by his wife or his concubine? When his son, Isaac, is born to his wife, Sarah, then the question becomes whom will Isaac marry so that the lineage is passed down correctly (Abraham does not want Isaac to marry a Canaanite woman)? Isaac marries Rebekah, who is the daughter of Abraham's nephew. The lineage is intact, but Rebekah, like Sarah, is barren. Again God intervenes, but this time there is not one son but two to inherit the blessing. Although on one level this is a story of the trickster Jacob stealing the blessing meant for his brother, on a deeper level it is about passing on the promise of God for the creation of a great nation. By receiving the blessing of his father, Jacob becomes the one to whom the lineage and the promise of God is passed on. At the end of this story Jacob is sent away, both to escape any reprisals by Esau but also to obtain a wife from his own kinsmen. Jacob will go and obtain as his wives the two daughters of Laban, Rebekah's brother.

> Our analysis shows how this story fits into the larger narrative and its overarching concerns for offspring to inherit the promise.

The Structure of the Story and the Role of Rebekah

This story can be outlined in the following way:

A Isaac and Esau—preparing to bless the eldest
  B Rebekah and Jacob—sending Jacob to obtain the blessing by deception
    C Jacob and Isaac—receiving the blessing by deception
A' Isaac and Esau—no blessing for the eldest
  B' Rebekah, Jacob, and Isaac—sending Jacob away to marry
    C' Jacob and Isaac—blessing and promise of the land (the beginning of chapter 28)

Interestingly Rebekah is the instigator of the important action in this story. Her role is contrasted with Isaac's foiled attempt to bless his oldest son, with Esau's failed attempt to retrieve the blessing already given, and with Esau's meaningless attempt to marry a woman of his own lineage. Rebekah is the one who hears of Isaac's plan to bless Esau. Rebekah plans the deception and cooks the meal that Jacob will bring to Isaac. Rebekah informs Jacob of Esau's plans for revenge. Rebekah plans Jacob's trip to her brother and convinces Isaac that Jacob should go there to seek a wife. Earlier at the birth of Esau and Jacob, Rebekah consults the LORD and receives the message that the elder will serve the younger (25:23). In the narrative Rebekah is the only one who knows the will of God for the two sons. None of the males knows God's will, but Rebekah does and works to bring about God's plan. In the end, God's promise is passed on to the one to whom God intended it. This happens through the careful listening and quick thinking of Rebekah. Although authors often speak of Jacob the trickster (and in chapter 30, Jacob will outwit Laban) here Jacob is passive and his mother is the trickster. Given the concern for God's power in Genesis, we can see that the chosen one of God is not capable and clever on his own, but obtains the promised blessing by the power of God working through his mother. The women of Genesis often play roles crucial to the continuation of the promise according to God's plan. One of the most notable of these women is Tamar in Genesis 38. This is one of the reasons that some have speculated that the Yahwist writer was a woman.

The narrative structure of the text and the role of the characters give us insight into the meaning of the text. By paying attention to the intervention of Rebekah, we come to realize the plan of God.

World in front of the Text

Reading the Signs of the Times

In the midst of a difficult pregnancy, Rebekah consults God, who informs her that her twin fetuses are two nations warring against each other in her womb. God tells her that the elder will serve the younger. When her sons are grown, she overhears her husband telling his eldest son that he will bless him. Rebekah quickly sets into motion a plan to subvert the plans of her husband, which she knows are not the will of God. Later, when she gets news of Esau's plans to kill Jacob, Rebekah works out a deal with Isaac to send Jacob to her brother Laban's house to obtain a wife. The story is of a woman who pays attention to what is going on in and around her, consults God, comes to know the will of God, and acts to make it happen. She acts much as a midwife for Isaac and Jacob to bring about the blessing that is intended by God. She cannot give the blessing or receive the blessing but she can make sure that it is passed on according to God's plan. This story can serve as an example for us in reading the signs of the times, keeping our ears to the ground in social and political affairs, listening to the will of God for ourselves and for the world, and working to bring about God's will. It might be that we are not the ones who are called by God for a special role in history, but we must still act as support for those who are.

> The role that a character plays in a biblical story can be translated into a contemporary situation. In this case, Rebekah's role in making sure that God's choice of Jacob to inherit the promise is accomplished can translate into a role for Christian readers of this text in the twenty-first century.

The Law

INTRODUCTION

World behind the Text

The Idea of Covenant and Law

Exactly how far back the idea of covenant goes in Israelite religion is a matter of some debate, but certainly by 840 B.C.E. Hosea describes the relationship of Israel and Yahweh in terms of covenant. The Hebrew word for covenant is *berit*. It refers to an agreement between two parties that is confirmed by a ritual. Some have argued that the covenant idea in Israelite religion is very old, and its form was taken over from contemporary Hittite treaties. The particular form of treaty that the Israelites used as a model for the religious covenant with God was the vassal treaty, which included the following elements:

1. Preamble—the name of the sovereign making the treaty
2. Historical prologue—what the sovereign has done for the vassal in the past
3. Obligations—the requirements placed on the vassal
4. Deposit of the treaty in the temple
5. Witnesses—usually the gods
6. Curses and blessing—depending on the faithfulness of the vassal to the treaty

The elements of Israel's covenant that match each of these elements are spread throughout the Pentateuch. There is no one text in the Pentateuch that contains all the elements in sequence. (Deuteronomy 27–29 comes closest to containing all the elements of a covenant.)

World of the Text

Types of Law

What concerns us most in this section are the law codes in the Pentateuch, which are understood as part of the covenant obligations. The obligations of the covenant come in two different forms. Apodictic laws were general statements of either requirements or prohibitions that were universally binding. The most widely known apodictic laws are the Ten Commandments. They are in the form of general prohibitions and not specific cases. Even statements that state, "whoever does this must be put to death," are general apodictic laws.

The second kind of law that we find in the Pentateuch is casuistic or case law. These laws contain statements of the specific crime and indicate a specific punishment. The cases in this kind of law are unique to one particular circumstance. Look, for example, at Exodus 21:20: "When a slaveowner strikes a male or female slave with a rod and the slave dies immediately, the owner shall be punished." We find examples of both kinds of law in the law codes and covenants from the ancient Near East.

World in front of the Text

Covenants Old and New

The idea of covenant is one of the most important in the Old Testament. Many Old Testament theologies have made the covenant their focus. We find the prophets concerned with the people's infidelity to the covenant. Jeremiah is so convinced of the people's inability to be faithful to the covenant that he looks forward to the day when God will make a new covenant with Israel. Because this new covenant will be written on the hearts of the people, they will be able to keep the law. This is not so much a change in the covenant itself, but in the people. God is going to create a new people who have the covenant written in their hearts (Jer 31:31–34). Ezekiel picks up Jeremiah's image and uses it to describe a situation when the exiles of Israel and the exiles of Judah return and are reunited as one nation. Then they will no longer be unfaithful to God. God "will make a covenant of peace with them; it shall be an everlasting covenant with them" (Ezek 37:26). In Luke's description of the Last Supper, Jesus announces, "This cup that is poured out for you is the new covenant in my blood" (22:20). In Galatians 4:24 Paul speaks of two covenants: one from Mount Sinai and one from Christ. The Letter to the Hebrews is perhaps the most explicit in contrasting the first covenant with the new covenant in Christ, which delivers us from sin once for all (Heb 9:26). The self-understanding of Christianity, which came to designate the Hebrew scriptures as the Old Covenant and the Christian scriptures as the New Covenant, came from Jeremiah. Jeremiah's hope for a new covenant was based on his commitment to the covenant presented in the Torah.

EXODUS 21, 34; LEVITICUS 20; DEUTERONOMY 5

To give a sense of the broad importance of covenant and law in the Old Testament, I have chosen to examine a text from each of the four sources of the Pentateuch: Yahwist (Exod 34), Elohist

(Exod 21), Deuteronomist (Deut 5), and Priestly (Lev 20). In keeping with our approach to reading the Bible, we will examine the texts in the order in which they occur in the Bible and not in the supposed order of their composition.

World behind the Text

Elohist Law (Exodus 21)

Although there is a "Ten Commandments" in the Elohist source, we have chosen to study an additional group of laws that represents more clearly the mindset and social context of the Elohist source. It is generally agreed that although many of these laws are older even than the Elohist, they have come down to us here as part of that source. We find in these laws a concern for the rights of different members of the community, especially those with little or no power. The first group of laws is about how male and female slaves are to be treated. These laws were meant to protect the rights of the slave. To understand the law about female slaves and why their treatment differs from male slaves it is important to understand what role a female slave would have. It is clear from the text that when a female slave was obtained, she was obtained to be a wife or concubine. There were three cases when her situation was in jeopardy. If the purchaser decided not to make her his wife, then she could be redeemed (bought back by the father). A female slave was not just property that could be sold to anyone, she was meant to be the wife (or concubine) of an Israelite. If she was purchased to be the wife of the purchaser's son (and so was not made a wife immediately), she was to be treated as his daughter. Finally, if the purchaser obtained another wife, he was required to continue to treat this slave as a wife (giving her conjugal rights as well as food and clothing). If he did not want to do that, he was required to give her her freedom. She was not simply his property to be sold.

The second group of laws deals with violence. The first case given concerned a person who strikes a mortal blow. There was a distinction between premeditated murder and a murder by accident (causing the death by an act of God). For an accidental murder, the murderer could flee to a city of refuge. To understand the significance of the cities of refuge, the modern reader must understand "bloodguilt" and the "avenger of blood." In ancient society, if a person was killed, a kinsman of the murdered man (the "avenger of blood") had the right and duty to kill the murderer. No matter what the situation, the one who had caused the death of another person had "blood guilt." The dead person's blood was on the murderer's hands. The family of the dead person had the obligation to restore equilibrium by shedding the blood of the murderer (see Gen 9:5–6). There was no trial required. The dead man's family, through the "avenger of blood," simply took the life of the murderer. The law of asylum (discussed in Num 35:9–29; Deut 4:41–43; 19:1–13) was instituted to deal with the case of accidental murder (manslaughter). There were three cities set aside within Canaan as cities of refuge: Bezer, Ramoth, and Golan. If the murder was an accident, the person who committed the murder could flee to a city of refuge. The "avenger of blood" himself committed murder if he went into the city of refuge and killed the person. According to Numbers 35, the person was required to stay in the city of refuge until the death of the high priest. If he came out before then, the "avenger of blood" was allowed to execute him without incurring bloodguilt. Apparently after the high priest had died, the person was free to leave with no fear of being executed. If the murder was intentional and the perpetrator fled to a city of refuge, the city of the perpetrator was responsible for retrieving the person from the city and handing him over to be executed. The purpose of the law of the "avenger of blood" was to limit blood feuds. There was to be no escalation in violence—a life was demanded for a life taken. The law of asylum was meant to provide for the situation of accidental murder. It allowed for a stay of execution until it could be figured out whether the murder was accidental.

In verses 23–25 we find the full statement of the *lex talionis* (the law of tit for tat): "you shall give life for life, eye for eye, tooth for tooth, hand for hand, foot for foot, burn for burn, wound for wound, stripe for stripe." The purpose of this law was twofold. First, it required that all perpetrators be treated the same way. Anyone who knocked out a tooth had his tooth knocked out. A rich person's tooth did not require a greater punishment than a poor person's. Second, the law was meant to keep blood feuds from escalating. If a person knocked out the tooth of another, the other might retaliate by breaking the first man's jaw. Then the first man's family might retaliate by killing the second man, whose family retaliates by killing the first man and all his children. The *lex talionis* restricted the violence to what was considered a fair reprisal.

Yahwist Law (Exodus 34)

The first concern of the Yawhist law is for idolatry. Yahweh reminds the people that he drove the Canaanites, Hittites, and Perizzites out of the Promised Land. The Israelites must not make any covenants with these people. The concern is that these people will lead them into idolatry. The people are commanded to tear down any of the places of worship related to these people: altars, sacred pillars, and sacred poles. This concern probably reflects the centralization of worship during the time of David. In a move toward greater national identity and unity, David institutes a policy of religious cleansing. Worship is centralized in Jerusalem and other shrines and altars are destroyed. To create national identity, the people are encouraged to see themselves as separate from the surrounding peoples. Even intermarriage is discouraged.

The second major concern of the Yahwist law is cultic: feasts, ritual, and worship. Whereas some of the laws in Exodus 34 repeat laws of the "Ten Commandments," the laws about feasts stand out as unique. During the time of the Yahwist writer (during or just after the reign of Solomon) the Temple was built, and the major feasts were codified as feasts of pilgrimage to the Temple. The three main feasts were Passover, Weeks (or Pentecost), and Booths. These were originally agricultural harvest feasts, but the Israelites transformed them into remembrances of historical events by subordinating their agricultural features to aspects of historical events. The Feast of Passover was originally the feast of unleavened bread, which celebrated the grain harvest in the early spring. To celebrate this agricultural event, all bread and yeast were thrown away, and the new grain was made into unleavened loaves to indicate a new beginning. The Israelites subordinated this ritual to the event of leaving Egypt in such a hurry that there was no time to leaven the bread. Thus the feast is often referred to as the Feast of Passover and Unleavened Bread. Similarly, the grape and olive harvest in the fall was celebrated by spending a week living in tents in the orchards harvesting the crop. The Israelites subordinated the agricultural necessity of living in tents to the historic event of their wandering in the wilderness for forty years. This was the Feast of Booths. The agricultural feast of the grain harvest in late spring was called the Feast of Weeks because it was seven weeks after Passover. (Later it became known as the Feast of Pentecost because it was fifty days after the Feast of Passover.) It was transformed into a celebration of the giving of the law on Mount Sinai. These three great feasts were the pilgrimage feasts, during which every male Jew was supposed to travel to Jerusalem to celebrate every year. This requirement was an effective means of centralization of worship, power, and identity in Jerusalem.

Priestly Law (Leviticus 20)

The Priestly writer, writing during the time of Exile but compiling more ancient laws, reveals many characteristics in chapter 20 that resonate with the historical situation of the Exile. The first law concerns the worship of Molech, a Canaanite god to whom children were sacrificed in a burnt offering (a holocaust). The place where Molech was worshiped in Jerusalem was in the Valley of Ben-Hinnom (also the location of the garbage dump of the city). The person most often associated with this worship is Manasseh, king of Judah from 686 to 642 B.C.E. He is often the model for the worst sins of Judah for the Deuteronomistic historian, the Priestly writer, and the later prophets (see Lev 18:21; 2 Kgs 21:6; 23:10; Jer 7:31–32; 19:5–6). The worship of Molech is often associated with mediums and fortune-tellers as it is here.

The second section of laws in chapter 20 is developed from the Ten Commandments. It begins with cursing one's parents (honor your father and mother) but then develops at great length the sixth and tenth commandments. It details all the possible ways that one could sin against marriage: by engaging in sexual relations with a neighbor's wife, father's wife, a man, a mother and daughter, an animal, and so forth. For each specific case there was a specific punishment: put to death, burned to death, cut off from people, and made to pay a penalty. The Priestly writer, as can be seen in Leviticus, was very concerned about sexual sins, not only because of the sins of the past, but also because of the temptations to the people of Judah in exile in Babylon, where perhaps some of these actions were acceptable. The reason given for these laws was that the people should be holy, pure, and set apart as God was holy. They should not be like the wanton people among whom they were exiled. The concern at the end of the chapter for distinguishing clean from unclean animals emphasizes the need for being a pure and clean people before God. It was also a way that the Jews in exile could distinguish themselves from their pagan neighbors. It should also be noted that the priestly laws seem to rely on Deuteronomy. Verse 22, which exhorts the people to "keep all my statutes and all my ordinances, and observe them, so that the land to which I bring you to settle in may not vomit you out," uses language taken from Deuteronomy. The Deuteronomist wanted to get the people to keep the law so they would not lose the land. The Priestly writer, on the other hand, was explaining that the people had lost the land because they had not kept the law.

Deuteronomic Law (Deuteronomy 5)

The laws in the book of Deuteronomy are not new and unique. The Ten Commandments in Deuteronomy 5 can be found first almost word for word in Exodus 20 (a text from the Elohist source). What is unique about Deuteronomy is how the laws are transformed by the theological context into which they are set. They are part of a reminder given by Moses, but a reminder that has its own unique theological flavor. We can find in this chapter four themes that are especially characteristic of the Deuteronomic writer. First, the Deuteronomist emphasized the fear of the LORD (this theme is also found in the Elohist). God was awesome and transcendent and could not be approached by humans (vv. 24–26).

Second and following from this, Moses was considered the mediator between God and the people (v. 27). The importance in
Judaism of Moses as the great teacher and mediator between God
and God's people was attributed in large part to the
Deuteronomist. For the Deuteronomist, God chose special repre-
sentatives to mediate between God and the people. The
Deuteronomist understood that in his own day, the prophets and
priests were the successors of Moses and served this function.
Third, the Deuteronomist was concerned that now (in 650 B.C.E.,
after supposedly living by the law for the last six hundred years) the
Israelites would take the law seriously. God says, "If only they had
such a mind as this, to fear me and to keep all my commandments
always, so that it might go well with them and with their children
forever!" (5:29). The Deuteronomist was concerned that if the
people of Judah did not start obeying the law, they would be punished like the northern kingdom. All through the book of
Deuteronomy, Moses exhorts the Hebrews to "be careful to do as
the LORD your God has commanded you" (5:32; see also 4:1,9; 5:1;
6:3; 8:1; 11:1; 12:1). Related to this is the constant reminder in the
Book of Deuteronomy to hear (5:1). It has been suggested that,
after its discovery in the Temple, the Book of Deuteronomy was
read aloud every fall at the New Year's festival for the people of
Judah to hear and renew their assent to the covenant with Yahweh.

Finally, the necessity of keeping the covenant is related to
the gift of the Promised Land God had given to them.
Repeatedly in Deuteronomy, God emphasizes that the land,
which they are about to enter and occupy, was promised to them
by God and was being given by God according to the terms of
the covenant. If they failed to keep their part of the covenant,
the land would be taken away from them. This is usually
expressed in a conditional statement: keep the commandments,
"so that you may live, and that it may go well with you, and that
you may live long in the land that you are to possess" (5:33; see
also 4:40; 6:3; 11:31–32). At the end of the Book of
Deuteronomy, the blessings and curses that come with obedience or disobedience to the covenant are enumerated. The final
curse for not keeping the covenant was exile from the land
(28:36–37, 63–68). We can see that the Deuteronomist was very

concerned about the fate of Judah, given that the northern kingdom of Israel had lost their land and been taken into exile. The
laws of Deuteronomy, although not in themselves significantly
different from earlier laws, were placed in the context of land,
covenant, and the necessity of obedience because of the historical situation of the fall of the northern kingdom.

World of the Text

Exodus 21

Exodus 21 is not a separate and discrete unit but is part of a
larger unit. In Exodus 21:1 God begins to enumerate for Moses
the laws that he is to lay before the people. These laws (referred
to in 24:7 as the Book of the Covenant) continue all the way to
23:33. Most scholars believe that 20:18–26 should be read as
the introduction to the Book of the Covenant and 23:20–33 as the
conclusion. Both the introduction and the conclusion focus on
the holy presence of God and the prohibition of idolatry. Thus,
the laws of the Book of the Covenant, although secular in nature
(dealing with slaves, injury, property, loans, etc.), are placed in the
context of Israel's covenant relationship with God. The social laws
of Israel are understood in the context of their worship of God.
Chapter 21 is divided by topic into three kinds of laws: laws
regarding slaves, laws regarding personal injury, and laws regarding property damage. The laws are mostly casuistic, in that they
have the form of a particular crime followed by a specified punishment. There are, however, some apodictic laws, laws that are
condemnations of general crimes, sometimes with a general reference to the death penalty or expulsion from the group. Verse 17
is a good example of an apodictic law: "Whoever curses father or
mother shall be put to death." The situation described in vv.
18–19, however, would be an example of casuistic law: "When
individuals quarrel and one strikes the other with a stone or fist so
that the injured party, though not dead, is confined to bed, but
recovers and walks around outside with the help of a staff, then
the assailant shall be free of liability, except to pay for the loss of
time, and to arrange for full recovery." Our interpretation of a

particular law should be influenced by whether it is apodictic or casuistic. Apodictic law serves to inform the reader of a general principle of morality, whereas casuistic law is meant to give the reader an example of how specific laws might be judged and carried out. What we do not find in the Old Testament is a complete law code, listing all possible offenses and punishments.

Exodus 34

Exodus 34 is made up of three sections, with only the middle section containing laws. The context of these Yahwist "Ten Commandments" is very interesting. Anyone familiar with Exodus will know that God gave Moses the Ten Commandments on the mountain earlier, in chapter 20. The Ten Commandments constitute the centerpiece of a covenant between God and God's people that is ratified by the people in chapter 24. God then tells Moses to come up to the mountain so that God can give him "the tablets of stone, with the law and the commandment, which I have written for their instruction" (24:12). When Moses goes up to the mountain, God instructs him for another seven chapters before he gives him "the two tablets of the covenant, tablets of stone, written with the finger of God" (31:18). When Moses comes down from the mountain, however, he finds the people worshiping a golden calf and throws the tablets to the ground, destroying them (32:19). This is the context for the story of the giving of stone tablets for the second time. Exodus 34:1–9 is a description of Moses' call to go up the mountain to God a second time and his meeting with God. Exodus 34:10–26 lists the laws that God gives to Moses (the focus of our study). Exodus 34:27–35 is a description of Moses writing these laws on the tablets (note that it is Moses who writes them this time and not God) and his bringing the tablets back down to the people.

The text of Exodus 34:10–26 can be divided into two interrelated parts. The first part describes how God will drive out the peoples of Palestine and commands the people to tear down those people's altars and not worship their gods. The Hebrews are prohibited from making any covenants with these people, from marring any of their children, and from making molten gods. The second part of this text deals with the kind of worship that the Hebrews are to perform. This section lists three main feasts: the festival of first fruits of wheat harvest (Passover, celebrated in early spring), the festival of weeks (or Pentecost, celebrated in late spring), and the festival of ingathering at the turn of the year (Booths, celebrated in the fall at the end of the year). After commanding the celebration of the third feast (fruit harvest), God tells the people that they must appear before the LORD (at the Temple in Jerusalem) three times a year. This journey to Jerusalem is possible and sensible only because God has promised to drive out of the land all the enemies of the people. There will be no one to covet the land when the Hebrews travel to Jerusalem to worship Yahweh three times a year (34:24). In this way the author reminds the people in this second part, which deals with the requirements of worship, about the first part, which prohibits any kind of association with the peoples that God is driving out of the land. The three great pilgrim feasts of Judaism are not only meant to worship God, but to remind the people of the land that has been given to them and the freedom and security they have in that land.

> By noticing how the author joins two sets of laws into a larger unit, the reader can see the logical connection between the laws.

Leviticus 20

A simple way to identify a discrete unit in the Bible is by the introductions that are used to set off separate units. Leviticus 20 begins with, "The LORD spoke to Moses," and the words of God in this unit continue to the end of chapter 20. Then at the beginning of chapter 21 this same introduction appears again, letting us know that this is a separate set of laws. By this simple structuring technique, the author is encouraging us to interpret chapter 20 as a discrete unit. The unity of the section is further enhanced by its concentric structure. The chapter begins in 20:1–6 with a condemnation of worship of Molech and of mediums and wizards (A). The chapter concludes in 20:27 with a condemnation of mediums and wizards (A′). This second condemnation of mediums seems out of place when the chapter is read linearly, but when the reader becomes aware of the concentric structure of the text, this condemnation of idolatry is seen as the context in which the whole of the chapter is to be interpreted. The second element in the structure is the command in 20:7 to "Consecrate yourselves therefore, and be holy; for I am the LORD your God" (B). Immediately before the concluding condemnation of idolatry, God says in 20:26, "You shall be holy to me; for I the LORD am holy" (B'). The third element is God's command in 20:8 to "Keep my statutes, and observe them" (C). The third to the last element is a much longer discussion in verses 22–25 about observing the commands of God, but it opens with the line, "You shall keep all my statutes and all my ordinances, and observe them" (C'). The center section (D) is the listing of the laws about purity and holiness (20:9–21). The laws in chapter 20 are mainly casuistic laws governing sexual activities. We can see that the context for these sexual laws is idolatry (elements A and A'). The author is not just a prude or a pervert obsessed with sex, but rather is concerned for the life of the people of God. In the experience of Israel, foreign gods have constantly been associated with impure sexual practices and with national unfaithfulness to God understood as marital infidelity. The reason the people are required to observe sexual purity is the purity (holiness) of God (elements B and B'). It is because of the identification of the people with their God (both being holy) that the people are exhorted to keep these laws (elements C and C'). Thus, the concentric structure of this text helps us to appre-

---

Structure of Leviticus 20

A Warning against Molech and mediums and wizards (1–6)
  B Be holy, for I am the LORD (7)
    C Keep statutes and observe them (8)
      D Laws (9–21)
    C' Keep statutes and observe them (22–25)
  B' Be holy, for I the LORD am holy (26)
A' Condemnation of mediums and wizards (27)

---

ciate better its meaning. Without recognizing the careful structure of this text, a modern reader might misread this text as simply a weird list of laws against all kinds of sex.

Deuteronomy 5

Deuteronomy 4:44–49 probably serves as a conclusion to the laws that precede these verses. Chapter 2 describes the defeat of Sihon, king of the Amorites, and chapter 3 describes the defeat of Og, the king of Bashan. Verses 41–49 of chapter 4 summarize the laws in chapter 4 that Moses proclaimed to them in the land of Sihon and in the land of Og (vv. 46–47). Therefore, Deuteronomy 5:1 begins a new section with Moses summoning all Israel. It is more difficult to decide where this section ends. It is not clear whether 6:1–3 is a conclusion to the laws in chapter 5 or an introduction to the laws in chapter 6 and following. Because chapter 5 seems to end with an exhortation to obey the covenant (vv. 32–33), it is reasonable to assume that 6:1 begins a new section. As with many of the other texts we have seen, chapter 5 has a concentric structure, but one that is strikingly unbalanced in its parts. The chapter begins in 5:1–3 with the exhortation to hear the statutes and ordinances, learn them, and observe them (A). The chapter ends in 5:32–33 with a similar exhortation to be careful to do as God has commanded (A′). Although there is not a strict verbal parallelism between these two parts (A′ does not repeat the words, "hear," "statute," "ordinance," or "observe" but instead uses the related words, "be careful," "commanded," and "path"), there is a thematic parallelism. In 5:4–5 Moses reminds the people that when God spoke to them on the mountain they were afraid and so Moses stood between Yahweh and them to announce to them Yahweh's words (B). After Moses reminds them of the Law that he announced to them on the part of God (the Ten Commandments and element C), he continues in 5:22–31 with a fuller description of the people's experience of encountering the terrifying fire of God and his own role as mediator between Yahweh and the people (B′). Although there is verbal parallelism between the "B" elements ("fear," "fire," "the words of the LORD"), they are noticeably unbalanced in terms of size.

Element "B" consists of only one verse, whereas element "B'" contains ten verses. This imbalance between the elements alerts the reader to the importance for this author of the "B'" element. Moses' role as mediator, in terms of amount of material, is comparable to the Ten Commandments, which are at the center of the text. Finally, the center of this structure is the Ten Commandments presented in vv. 6–21 (C). As the center of the structure, the Ten Commandments are the focus of the text, but they are presented in the context of the terrible and awesome glory of God that requires a mediator. The focus is not only on the law, which God has given to the people, but also on Moses' role as mediator. The law, coming from the awesome and terrible glory of God, must be mediated by spokespersons and intermediaries (such as prophets and priests). Placing the Ten Commandments in the context of the terrible glory of God that requires a mediator serves to strengthen the exhortations to the people at the beginning and the end of this section to be careful to observe these laws.

World in front of the Text

Exodus 21: Social Justice

The casuistic laws that are in the Elohist source are mostly laws concerning those who do not have the power and voice to protect their own interests: slaves, widows, and orphans, for example. These laws remind us of the importance of society making every effort to protect the interests of its weakest members. Very often in these law codes, God reminds the Israelites that they must look out for the weaker members of society because they were once the weakest members of society (slaves in Egypt) themselves. The social justice concerns of the Elohist law codes are the background for the later prophets' emphasis on the importance of social justice for the survival of the kingdoms of Israel and Judah. It is from the prophets that Christians have learned social justice. The social teaching of the Catholic Church finds it roots in the Covenant and in the prophets who interpreted it.

Exodus 34: Ecumenism and Pilgrimage

In reading Exodus 34, a modern reader can be challenged on two fronts. First, this text should encourage among Christians a discussion about our relationship to persons of other faiths. The Yahwist's attitude to the indigenous peoples of Palestine and to having any relationship with them strikes us as isolationist and cultlike. Yet we do know that there is need for recognizing differences and not becoming assimilated to beliefs and rituals that are at odds with our faith. Paul's letters to his communities reflect the early Christians' struggles with just such issues. Paul saw a need to separate from the behaviors, beliefs, and rituals of the pagan Gentiles, but at the same time, he encouraged his communities not to separate from the world entirely. They could remain married to an unbelieving Gentile, and they could go to a meal at an unbeliever's house. Vatican II grappled with this same issue in more recent history.

Second, the text tells us about a law to go on pilgrimage to Jerusalem three times a year and reminds the people that God has given them the land and the security to be able to do this. Christians in the United States might want to reflect on all the blessings of peace, security, and wealth that they have been given. These blessings allow us the opportunity to worship God in special ways. The security of our lives offers us the opportunity to dedicate whole days to some kind of "pilgrimage" to worship God (a retreat perhaps). Although the word of God does not demand that we must all travel to Jerusalem three times a year, if we are to take the word of God seriously we might realize that we are challenged to trust in God's providence long enough to journey to God's presence.

Leviticus 20: The Holiness of God

The motivation for the sexual laws of purity and holiness in Leviticus is the holiness of God. This could be interpreted to mean that God has nothing to do with the evil material world. God is completely set apart from the profane world, although from Jesus we know that this is not the case. God is in the midst of the world. God's kingdom is here among us. Christ is both human and sinless (holy). We are called to be a holy people as

God is holy—but we are also called to be a people in the world as God is in the world. We should not interpret Leviticus 20 as meaning that we should become sexual vigilantes, denouncing the sexual sins of the world (of which there are many). Rather, Leviticus 20 invites us to come to know the holiness of God and seek to imitate that holiness in our present situation. God is holy by not playing favorites, by caring for the poor, by rejecting violence and coercion, by being above petty rivalries, and by seeking the salvation of all of creation.

Deuteronomy 5: Mediators of God's Law

Because of the structural emphasis placed on Moses as mediator in Deuteronomy 5, we are led to reflect on the need for mediation between God and humans. According to Paul, humans were all enemies of God and separated from God with no hope for being able to change this situation. Even the laws that Moses mediated were powerless to change this situation. It is only Jesus, as sinless Son of God, who is able to be a real mediator between God and humans. Paul derides Moses' role as mediator by maintaining that Moses actually received the law not from God but from angels (Gal 3:19). In Paul's reading, Jesus is the full and perfect mediator between the glory of God and sinful humanity. When we are in Jesus Christ, we become one with God and so there is no longer a need for a mediator. "Now a mediator involves more than one party; but God is one" (Gal 3:20). For Paul mediation is replaced by incorporation. The Christian understanding is that once we are incorporated into Christ we are able to approach the throne of God, hear the voice of God, and see the face of God. The mediation of Moses, priest, or prophet is no longer necessary.

Learning Achievements

After studying this chapter, students should be able to:

- Outline the Documentary Hypothesis, describing the four sources, their historical context, and their literary features.

- Define the literary genre of myth as it is applied to the Old Testament, discussing the truth-value of a myth and the relation of Old Testament myths to other Near Eastern myths.

- List the ancestors of Israel, the matriarchs and patriarchs.

- Outline the basic story of Exodus.

- Describe the difference between apodictic (general prohibitions) and casuistic (case) laws.

- Discuss the importance of law and social justice for the Old Testament.

Recommended Reading

Blenkinsopp, Joseph. *The Pentateuch*. New York: Doubleday, 1992.

Brueggemann, Walter. *Genesis: A Bible Commentary for Teaching and Preaching*. Louisville, Ky.: Westminster John Knox, 1982.

L'Hereaux, Conrad. *In and Out of Paradise: The Book of Genesis from Adam and Eve to the Tower of Babel*. New York: Paulist, 1983.

Van Wolde, Ellen. *Stories of the Beginning*. New York: SCM Press, 1996.

Chapter 4
HISTORICAL BOOKS

Introduction

World behind the Text

Deuteronomistic History

The bulk of the Historical Books (called the Former Prophets in the Hebrew Bible) belongs to a collection of books known as the Deuteronomistic History (DH). The books are Joshua, Judges, 1 and 2 Samuel, and 1 and 2 Kings (in the Hebrew scriptures, Samuel and Kings are each on only one scroll). The language and theology of these books indicate that they were probably all written by the same person or group of persons at one particular point in Israel's history. The conjecture is that they were written at the time of the Exile by a group of priests who were deeply influenced by the Book of Deuteronomy. The underlying theology behind this history focuses on the covenant that God made with Israel, a covenant that included the giving of the land of Canaan. It was the duty of Israel to love God and be faithful to the covenant (for the Deuteronomistic historian this primarily involves rejecting idolatry). If Israel was not faithful to the covenant, then she would lose the land. Although the narrative is complex and well constructed, a simple example from the Book of Judges will illustrate the theological principle that informs the text. In an almost tiresome manner, the author repeats essentially the same story over and over. Israel sins against God by being unfaithful, God hands Israel over to her enemies, the Israelites suffer under oppression and foreign rule, Israel repents and calls on God, God raises up a judge to deliver them from oppression, and they are delivered. Then the cycle starts all over again.

Each sin is followed by punishment, and each repentance is followed by deliverance. This strict correlation between sin and punishment, obedience and reward is known as the *Deuteronomistic Principle*. It is clear that ideology (theology) motivated the writer of this text. Although the author was not making up history, and although the story was constructed to follow events chronologically, the historical facts were not the primary concern of the author. The author's intention was not to create readers who knew all the historical facts of Israel's history during its time in the land of Palestine. Rather the author's intention was to create readers who understood the divine principle at work in the historical events.

In addition to the DH, the Historical Books also contain 1 and 2 Chronicles, Ezra, Nehemiah, Esther (which are part of the Jewish Bible), Tobit, Judith, and 1 and 2 Maccabees (which are contained in the Catholic and Orthodox Bibles). For Catholics, Tobit, Judith, and Maccabees are considered part of the canon but are called Deuterocanonical (secondarily canonical). For Protestants, these books are not part of the canon, but are often included at the end of the Bible and called the Apocrypha. For the most part, all of these books are later and derivative of the great Deuteronomistic theology.

World of the Text

The Narrative of the History Books

The Historical Books of Joshua, Judges, 1 and 2 Samuel, 1 and 2 Kings, 1 and 2 Chronicles, Ezra, and Nehemiah form a relatively continuous chronological account of the history of Israel from the end of the Exodus (when the Hebrews reach the land of Canaan) until the time of the rebuilding of Judah after the Exile (around 400 B.C.E.), with 1 and 2 Chronicles retelling most of the history already found in 1 and 2 Kings. Chronicles adds a few verses about Cyrus and the end of the Exile. Although these books cannot be called "history books" in the modern sense of the term, they are theological interpretations of historical events presented in chronological order. They are the history of the people of Israel as they interpreted it in light of their covenant with God.

The books of Ruth, Tobit, Esther, and Judith can more aptly be called historical novels, with Tobit, Esther, and Judith being of the subgenre of "tales of successful courtiers." The last books in the Historical section are 1 and 2 Maccabees, which tell the story of the Maccabean revolt against the Seleucid overlord Antiochus IV in approximately 167 B.C.E. These books come closest to religious propaganda.

World in front of the Text

Seeing God at Work in History

There are several insights that a reader of the historical books might gain from the collection of writings in the Historical Books. First, it is clear that the Deuteronomistic historian is working with older documents (the Court History of King David being one example). The DH takes this material and weaves a fabric of theological reflection that is meant to make sense of Israel's checkered history and its disastrous downfall. It is clear that for the biblical writers facts are not enough. The DH is interested in interpretation. Similarly, the Chroniclers have the DH but want to retell the same history, giving a new theological spin to it because of the new historical circumstances (after the return from Exile and during the reforms of Ezra, around 400 B.C.E.). In the course of Jewish history as the Historical Books were used, preserved, and became part of the canon, both of these accounts of Israel's history were included even though they covered essentially the same material. This tells us that the Jewish (and later the Christian) community felt that two different accounts of the same material could represent the word of God. God's inspired word about the history of God's people is not singular and uniform. There are numerous God-inspired ways for a community to reflect on the same events of history depending on the community's specific circumstances.

Deuteronomistic History

INTRODUCTION

World behind the Text

The Agenda of the Deuteronomistic Historians

We have concluded that the DH was written during the time of the Exile, and in it the authors tell the history of Israel from the perspective of the end—Israel has lost their Temple, their king, and their land. Why has this happened? The Deuteronomistic historians are convinced that the reasons for this great catastrophe are not mere chance or the failure of God, but the failure of the people of Israel and Judah. They tell the story of Israel and Judah with their focus on what led to the Exile. They read back into the history a moral judgment on all that has happened. When Israel was faithful to the covenant, they prospered and were blessed. When they were unfaithful to the covenant, they were punished. When their unfaithfulness finally reached its limit, they were purged from the land (not really by the Babylonians but by their God, Yahweh).

World of the Text

Israel's Story in the Land

The Book of Deuteronomy, which is presented as the last will and testament of Moses before he dies and hands over to Joshua the leadership of the people, concludes with the death of Moses. The DH takes up where Deuteronomy leaves off and tells the story of Joshua leading the people into the Promised Land. The Book of Judges tells the time of the conquest and settlement of the land under the leadership of the judges. The Books of Samuel tell the story of Samuel, the last of the judges, and his commission by God to anoint first Saul and then David as kings over Israel. The whole of the reign of David is recounted in these two books. The Books of Kings begin with the reign of Solomon and continue to the end of the kingship and the Exile in 586 B.C.E.

World in front of the Text

Suffering as a Crucible for Theology

The crisis of the Exile and all the suffering that accompanied it are the sources of Israel's greatest theological reflection, not only in the DH but also in the prophets, the psalms, and the Priestly writer. It is pain and suffering, loss, and destruction that bring about in the Jewish people the most profound and humble reflections on their relationship with God. For modern, first-world Christians this might suggest that we look to those Christians, especially in the third world, who are suffering and who face grave crises as the ones who have much to teach us about God.

JUDGES 4—5

World behind the Text

Different Versions of the Battle with Hazor

The book of Judges is part of the DH, written during the time of the Exile to make sense out of the destruction of the nation and the loss of the land. Its theology and literary features reflect an exilic or postexilic context. However, the story concerns the period of 1200–1050 B.C.E. This period of history in Israel is the subject of much study and debate. However, new archaeological evidence is helping us clarify the picture. The DH itself gives us two contrasting pictures of the "conquest" of the Promised Land. The Book of Joshua tells a story of the military conquest of the land under Joshua in the course of one generation. The Hebrews captured and destroyed the city-states of the Canaanites, Perrizites, Amorites, and Jebusites and took sole possession of the land. The Book of Judges tells a different story, in which the Hebrews do not march in and conquer the land. Rather, they settle in the land and, as they grow in size and power over the next two hundred years, come into periodic conflicts with the neighboring peoples, especially the Canaanite and Philistine city-states. Most scholars believe that the Book of Judges offers the more accurate picture of the process of the "conquest." It probably took place over a period of centuries and involved peaceful settlement, assimilation, and intermittent skirmishes, which intensified at the time of Saul. The archaeological evidence points to a peaceful settlement rather than an all-out conquest of the land. A few cities from this period were destroyed, but there is more evidence for the expansion of existing cities and new settlements.

In our story in Judges 4–5, the Israelites have been suffering under Jabin, king of Hazor. Hazor was a city-state located north of the Sea of Galilee near the Jordan River valley and in the territory that was assigned to the tribe of Naphtali. Because of his superior military technology (he had nine hundred iron chariots) Jabin is able to oppress the northern tribes for many years. This story would seem to take place only a few generations after the death of Joshua (Deborah is one of the first judges in the book). However, the Book of Joshua tells a different story of the defeat of Jabin, king of Hazor. In that book, Jabin joins forces with other northern kings and wages war against Joshua and the Israelite army (Joshua 11). That story tells us that all in the Canaanite armies were killed; Jabin, king of Hazor, was put to the sword, and the whole city of Hazor was destroyed. This would have happened less than one hundred years before the time of the story that is told in Judges. We do not know for certain that the Israelites went to war against Hazor, but if they did, the version of that war found in Judges is probably closer to history than the version in Joshua.

Mustering the Tribes

The time of the judges coincides with the time of the confederacy of the twelve tribes. Once the Hebrews had settled in Canaan, they formed a confederacy. Each tribe was autonomous in most of its dealings, but all were responsible for the protection of the whole from outside invasion. If one tribe was attacked, it was the responsibility of all the tribes to come to its aid. We see this agreement reflected in the older poem of Deborah in chapter 5. A concern in the poem, not found in the prose narrative, is that some cities and tribes were negligent in not coming to join in the war against the Canaanites. Joining in the battle are the tribes of Ephraim,

Benjamin, Manasseh, Zebulun, Issachar, and Naphtali. The tribes noted for not joining in the battle are Reuben, Gad, Dan, and Asher. The tribes of Judah and Simeon were probably too far south to have been summoned. They are not mentioned in either list.

As we noted earlier, the city of Hazor is located in the territory assigned to the tribe of Naphtali. It is therefore logical that Barak, the general whom Deborah summons, is from the tribe of Naphtali, living in the village of Kedesh, about eight miles north of Hazor. In the prose account in chapter 4, Barak summons only the two tribes of Naphtali and Zebulun. The tribe of Zebulun occupied the area south and west of Naphtali. The poem would seem to indicate that all of the tribes except Judah and Simeon were summoned. Deborah is of the tribe of Ephraim, which lies far to the south. The narrative says that she judged Israel from a palm tree located between Bethel and Ramah. This would put her only fifteen to twenty miles from Jerusalem, but eighty to ninety miles from Kedesh.

Deborah is identified as a prophetess. This story makes much of the fact that it is a woman who directed the battle and another woman who killed the opposing general. These events were considered as unique signs of God working even in the lowliest and least powerful, although a woman having the role of a prophet was not unusual in early Israel. Isaiah's wife was called a prophetess (Isa 8:3).

World of the Text

The Story of Barak, Sisera, Deborah, and Jael

In our study of the story of Deborah, we will do a narrative close reading of the text, looking at how as a reader we are led by the narrator to understand the deeper message of the story. The most interesting feature of the story is that Deborah, a woman, summons Barak, a military leader. However, she has the credentials to do this because she is identified as a prophetess. When Barak arrives, she tells him what the LORD, the God of Israel, commands. As a prophetess, she knows what God commands and has the authority to speak on God's behalf. We, the readers, accept this because the narrator, who is omniscient and reliable, tells us, but

Barak questions Deborah. The text does not tell us what he is concerned about or what it is that he does not trust about her words. He tells her that if she will go with him, he will go; but if she will not go, he will not go. One possibility is that if she is willing to put her life on the line, then he knows she herself truly believes that this word of God can be trusted. Another possibility is that he feels that he will need her present to continually intercede with God for their cause. A third possibility is that if Deborah, who is an Ephraimite, goes, then the tribe of Ephraim will join the fight. As we saw earlier, the poem indicates that more tribes were involved in the fight than just the two mentioned in the prose text. So at this point the reader trusts and knows more than Barak. We are confirmed in our trust when Deborah replies that she will surely go. Her prophetic words telling what God will do are certainly reliable, and she is willing to put her life on the line for them.

However, we learn something more in her response. Apparently Barak should not have asked this, but should have trusted. Because he has not trusted but has required Deborah to go along, Deborah tells him that he will not gain the glory for the expedition. Instead, God will sell Sisera (the enemy general) into the hand of a woman. At this point in the narrative, the reader might suppose that the woman in question is Deborah. She is the only woman in the story, and because Barak has required her to accompany the expedition, it only makes sense that the victory will end up being to her glory. The narrative then tells of three different people and the actions they each take. Barak summons ten thousand men to march with him. Deborah goes up (goes out to war) with him. A man named Heber, who is a Kenite and not an Israelite, has left his people and moved to Israelite territory (near Barak's home town of Kedesh). The first two bits of information (about Barak and Deborah) fit with the logic of the story line and are expected by the reader, whereas the third piece of information (about Heber) does not seem to fit with the story. It seems to the reader that the narrator is rambling. If the reader has come to trust the narrator, however, the reader will probably guess that this information will be important later, although the reader does not yet know how. This is a place where the narrator knows more than the reader does and reminds the reader that the narrator is in charge of the story. It also creates suspense. The reader wants to find out how Heber figures in this story.

Verses 12–16 describe the battle. These verses are constructed in such a way as to contrast Sisera and Barak. It is reported to Sisera what Barak is doing, so Sisera assembles for battle. In contrast, Deborah tells Barak what God has planned, so Barak goes down to engage Sisera in battle. Then the LORD takes over and wins the battle. In the midst of the battle Sisera dismounts from his chariot and flees on foot (a humiliating thing for a general to do). In contrast, Barak pursues the chariots and army and slays the entire Canaanite army. The text tells us that "no one was left" (4:16). This highlights the fact that Sisera deserted the army to flee on foot. The structure of the battle has three sections. The contrast between Sisera's self-will and Barak's obedience to the word of God constitutes the first section. The middle section contains God's victory. The last section contrasts Sisera's humiliating desertion from the army with Barak's pursuit and annihilation of the entire Canaanite army. The reader though is wondering where is the woman who will get the glory. Deborah has not played a heroic role in the story of the battle. Certainly more glory is given to Barak in this battle than to Deborah, but if we remember the words of Deborah, "for the LORD will sell Sisera into the hand of a woman" (4:9), we might begin to guess that there is more to the fate of Sisera than we yet know.

Verse 17 takes up the story of Sisera. We are told that he has fled to the tent of Jael. It is part of the genius of the writer to remind us that he fled on foot. The humiliation of Sisera is kept before us. We are told that Jael is the wife of Heber the Kenite who was mentioned earlier. Now the strands of the narrative are coming together. Jael goes out to greet him and tells him to have no fear. She covers him with a rug. We are not told that she knows who he is or what has happened to him, but she acts as if she does. He asks for water, but she gives him milk instead. This is a central plot twist in the story. From one point of view, she is generous and even a bit extravagant. However, she does not give him what he asks for. Then he tells her to stand guard and tell anyone who is seeking him that he is not there. Again, she does not do what he asks, but this time her actions cannot be construed as generous.

Instead of standing guard, she takes a tent peg and drives it into his temple, killing him. Now, the gift of the milk becomes clear. She gave him milk as a sedative to put him to sleep so that she could kill him. We also remember that Heber, Jael's husband, had pitched his tent near Kedesh (4:11), but also that he was at peace with Jabin, king of Hazor (4:17). Here, Jael "pitches her tent" with the Israelites by not holding to the peace treaty Heber has made with Jabin. In terms of the narrative, it is not an accident that the murder weapon is a tent peg.

The narration then returns to where it left off in v. 16. Barak, who has killed all the army, now goes in search of Sisera and arrives at Jael's tent. Jael again goes out to meet the visitor, but now tells Barak she will show him the man he is seeking. Barak enters the tent and sees Sisera dead with the tent peg in his temple. Note how the narrator concludes this story. "So on that day God subdued King Jabin of Canaan before the Israelites" (4:23). What is fascinating about such a conclusion is that the reader has been focused more narrowly on the humiliation of Sisera and also the loss of glory for Barak because Jael has killed the great general. The narrative has led us to see and feel these humiliations, but they are to be understood as part of the larger picture of God's victory over the enemies of his people Israel.

> Here we pay attention to the narrative clues. The narrator gives information that seems irrelevant or unfulfilled until later in the story. The reader is encouraged to be on the lookout for the relevance or fulfillment of the earlier information.

God Works in Mysterious Ways

What is the meaning we get from this close reading? With a narrative reading of a text, what we obtain is not so much a meaning that can be stated in a simple declarative sentence as a meaning that is experienced by the reader. What we notice is that the text has played with us in giving us clues but hiding the essential information until the end. It is not revealed until the end who the woman is who will be Sisera's downfall. We are introduced to her husband early in the story, but we do not know at that point why this information has been given to us. Even when we meet Jael, we are at first led to believe that she is positively inclined toward Sisera. Her family is not Israelite, she offers to hide Sisera, and she generously gives him milk to drink instead of water. Why does the text lead us on in this way? One of the themes of the DH is the surprising way that God works. For the Deuteronomistic historian, human power and prestige are of little value. The real power is with God. Story after story in the DH is about a lowly, powerless, or unexpected person who is used by God to win a victory. Jael is a woman who is not even an Israelite. The judge, Ehud, is a left-handed man, who by trickery brings victory to Israel. Gideon even says to God, "How can I deliver Israel? My clan is the weakest in Manasseh, and I am the least in my family" (Judg 6:15). Later when Gideon is assembling men to go out to battle, God keeps telling him that he has too many. "The troops with you are too many for me to give the Midianites into their hand. Israel would only take the credit away from me, saying, 'My own hand has delivered me'" (Judg 7:2). The reason the Deuteronomistic historian leads us along without revealing all the information to us is to surprise us with the work of God at the end. The writer wants the reader to feel the surprise of God working through the unexpected, the lowly, and the weak.

> A close reading of how the narrative develops helps us to experience the message that the ancient storyteller intended. Paying attention to the rhetorical strategy of the author allows us to experience the surprising nature of God's work and the futility of human strength.

World in front of the Text

The Lowly Hero

This text can be read in several different ways that challenge and inform a reader in the present day. First, the text forces the modern reader, especially one in the rich and powerful Western world, to come face to face with a God who is not impressed by power, wealth, prestige, and importance. Those who would heed God's call and be faithful to God's way of working in history must give up power and prestige and rely on the power of God, knowing that God will probably work through the lowly and unexpected person.

The Demise of Patriarchy

Second, the message about women, when taken in the historical context of the story or of the author, is astounding. The text breaks with the natural tendency of the world at that time to present God working in history exclusively through men. Women did not normally play a role in the history of the people or in speaking the word of God. For two women to play such central roles in a military victory is astounding. Note how, in keeping with a patriarchal culture, we are introduced to Heber the patriarch of a family, but, when this information becomes relevant, the story has nothing to do with Heber but only with Jael. What is astounding is that Jael acts not out of patriarchal motivation (her husband's family is not at war with the Canaanites) but out of her own self-identity (her name is Jael, which means Yahweh is God). As a member of her patriarchal family, Jael has no reason to act in this situation, but as an individual who bears the name of Yahweh, she acts in accord with her name. Unlike her husband who tried to pitch his tent in God's promised land and yet be at peace with Israel's enemies, Jael pitches her tent with God and God's people by driving the tent peg through the enemy general's temple. The text goes out of its way to mock Sisera for being slain by a woman, and it also mocks Barak for needing the support of a woman to trust the word of God to go into battle. At one level, it could be argued that this mockery only reinforces the negative view of women as not worthy of being historical actors. However, it is also possible to read the text as mocking not only Sisera and Barak, but also all those who place such stock in the male domination of history and the male domination of interpreting and proclaiming God's plan.

A Living Bible

Third, this story reflects a triple tradition. The prose story of Deborah uses an older poetic account of the same story, which the DH places into the prose narrative as a song that Deborah sings in celebration of the victory. The story of the defeat of Hazor, however, is also found in a contradictory version in the Book of Joshua. The different versions are incorporated into one overall framework, and the differences and even contradictions are ignored. The text does not have to explain why there are differences or try to coordinate the three versions so that they are the same. The poetic version is concerned with the tribes that have refused to join in the battle, which is not part of the prose story. The prose story places great emphasis on the humiliating desertion and fleeing of Sisera. This is not part of the poem. Instead, the poem adds a rather lengthy section about the wife and mother of Sisera who wait at home and imagine why he is delayed. This is a wonderful touch of irony in the poem that is completely absent from the prose text. The version in Joshua describes a complete destruction of all Israel's enemies at the time of Joshua, whereas the version in Judges is the story of an unlikely hero using cleverness and deception to win a victory for God. What the modern reader can come to appreciate in all of this is that scripture itself is comfortable with a variety of ways of looking at the same story. Any given story can take on a number of different meanings in different contexts. Also, the Bible itself is a living text. An ancient poem that is concerned with the problem of the equal participation of all the tribes in the confederacy is taken over by a later community and reworked to deal with their contemporary concern to show how God humbles the powerful and uses the lowly ones to do God's will. The Bible teaches us how to use the Bible. We should not be afraid to retell the stories of the Bible in ways that make them come alive and have application for our own time and place.

Historical Novels

INTRODUCTION

World behind the Text

Ruth, Esther, Tobit, and Judith

In the Jewish scriptures, there are two historical novels, Ruth and Esther. The Catholic canon of the Old Testament adds two more: Tobit and Judith. These books describe the faith of a particular person who acts in accord with God's will and brings about the salvation of the nation or the blessings of God on his or her family. These texts appear to be quite late in the postexilic period except for the Book of Ruth, which could be from the preexilic period. These novels are not concerned about historical details, often getting them quite wrong. Esther and Tobit show how Jews can act in a way that is faithful to God and still be successful in a foreign land. Ruth shows how a foreign person can be faithful to God and join the chosen people. Judith shows how a person faithful to God can gain salvation for the whole nation. Three of the stories are about women who do what men have been unwilling or unable to do.

World of the Text

The Genre of These Books

To call these books historical novels is actually misleading because the novel really did not come into being until our modern era, but neither are they traditional folktales. Their length and their unified plot make them different from folktales. The folktales of Jacob each have a different plot and are simply linked chronologically. These four books all introduce a problem or crisis at the beginning of the book that is developed and eventually resolved in the story. All of the books are written in prose and use traditional techniques of foreshadowing, repetition, and surprise to make the stories artistically pleasing. What is unique about all four of these books, but especially Judith, Tobit, and Esther, is the lack of concern for historical accuracy. They are clearly written to edify an audience and not to give information about history. Of all of them, the Book of Tobit has the most direct intervention of God, with an angel accompanying Tobias on his journey, although as a rule, all of the books are human-centered stories about the trials and courage of exemplary Jews in a time of crisis.

World in front of the Text

Women in the Margins

Three of the four books we have identified as historical novels are about women. However, each of the stories contains another woman who is not as central to the story. In Ruth there is Naomi, in Judith there is her maid, in Tobit there is Sarah, and in Esther there is queen Vashti. Modern hermeneutics often finds that what is not said can be as important as what is said, a character that is nearly invisible can be highlighted and given new importance, and gaps and inconsistencies in the story are sources for fruitful speculation. This is similar to the rabbinic method of midrashic interpretation. The Book of Tobit, focuses on Tobias, who goes on the journey to Rages accompanied by the angel Raphael, marries Sarah, defeats the demon, and returns home with the money that his father had sent him to collect. A feminist hermeneutic of this story might move Tobias to the side and focus on Sarah and her plight. The demon that wants her for himself, kills her husbands, and makes her seem to be a threat to men could be read as the demon of culture that still plagues women today.

In the Book of Esther, Esther is made queen of Persia after the previous queen, Vashti, is deposed for insubordination. The king commands Vashti to "show her beauty" before all his guests, and she refuses. By describing how, during the course of an extended feast, King Ahasuerus displays all his material wealth to his guests, the narrative implies that his wish to display Queen Vashti is a wish to display one more of his precious "objects." A feminist reading of this story might focus on the dismissed Vashti who stands up for her dignity and refuses to be considered an object. After Queen Vashti is deposed, a beauty contest is held to see who will replace her, and Esther wins. The narrative spends an inordinate amount of time describing how the contest will work and how each of the contestants is brought to the palace for one year to be "made over" with oils and cosmetics before being presented to the king. The story reads like an infomercial for beauty products. Male obsession with female "beauty" is evident throughout the story. In this reading, Vashti stands out as the protest against such objectification of women by men.

Hermeneutics, especially feminist or other minority readings, will often focus on something hidden in the text, something that is not the focus of the narrator but whose importance almost "inadvertently" slips past the narrator. A feminist hermeneutic does not claim that the author wished to present Vashti as a protest against the objectification of women, but only that a modern reader can find her as such in a careful reading of the text.

RUTH 3

World behind the Text

Setting

The story is set during the time of the judges (around 1200 to 1000 B.C.E.). We are not sure exactly when the story was written, although some have claimed that it comes from a postexilic setting. However, because there is nothing in the story that requires a postexilic dating, other scholars have maintained that this story is quite old and fairly accurate in its history. The Book of Ruth tells the story of how Boaz, the great-grandfather of King David, came to marry a Moabite woman. It is thought that making David's great-grandmother a Moabite would not have been something that a later writer (either preexilic or postexilic) would likely have done. (Deuteronomy 23:3 explicitly forbids allowing a Moabite into the Jewish community to the tenth generation.) Also, in 1 Samuel 22:3–4 David takes his parents to the king of Moab for safe keeping when he is a fugitive pursued by King Saul. Therefore, many consider that this story may be grounded in the historical fact of David having Moabite ancestry. Scholars who date this book in a later period see this story as a reaction against the prohibitions of the time of Ezra against marrying any foreign woman.

The Redeemer

An important role in the Old Testament is the role of the **redeemer,** the *goel.* The word is used a number of times in this story, and is translated as "next-of-kin." The redeemer was in fact usually a kinsman. In matters of marriage, property, or litigation, it was the right and duty of the next-of-kin to act on behalf of his relative. One of the most important roles of a redeemer had to do with obtaining offspring for one's brother. This is the concept of **levirate marriage.** In Israel, if a man died without bearing any children his younger unmarried brother was required to take the man's wife for his own and produce offspring. The firstborn son of the younger brother and the dead man's wife would be the son of the dead man and inherit his property. This principle does not seem to apply to just any relative of the man but only to his brothers. The concern was to keep the property in the family and to have inheritance through the eldest son. In our story it is not clear that Boaz or the other "next-of-kin" was required to marry Ruth and produce offspring for her husband Mahlon (because they are not Mahlon's brothers). However, at his marriage to Ruth, Boaz says he is taking her as his wife, "to maintain the dead man's name on his inheritance, in order that the name of the dead may not be cut off from his kindred and from the gate of his native place" (4:10). When Ruth asks Boaz to marry her, she says, "spread your cloak over your servant, for you are next-of-kin" (3:9). So Boaz's marriage to Ruth is seen in the story as a levirate marriage, and by marrying her he is acting as next-of-kin/redeemer (*goel*). Also when the child is born, it is taken by Naomi and treated as her own son, clearly meaning that he is considered not just the son of Boaz but also the son of Mahlon.

A second major duty of a redeemer had to do with keeping property within a family. The possession of the land given by God as an inheritance was a very important principle in Israel, especially during the time of the judges. If a man needed to sell his inherited land because of debt, his next-of-kin had the right and duty of the **redemption of the land** (Lev 25:25). That meant that the relative was allowed to buy the property back to keep the ancestral inheritance intact. In the Book of Ruth, this principle and the principle of levirate marriage are linked together. The "next-of-kin" has the right to buy the ancestral property of Naomi's husband, but if he chooses to claim that right, he must also marry Ruth and, apparently, his first son by Ruth would be the owner of that property. (The law itself does not make such a connection, but Boaz does, and no one in the story objects.) The relative who is first in line to do this in the Book of Ruth chooses not to. So Boaz marries Ruth and redeems the ancestral property of Ruth's husband.

Part of the deeper meaning of the Book of Ruth has to do with the layers of meaning given to the *goel* in the Old Testament. The redeemer is the next-of-kin who has obligations in marriage, property, and litigation, but the word *goel* (redeemer) is also used metaphorically of God. God is pictured as acting as a *goel*, a redeemer, a next-of-kin, for the Israelites. God acted as *goel* initially by redeeming the Hebrews from slavery in Egypt.

World of the Text

The Story of Ruth

In the Catholic canon, the story of Ruth comes right after the Book of Judges because the story is set during the time of the judges. The story of Ruth also serves as a good introduction to the Books of 1 and 2 Samuel by giving the genealogy of King David. The story is a compact narrative that develops in four main scenes. The first scene contains the setting of the story in Moab and the deaths of Naomi's husband and two sons. Naomi then decides to return to Israel and sends her two daughters-in-law back to their Moabite families. Ruth, however, refuses to go and accompanies Naomi to Israel. The second scene takes place back in Judah and is set in the barley fields when Ruth goes out to glean (pick up the leftover grain) the fields. There she meets Boaz and is given preferential treatment because of her reputation of kindness toward Naomi. That night she finds out from Naomi that Boaz is Naomi's kinsman. In the third scene, after the barley harvest is finished, Naomi sends Ruth out to the threshing floor to spend the night with Boaz. Although there are clear sexual overtones in this scene, the intention is to encourage Boaz to marry Ruth and not to force him into a compromising situation in which he is forced to marry Ruth. It is not completely clear whether Ruth's laying at the feet of Boaz and her request for him to cover her with the corner of his cloak are meant to indicate a sexual action that night, although given that Boaz wishes to give another relative the prior right to marry Ruth, it would seem that no relationship was consummated that night. Boaz agrees to marry Ruth, but says that someone else is a closer kin and has the prior right to marry her. The fourth scene takes place at the city gates the next day when Boaz discusses the issue of Naomi's property with the "next-of-kin." It seems that this person is willing to purchase Naomi's property until he finds out that he must also marry Ruth, with the implication that Ruth's son by him will be the inheritor of this property. The other man then declines both offers, and Boaz marries Ruth who bears him a son, Obed, the grandfather of David. The story concludes with the genealogy of David going all the way back to Perez. It is possible that the genealogy goes back to Perez because Perez's mother was Tamar. Tamar is also a foreign woman, is herself involved in a levirate marriage, and takes steps to make sure that she obtains offspring for her first husband. Tamar's husband, Er, dies and so she is married to his younger brother who also dies. When there is a long delay in marrying her to the youngest brother, she realizes that it will never happen and so takes it on herself to seduce her father-in-law, Judah (by pretending to be a prostitute), and so ensures her place in the line of Judah. She gives birth to a son, Perez, who will become the ancestor of King David. Ruth and Tamar are both foreign women who make sure that God's promise continues uninterrupted in the offspring of Israel.

Scenes one and four are contrasting parallels. Naomi, who is empty and alone and sends away her daughters-in-law in scene 1, has a daughter(-in-law) who is married to her kinsman and a grandson in scene four. Scenes two and three both focus on the exchanges between Boaz and Ruth.

Ruth and Naomi: Your People Shall Be My People, and Your God My God

Ruth 3 is the third scene of the story and is made up of three sections: Naomi's instructions to Ruth as to what to do, Boaz's discovery of Ruth next to him and their conversation, and Ruth's return to Naomi to report the outcome. Naomi's plan that is carried out by Ruth serves as a bracket around the scene. We are reminded of the plans that Rebekah makes that Jacob carries out in Genesis 27. The story gives a special prominence to Naomi by continually emphasizing that Ruth is committed in every way to her mother-in-law. In 1:16 Ruth tells Naomi, "Where you go, I will go; Where you lodge, I will lodge; your people shall be my people, and your God my God." As an explanation of why he is treating Ruth with so much kindness and generosity, Boaz tells her, "All that you have done for your mother-in-law since the death of your husband has been fully told me, and how you left your father and mother and your native land and came to a people that you did not know before" (2:11). When Ruth gives birth to her son, the women of Bethlehem speak of God's blessings to Naomi by giving her an heir. They tell her that he will be a comfort and support for her, "for your daughter-in-law who loves you, who is more to you than seven sons, has borne him" (4:15). Ruth's love for and loyalty to Naomi represent her faithfulness to Yahweh even though she only knows Yahweh through Naomi.

What is striking in this story is that even though God is not a direct actor in the story, God's presence in the characters' lives is never out of view. Repeatedly, God is seen as the one to whom every situation can be attributed. Yahweh has ended the famine in Israel by providing food. Yahweh is the one who will acquire new husbands for Naomi's two daughters-in-law. Noami says that the Almighty is the one who has made her life bitter. Boaz greets his harvesters with a blessing of Yahweh, and asks that Yahweh reward Ruth. Naomi blesses Yahweh when she hears that Ruth has been working in Boaz's field. When Boaz wakes up to find Ruth sharing his bed, he again prays that Yahweh will bless her. When Boaz marries Ruth, the elders at the gate pray that Yahweh will make Ruth like Rachel and Leah in giving Boaz many sons. It is Yahweh who enables Ruth to bear a son, and Yahweh whose name is blessed by the women when the son is born. Even all the things that make the plot possible (the laws of gleaning, levirate marriage, and redemption of property) are the laws of God. The reader can never forget that the setting for this story is in a community completely aware of and faithful to the guiding presence of Yahweh—and yet Yahweh is not an actor. The actors are Naomi, Ruth, and Boaz. By the decisions they make and the actions they take, these characters do the will of God and further God's plan of salvation for God's people. The reader is led to see that it is human actions, and even humans taking matters into their own hands, that bring about the plan of God. What is even more amazing is that Ruth, the central character, who fulfills the laws of God and who brings about the inheritance of God's people, is a foreign woman.

By repeatedly mentioning prayers and blessings, the author makes the reader aware that this story is not simply about how Ruth found a husband. The story is ultimately about Yahweh's plan for his people and how that plan includes a foreigner. By paying close attention to the subtext of the story, we see Yahweh at its center.

World in front of the Text

Steadfast Love

In Judaism the Book of Ruth is read during the Feast of Weeks (*Shavuot*), which coincides with the late spring barley harvest. This of course is the time that the story of Ruth takes place. Probably even more than that, the story is about Ruth joining the Jewish community and taking on herself the duties of the law. The Feast of Weeks celebrates the giving of the law at Sinai and the people's taking on the duties of the law.

Commentators on the Book of Ruth generally point to its relevance for readers as an example of *chesed*, another important word used in the book. *Chesed* is often translated as loving-kindness, the love that goes beyond duty. *Chesed* is steadfast, enduring love, the love God has for God's people. In the Book of Ruth, Ruth shows *chesed* to her mother-in-law, Naomi (and to the inheritance of her dead husband). Also, Boaz shows *chesed* to Ruth. It is this loving-kindness and going beyond what is required that brings about community and new life. Related to this is the theme of the friendship between Naomi and Ruth. This is the one story of the Bible that has two women as the main characters, and two women who are not in competition (such as Sarah and Hagar or Rachel and Leah) but who have a bond of friendship that is truly remarkable.

Universalism

Many commentators have seen this story as a deliberate critique of the policies of Ezra who required the postexilic Jews to divorce their foreign wives. We noted above that the story is possibly much older than the time of Ezra (440 B.C.E.). Whenever the book was written, however, it stands as a challenge to the kind of narrow thinking that believes that only persons of a certain ethnic background can be the people of God. Ruth is an example of one who is faithful to the law, who goes beyond the requirements of the law in showing *chesed*, who "builds up" (by having children) the people of Israel (in fact becomes the ancestress of their greatest king), and who nonetheless is a stranger and alien. Her story reminds us that the story of Abraham, the story of the Exodus, and the story of Israel for all time (seen particularly in Paul's story of the new Israel) is a story of God calling the alien and the stranger to follow and be God's people. The announcement of Ruth to Naomi ("Where you go, I will go; Where you lodge, I will lodge; your people shall be my people, and your God my God") is one of the most profound statements of discipleship ever written. It is not who we are by birth but who we are by commitment and action that matters to God.

Learning Achievements

After studying this chapter, students should be able to:

- Describe the content and context of the Deuteronomistic History.

- Define Deuteronomistic theology.

- Do a close reading of a narrative, knowing how to pay attention to the clues that the narrator gives the reader.

- Discuss the genre of historical novel in the Old Testament.

- Do a hermeneutics of reading in the margins, by focusing on minor or marginal characters.

- Explain the role and importance of the redeemer in the Old Testament.

Recommended Reading

Kates, Judith A., and Gail Twersky Reimer. *Reading Ruth: Contemporary Women Reclaim a Sacred Story*. New York: Ballantine, 1994.

Linafelt, Todd, and Timothy Beal. *Ruth and Esther: Studies in Hebrew Narrative and Poetry*. Berith Olam. Collegeville, Minn.: Liturgical Press, 1999.

Schneider, Tammi. *Judges: Studies in Hebrew Narrative and Poetry*. Berith Olam. Collegeville, Minn.: Liturgical Press, 2000.

Sternberg, Meir. *The Poetics of Biblical Narrative: Ideological Literature and the Drama of Reading*. Bloomington, Ind.: Indiana University Press, 1987.

Chapter 5
WISDOM BOOKS

Introduction

World behind the Text

Wisdom Books or Writings

The first issue we need to deal with in discussing the Wisdom Books is the difference between the Wisdom Books of the Catholic and Orthodox Old Testament and the Writings of the Jewish scriptures. The Writings (*ketubim*) come after the Prophetic Books at the end of the Jewish scriptures, whereas the Wisdom Books in the Old Testament precede the Prophetic Books. The Writings contain works of all different types. Ruth is a historical novel. Daniel is apocalyptic prophecy. Ezra–Nehemiah and Chronicles are historical narratives. Lamentations contains poetic hymns of complaint. Many of these books are contained in other sections of the Christian Old Testament. Ruth, Chronicles, and Ezra–Nehemiah are part of the Historical Books. Daniel and Lamentations are included in the Prophetic Books. The collection known as the Wisdom Books in the Old Testament is more focused on just wisdom books than is the Jewish collection of Writings. Still, the Books of Psalms and the Song of Solomon (also called Song of Songs) in the Old Testament are not exactly wisdom books, and so the designation of this grouping of texts as Writings might be more apt. However, the Christian tradition, in designating all of the books as wisdom, points to their shared form (poetry characterized by parallelism) and content (nonprophetic exhortations to live the good life in accord with the will of God). The Wisdom Books also contain most of the extra books that are in the Catholic canon. Wisdom and Sirach are two important books in the Old Testament that are not found in the

109

Jewish scriptures. Both of these books were written at a late date and were found only in the Greek. Sirach (also called Ecclesiasticus) seems to have been originally written in Hebrew, but is found only in the Greek translation.

Foreign Wisdom Traditions

The wisdom literature in the Old Testament owes its origins to a variety of sources and influences. Although many of the wisdom books are quite late, the traditions of wisdom are widespread and very early. Wise sayings, proverbs, reflections on life, morals, hymns, and praises of wisdom are found in many different cultures. The traditions of Hebrew wisdom are related to the traditions from Egypt and Babylonia. Egyptian wisdom texts are the most numerous texts we have from the second millennium B.C.E. These were mainly intended as instructions on life for young men at court. Perhaps the most important influence on Israelite wisdom was from the Canaanites whom the Israelites displaced or assimilated. There are numerous direct links between the wisdom texts in the Bible and Phoenician sources. Biblical wisdom was later influenced by Persian (Zoroastrian) traditions of wisdom. Finally, for many of the books found in the Christian Old Testament (less so for the Hebrew scriptures) Hellenistic traditions of wisdom constitute a major influence. Still, the wisdom tradition in Israel was not simply the result of direct borrowing. Like the surrounding nations, Israel had a long and rich tradition of wisdom.

Hebrew Wisdom Traditions

Even outside the Wisdom Books there is a clear and ancient tradition of wisdom in the Old Testament. The stories of Joseph as interpreter of dreams and Samson as giver and solver of riddles (Judg 14:12–19) reflect Egyptian and Mesopotamian wisdom traditions. The Deuteronomistic History speaks of both men and women who are given the title of "wise" (see 2 Sam 14:2; 20:16). Solomon is of course the most famous of Israel's wise (see 1 Kgs 3). As the epitome of the wise person, he was assigned authorship of many of the collections of wisdom sayings. Although his authorship of all this material is doubtful, his foundational role of supporting, promoting, and exemplifying the wisdom tradition is not doubted. By the time of Jeremiah, there seems to have been three groups of professionals in Judah entrusted with roles of training and instructing the people: the prophet, the wise one, and the priest (Jer 18:18).

There are four different settings reflected in the wisdom material: the home, the court, the Temple, and schools. Whereas scholars have suggested that the original setting of wisdom traditions may have been in the home, the texts as we have them now reflect all four settings. The sayings of wisdom would be passed down from parents to children in an effort to strengthen the life of the family. We see this especially in the Proverbs, but we also find that some of the other books of wisdom reflect a setting in the Temple (Psalms) or in the schools (Ecclesiastes, Sirach). The best evidence we have for the setting of wisdom in the royal court is from the historical narratives.

World of the Text

Hebrew Poetry

For the ancient Israelites poetry was much more than just a genre or form of writing; it was the way they thought. Modern Western thinking and writing is linear, practical, and scientific. The clearer a statement is, the more perfect it is for us. We want a statement to mean only one thing. This was not true for the ancients. Language for them was necessarily metaphorical and comparative. Complex and abstract thought could be expressed only with metaphors and poetry. The way to discuss any idea or object was to compare and contrast it to something else. For this reason, Hebrew poetry is primarily characterized by parallelism. Although any good scholar who reads Hebrew will tell you that there are many other characteristics of Hebrew poetry, parallelism is the one most readily experienced by a contemporary reader reading in a modern language. It is experienced as repetition in the text. The text says everything twice. Hebrew poetry is made up of lines, which are the basic sense unit. Each line has usually two, but sometimes three, measures to it. In the NRSV, the line begins at the margin and the second (and third) measure(s) is (are) indented. The parallelism of Hebrew poetry is primarily between the measures of a line of poetry. Parallelism in Hebrew poetry is usually in one of three kinds: synonymous, antithetical, or synthetic.

In **synonymous parallelism,** the second measure will say the same thing as the first measure but with other words. Sometimes one measure will express the thought in literal terms, and the other measure will be figurative (this is called emblematic parallelism, and for our purposes it is just a special kind of synonymous parallelism.) Look for example at Psalm 18:4–5:

> The cords of death encompassed me;
>   the torrents of perdition assailed me;
> the cords of Sheol entangled me;
>   the snares of death confronted me.

This is an example of synonymous parallelism. The cords of death and the torrents of perdition are the watery chaos that engulfed the world at the beginning of time. These terrible flood-waters are pictured as threatening to overwhelm the psalmist. The two measures in the first line say the same thing. The two measures in the second lines are also parallel. Sheol is the underworld, the place where all people go when they die. Sheol is often pictured as actively trapping or catching people. The cords of Sheol are like a noose in a trap. The phrase "snares of death" also pictures a trap that will bring the psalmist down to the underworld of death.

Now look at another example in Psalm 18:13–14:

> The LORD also thundered in the heavens,
>   and the Most High uttered his voice.
> And he sent out his arrows, and scattered them;
>   he flashed forth lightnings, and routed them.

This is an example of emblematic synonymous parallelism. The presence of God is often recognized in natural phenomena. Psalm 18 gives a description of a thunderstorm. Thunder and lightning are the literal phenomena, whereas God's voice and his arrows are metaphorically compared to the thunder and the lightning. Notice that in the first line, the literal phenomenon is in the first measure and the figurative metaphor is in the second. In the second line, the metaphor is first and the literal phenomenon is second. This is a chiastic structure: ABB'A.' We will discuss this kind of chiastic structuring below.

In a line that uses **antithetical parallelism,** the second measure has the opposite meaning of the first measure. This kind of parallelism is especially frequent in Proverbs, in that the biblical writers will often want to contrast the good with the bad, or the way of wisdom with the way of folly. Look at Proverbs 28:6:

> Better to be poor and walk in integrity
> than to be crooked in one's ways even though rich.

This is a clear example of the kind of antithetical parallelism found throughout the Book of Proverbs. The poor man's integrity is opposite of the rich man's crooked ways.

In **synthetic parallelism,** the second measure does not repeat or contrast with the first measure but adds a new thought or extends the first thought in a new direction. Look for example at Psalm 40:1–3:

> I waited patiently for the LORD;
> he inclined to me and heard my cry.
> He drew me up from the desolate pit,
> out of the miry bog,
> and set my feet upon a rock,
> making my steps secure.
> He put a new song in my mouth,
> a song of praise to our God.
> Many will see and fear,
> and put their trust in the LORD.

There are five lines in these verses. The last four lines are all in synonymous parallelism, but notice that the first line is not. The first measure of the first line says that the psalmist waits for the LORD. The second measure then describes what the LORD does. This then leads to the rest of the lines that describe what the LORD has done for the psalmist and what the results of that rescue are. The first line is considered synthetic parallelism. It is clearly meant as a couplet with the two measures in a kind of parallelism, although the parallelism is not a comparison or a contrast but rather a synthesis of two disparate elements—the psalmist's need and God's response.

There is also an artistic way of structuring parallelism that is common in Hebrew poetry. This is not a separate kind of parallelism but can be used with any of the three kinds of parallelism. **Chiastic parallelism** refers to the way parallelism is arranged in the form of an **X.** Look at Job 5:22:

> At destruction and famine you shall laugh,
>   and shall not fear the wild animals of the earth.

This is just a simple synonymous parallelism, except that the internal order of the measures is opposite. The first measure begins with the threatening situation of destruction and famine and ends with the psalmist's reaction of laughing. The second measure begins with the psalmist's reaction of not fearing and ends with the threatening situation of wild animals. If the threatening situation is designated by "A" and the psalmist's reaction is designated by "B," then the structure of this line is ABB′A′. This is chiastic parallelism and takes the form of an X.

A   B

B′   A′

The power of parallelism in Hebrew poetry is to show the relationships between things in the world. Comparison, contrast, and synthesis generate thought and meaning. The reader learns how to see things in new and deeper ways because of the parallelism used in poetry.

The reader should be aware that the two measures of a line of Hebrew poetry are meant to be read, chanted, or sung in rhythm. To this end, the number of syllables, the stresses, the accents, and the alliterations are important elements that contribute to the rhythm. These are lost in English translations. Another aspect of Hebrew poetry that should be noted is the use of typical poetic techniques such as simile, metaphor, idioms, and hyperbole. These should be recognizable for contemporary readers even in English translations.

Genres of Wisdom Literature

Wisdom literature in the Bible can be grouped into three major kinds of texts. The Wisdom Books contain songs and hymns (Psalms and Song of Solomon), practical advice (Proverbs, Wisdom, and Sirach), and reflections on the complexities of life (Job and Ecclesiastes). Each type of text also has its own typical genres. The Psalms have laments, dirges, hymns, coronation hymns, songs of procession, and so on. The books of practical advice mainly use aphorisms (short pithy sayings). In the reflective books, we find a folklore tale encasing a philosophical dialogue and a more sustained philosophical argument.

Themes of Wisdom Literature

Although the themes of wisdom literature are nearly as varied as the genres, there are a few important themes that characterize most of the Wisdom Books (Psalms will often be the exception). Wisdom literature is concerned more with humanity in general than with the Israelites or Jews in particular. It does not focus on the history of Israel, on God's acts of salvation, or even on the covenant but is concerned with the issues of the good life, correct behavior, and success in society. Although it would be false to say that the Wisdom Books are secular, the role of God in these texts is more implicit than in the other books of the Bible. Certainly the Wisdom Books are humanistic. Their focus is on human life and the questions raised by it: how to be successful, why is there suffering, what is the meaning of life, what is after death, and how do humans fit into creation?

Wisdom

Universal—Not just for Jews
Humanistic—Not explicitly about God
or God's actions in history
Experiential—Not derived from God's law and Covenant

World in front of the Text

Humanism

One of the features of wisdom literature is its strong sense that creation and humans are good and naturally gifted with the ability to know and serve God. The wisdom that is in all creation and the wisdom that humans acquire are natural gifts from God. God has built into creation and into humans the knowledge and understanding of God. Wisdom's positive view of humanity can serve as an antidote to the more negative evaluations found in prophetic and apocalyptic literature. Moreover it is in the Wisdom Literature that we find the clearest influence from other nations and peoples. Proverbs 22:17—24:22 are dependent on the Egyptian *Instruction of Amenemope* (some translations even include the name of Amenemope in the text). Even though there is much in the Old Testament that is very judgmental of other nations and their influences, we find in the Wisdom Literature an openness to wisdom wherever it is to be found.

Job

INTRODUCTION

World behind the Text

Postexilic Reflection

The Book of Job is very difficult to date for a number of reasons. No other books in the Old Testament are similar to it. Its language is unusual; some of it is archaic and some seemingly influenced by foreign cultures. Because it is not about Israel or an

Israelite (its main character is a nomadic chieftain living in the east), there are no historical references. It is probably the case that the folklore tale, which is the setting for the longer dialogues in the book, is a much older work. The dialogues that are the bulk of the book probably reflect a postexilic setting of around 500–400 B.C.E. The work is written by a person who is familiar with the deuteronomistic and wisdom traditions of Israel but is also critical of them. Perhaps because of the disastrous experience of the Exile and post-Exile, the traditional interpretations of Israel's sinfulness and punishment no longer seemed adequate. The author of the Book of Job challenges the too easy assigning of guilt to those who suffer calamity. The book probably went through several editions. The speeches of Elihu (chapters 32—37) and the poem about wisdom (chapter 28) do not fit well into the structure or into the narrative and seem to have been later additions to the book.

Satan

One of the characters in the opening section of the story is identified as the Satan. Although later writings identify Satan with the devil, the evil opponent of God, the Satan in early Jewish writings is not evil, nor an opponent of God. The word *Satan* in Hebrew means the adversary, but he is not God's adversary. The Satan is a member of God's heavenly court whose role is prosecuting attorney, or, as we might say in modern idiom, the "Devil's advocate." In this story Satan challenges God's perception of Job as an upright man. The Satan takes a very pragmatic approach to the relationship between God and humans. Humans who are blessed by God will honor God, and those who are not blessed by God will not honor God. The role of Satan in this story is as the instigator of the crisis that provokes the dialogues. Satan is proved wrong at the beginning and does not play any further role in the story.

World of the Text

A Prose Envelope for a Poetic Book

The structure of the Book of Job may be its most striking feature. The book begins and ends with a folktale of Job, a wealthy and

blessed man who because of the challenge of the Satan has everything taken away from him. He apparently withstands the challenge
and in the end has everything given back to him. This folktale prologue and epilogue are in prose. In the middle of this frame, we find
the poetic complaint of Job, his dialogue with his three friends plus
one, and his dialogue with God. This material is all in poetry. What
is striking is the discontinuity between the two parts. Satan plays no
role in the story after the opening. The Job of the poetry sections
does not correspond to the Job of the prose prologue and epilogue.
The Job of the folktale is patient and long-suffering, whereas the
Job of the poetry complains most bitterly and is ready to accuse
God of injustice and indifference.

The Book of Job has a very definite structure. In addition to
the prose envelope structure we just noted, the poetic middle of
the book also has a clear structure, although it is complicated by
what seem to be additions to the book. The first and main section
of the poetic dialogue in the middle of the book contains three
cycles of speeches by Job and his friends. The section begins with
the introductory complaint by Job. Then each of his friends gives
a speech with Job giving a reply to each one. This cycle of
speeches is repeated three times. At the end of the third cycle, Job
summarizes his case. We can diagram this section as follows:

> Job's Complaint Chapter 3
> 1st Cycle
>> Eliphaz's 1st speech 4—5
>>> Job's reply 6—7
>> Bildad's 1st speech 8
>>> Job's reply 9—10
>> Zophar's 1st speech 11
>>> Job's reply 12—14
> 2nd Cycle
>> Eliphaz's 2nd speech 15
>>> Job's reply 16—17
>> Bildad's 2nd speech 18
>>> Job's reply 19
>> Zophar's 2nd speech 20
>>> Job's reply 21

3rd Cycle
   Eliphaz's 3rd speech 22
      Job's reply 23—24
   Bildad's 3rd speech 25
      Job's reply 26—27
   A hymn to Wisdom 28
   Job's summary of his case 29—31

Notice that even this well-organized structure seems to disintegrate at the end. Bildad's third speech, which constitutes all of chapter 25, is actually only six verses long, and there is no third speech for Zophar. Has the text been compromised from its original structure, or was it originally intended this way? Perhaps this disintegrated structure is meant to point to the fact that the dialogue is disintegrating.

After this section (which constitutes the bulk of the poetic dialogues), we are introduced to another friend—Elihu. The narrative presumes that he has been there with Job and his three friends all the time, but we are never told of him at the opening of the dialogues when the other friends are introduced. Some consider Elihu's speeches to be a later addition meant to put a better face on the opposition to Job's scandalous challenge. After Elihu's four speeches (32—37), Yahweh addresses Job out of the storm in two separate speeches (38—39 and 40—41). In 42:1–6 Job, having gotten the meeting with God that he asked for, acknowledges that his evaluation of God was incorrect.

World in front of the Text

The Patience of Job

Given that the largest part of the Book of Job is composed of Job's dialogues with his friends, in which Job's argument is that God is unjust, capricious, and a bully, it is almost ludicrous that Job is held up as the model of patience and long-suffering. No other Old Testament character stands up to God and accuses God of injustice the way Job does. The reputation of Job as the epitome of patience was sealed for Christians in

James 5:11: "You have heard of the endurance of Job." Some commentators question whether James knew of the Job of the poetry or was speaking only of the Job reflected in the prose folktale.

JOB 6—7

World behind the Text

Cosmic War Myth

The background for understanding the words of Job in his first reply to Eliphaz is the cosmic war mythology of the ancient Near East. In this myth, the hero god goes to war against the force of chaos, usually a sea monster. In the Babylonian myth, Marduk goes to war against the watery abyss, Tiamat, and kills her with an arrow shot into her heart. In the Canaanite myth, Baal goes to war with Yam, the god of the sea. When Job complains in 6:4, "For the arrows of the Almighty are in me; my spirit drinks their poison; the terrors of God are arrayed against me," he would seem to be picturing God fighting against him as against the primordial sea monster. This is even clearer in 7:12 when Job says, "Am I the Sea [the Hebrew word is *yam*], or the Dragon, that you set a guard over me?" Job's complaint against God is not that he is perfect and should receive all blessing and no punishment. Job even admits in 7:20–21 that he is a sinner. What Job is arguing is that the suffering he is enduring is not commensurate with his small sins, which do not really threaten God or the order of the universe. God seems to be treating Job as an enemy of the order of the universe.

By comparing this text to religious texts from the ancient Near East, we understand better what the author of Job is trying to say. This is called History of Religions criticism, and it makes us aware of both the similarities and differences with other religious texts.

Turning Psalm 8 on Its Head

After questioning God as to why he is being treated as the primordial sea monster, Job asks God to just leave him alone. It is at this point that Job asks, "What are human beings, that you make so much of them, that you set your mind on them?" (7:17). This is almost a direct quote from Psalm 8:4, but the context and meaning are quite different in Job than in Psalm 8. In Psalm 8, the psalmist extols the greatness and majesty of God and marvels that God, the creator of all the universe, has thought so highly of human beings as to give them dominion over all creation. So when the psalmist says, "What are human beings that you are mindful of them, mortals that you care for them?" the psalmist is wondering at the positive esteem in which God holds humans. Job takes this line from Psalm 8 and uses it to question why God holds humans in such negative esteem, considering them such a threat and spending so much time monitoring what humans do. Job goes so far as to say that God will not turn away from watching him long enough for him to swallow his spittle. The author of the Book of Job turns the positive religious image of God watching humans to care for them into a negative image of God watching humans as a vindictive judge and enemy in war.

This is a good example of intertextuality in the Bible. Later books will often use material from earlier works. In this case, there is an ironic and critical use of an older tradition. The Book of Job calls into question the religious ideas taken for granted at that time.

In Dialogue with Deuteronomistic Theology

As we noted above, the bulk of the Book of Job is a dialogue between Job and his friends about the reasons for his suffering. The friends take the "tried and true" approach of Deuteronomistic theology that Job's sufferings are punishments for sin. The friends maintain that if Job will only repent, God will surely bless him. When we examined the Book of Deuteronomy and the Deuteronomistic History in Judges, we saw this theological principle at work. When Israel was faithful to God, God blessed them with peace and prosperity. When Israel was unfaithful to God, they were punished with famine, disaster, war, and suffering. This principle, which grew out of the experience of national destruction and exile, was originally meant to show that God had not been unfaithful to the covenant nor was God too weak to save the people from their enemies. Rather, the calamity that befell Israel and Judah was the result of their own sinfulness. In the time of the Exile, this was a hopeful message. If the people of Judah would only trust in God, God was strong enough and faithful enough to bring them out of exile and bless them with prosperity. As this theological principle became fixed and universalized, however, it was also recognized as being problematic. The Book of Job is a theological reflection on the viability of this theological principle as it applies to the human experience of suffering. Note that the book takes the discussion out of the context of Israel's covenant relationship with God and places it in the context of all humans before God. What is at issue is whether human suffering can be reduced to punishment for sin. This is the position of Job's friends. Job, however, maintains that the suffering he endures, and the suffering of most of humanity (see 7:1), is out of proportion to any supposed sinfulness. Humans seem to be created to suffer and die. In the final analysis the questions raised by Job go far beyond simply questioning the Deuteronomistic principle. The issue that Job raises is **theodicy,** the question of why there is evil and suffering in the world, and what role God plays in it. Is God the cause of evil? Is God unable to do anything about evil and suffering? Does God even care?

Theodicy (how God relates to the world) is an important term that any reader of the Bible should be familiar with. The word is not used in the Bible, but any discussion of the Bible will usually come around to this issue.

World of the Text

Going Toe to Toe with Eliphaz

The text that we are studying is Job's reply to the first speech of Eliphaz, who begins his speech by accusing Job of hypocrisy.

Job has instructed and comforted many, but now when it comes to him, he is impatient and dismayed (4:5). Eliphaz continues with the argument that the evil that befalls a person is the result of that person's own actions: "Think now, who that was innocent ever perished?" (4:7) and "misery does not come from the earth, nor does trouble sprout from the ground; but human beings are born to trouble" (5:6–7). Eliphaz goes so far as to recount a vision of the night in which it was revealed to him that no human is blameless before God. "Can mortals be righteous before God?" (4:17). Eliphaz then gives the advice that Job should appeal to God because God punishes the wicked but listens to those who turn to God for help. If Job will only do this, he will be able to laugh at adversity and hope for the future (5:22–26).

Job begins his reply by answering Eliphaz's charge of hypocrisy. Job uses images from nature to make his point that this is not simply a matter of his needing to be strengthened and upheld in trying times. He tells Eliphaz that his calamity is without measure. He maintains that he would not complain if it were not called for, asking, "Does the wild ass bray over its grass?" (6:5). In answer to Eliphaz's contention that no innocent person perishes, Job maintains, "I have not denied the words of the Holy One" (6:10). Then Job digresses slightly. Eliphaz had engaged in an *ad hominem* argument by accusing Job, the great leader and counselor, of himself being unable to take counsel. Job counters by accusing Eliphaz of not being much of a friend. He says that "those who withhold kindness from a friend forsake the fear of the Almighty" (6:14). Job claims Eliphaz is a fair-weather friend: "My companions are treacherous like a torrent-bed" (6:15). Job accuses Eliphaz of being such a lowlife he "would even cast lots over the orphan, and bargain over your friend" (6:27). After getting this out of his system, Job continues answering Eliphaz's arguments. In answer to Eliphaz's claim that no human is blameless before God, Job gives his own description of human beings before God. Instead of focusing on the majesty of God, Job emphasizes the piteous condition of humans by asking, "Do not human beings have a hard service on earth, and are not their days like the days of a laborer?" (7:1). Finally, in answer to Eliphaz's advice to throw himself on the mercy of God, Job counters by drawing a picture of an all-out cosmic war between God and humans, a war in which God holds all the cards (7:12). (Up to this point Job has been addressing Eliphaz, but from 7:12 on Job addresses God directly.) Job ends by saying that instead of his seeking God, God ought to seek him. Job can do nothing for God, but if God should ever want Job, "you will seek me, but I shall not be" (7:21).

> In this study, the method used was a correlation of Job's reply with the speech of Eliphaz that preceded it. The structure of the dialogue pairs a speech of a friend with a reply of Job. This structure invites us to read Job's reply against the speech of the friend. The parallelism between the two allows us to contrast the two points of view.

World in front of the Text

Face to Face; Not a Face-Off

The nature of humans in the eyes of God and the place of humans in God's overall plan are profound issues raised by the Book of Job. Our text (chapters 6—7) must be interpreted in light of the whole of the Book of Job. The main point of the Book of Job is not universally agreed on, although it seems that the author of this book rejects a simplistic understanding of evil and suffering as the result of human sinfulness and the punishment of God. God's answers to Job in chapters 38—41 do not even deal with the issue of human suffering, which seems to have been the major issue of all the dialogues. God's "answer" to Job seems to be that "What you consider to be evil and chaos is part of my creation and just the way things are." God tells Job that he is correct to reject the arguments of his friends that all suffering and calamities that befall humans are punishments for sin. However, Job is mistaken in thinking that God is at war with humans or is capricious and unjust. God's answer to Job then is simply meeting him face to face. From the point of view of humans, the world contains catastrophic, terrible, and unexplained suffering and evil. From the point of view of God, the world does not look quite the same. The terrible sea monsters are God's pets, and catastrophes are just the way nature works. Yet God is not a God cut off from humans and unconcerned. God has heard Job's complaint and comes to speak with him. The message of the Book of Job seems to be that the answer to the question of suffering is less important than the fact that God is a God who listens to humans and meets them in conversation. However, Job achieves this face-to-face meeting with God only because he is willing to take the risk of rejecting the easy answers of religious tradition and confronts God directly.

Psalms

INTRODUCTION

World behind the Text

Where Do the Psalms Come From?

The Book of Psalms contains a collection of psalms written over a period of centuries. It is actually a grouping of five separate collections of psalms. The final grouping into the five "books" of psalms that are in the Bible was probably compiled in the postexilic community in Jerusalem around 500 B.C.E. Many, but not all, of the psalms contain an ascription at the beginning. (Some translations make the ascription the first verse and others, such as the NRSV, begin numbering the verses after the ascription.) The psalms are "of David," "of Asaph," "of the sons of Korah," and more. The ascription "of David" most likely means "for him," "about him," "in his honor," or simply "in his style" and does not indicate that David was the author of the psalm. So, although David has traditionally been considered the author of the psalms, he is perhaps the author of only a few of them but the inspiration for many more.

Psalm 4 is a good example of a typical ascription. The ascription reads: "To the leader: with stringed instruments. A Psalm of David." As we can see from this example, the ascriptions of many psalms also describe who is to sing it and the tune to which it is meant to be sung. The primary setting for all of the psalms in their final form is worship in the Temple. Although some of the individual lament psalms may have begun as private prayers, their being added to a collection of psalms meant that they were being used in public liturgies. Many of the psalms reflect the situation of the Babylonian Exile, whereas others reflect the time of the kingship while the first Temple was intact.

World of the Text

The Shape of the Book

Psalms is divided into five separate "books" (1—41, 42—72, 73—89, 90—106, 107—150). Each of the separate books ends with a benediction that is not part of the psalm to which it is attached but is meant to conclude the book as a whole. The last book does not have a benediction attached to its last psalm. Instead, the whole of Psalm 150 is meant to be the benediction that closes the entire collection. This division of the collection into five "books" is no doubt meant to imitate the collection of the law in five books (the Pentateuch).

Literary Types

The psalms are not a homogeneous group. There are at least six major different types of psalms: Laments, Hymns, Thanksgivings, Royal Psalms, Wisdom Psalms, and Liturgical Psalms. (There are different ways to classify the Psalms, but this classification is common.) Laments are the most frequent type, constituting about one-third of the book. Laments can be either personal or communal (though as we noted earlier even psalms that are personal end up being used in communal settings) and contain a description of the terrible situation of the petitioner, a plea for help, and usually a statement of confidence that God will intervene. Hymns are psalms that praise God for God's actions and attributes. Very often God's majesty, as evidenced in nature, is the cause for praise. Thanksgiving Psalms are hymns that thank God for deliverance from a specific situation. The Royal Psalms are varied in type. They share the common feature of being about the king. They can commemorate and bless the enthronement of the king, ask for blessings for the king, or thank God for deliverance of the king. The Wisdom Psalms differ from the other psalms in being intended for teaching more than for worship. They are concerned with the themes found in the other wisdom books: evil, death, and suffering. Finally the Liturgical Psalms are those psalms that focus on Jerusalem (the Zion Psalms), that speak of pilgrimage to Jerusalem (the Ascent Psalms), or that focus on covenant renewal.

Literary Features of the Psalms

The Psalms are some of the finest poetry in the Old Testament and use the methods of poetry described in the introduction to the Wisdom Books: parallelism, rhythm, and metaphor. Another feature of the poetry of the Psalms that is not found in other poetry of the Old Testament (except in a few cases in Proverbs) is the use of the **alphabetic acrostic.** A psalm is an acrostic if it begins each line with a different letter of the Hebrew alphabet. The psalms that use this form are Psalms 9—10, 25, 34, 111, 112, 119, and 145. (This form is not reproduced in English translations.)

World in front of the Text

Psalms: The Prayer of the Church

The psalms have always been at the center of the way Jews and Christians pray. The psalms were used in the great pilgrim feasts at the Temple and later were used in prayer and study in the synagogue. The psalms were the heart of the monastic Liturgy of the Hours in the Middle Ages and after and have always been a part of the Mass. Psalms were set to music, or their words and images were used as lyrics for new hymns and songs in Christian liturgy. It would not be an exaggeration to say that the Book of Psalms is the single most important and influential book of the Bible for liturgy in both Judaism and Christianity.

PSALM 22

World behind the Text

The Situation

The ascription of this psalm tells us the melody (The Deer of the Dawn) to be used in singing the psalm. Although we no longer know the melody, it is important to appreciate this text as a song that would have been sung in a liturgical setting. It is part of the first book of psalms and is attributed to David.

It is difficult to know what is the original situation described in this psalm. Is this an individual lament that describes the situation of an Israelite who is hated by his fellow Israelites? This is something that Jeremiah experienced. Verse 9, especially, might imply that the issue is religious trust. It is also possible that the psalm is about the king who is experiencing the scorn of his neighbor kings who mock his trust in God. There is enough war imagery in the psalm to make this a plausible suggestion.

World of the Text

A Lament Psalm

The elements of a lament psalm are an Invocation, a Description of the Predicament of the Speaker, a Confession of Confidence, a Petition, and a Command to Praise. Psalm 22, as a lament psalm, contains each of these elements but doubles some of them. It can be outlined as follows:

Invocation (vv. 1–5)
Description of the Predicament (vv. 6–8)
Confession of Confidence (vv. 9–10)
Petition (v. 11)
Description of the Predicament (vv. 12–18)
Petition (vv. 19–21)
Command to Praise (vv. 22–31)

The Invocation not only calls on God but also expresses the past experience of Israel in being rescued by God. The Description of the Predicament of the speaker is in two sections each followed by a Petition (the first section is also followed by the Confession of Confidence). Both Predicaments contain descriptions of the speaker and of the enemies. The first Predicament (vv. 6–8) focuses on the speaker's place in society: he is a worm and the enemies mock him. He is considered subhuman and mocked for his trust in God. It may be that the Confession of Confidence follows this description as a way to counter the enemies' taunt about letting God rescue him.

The second Predicament is more complicated. It alternates between descriptions of what the enemies are like and what the speaker is suffering. First, the enemies are pictured as wild animals: bulls and lions (vv. 12–13). Then the speaker describes his own experience in two ways. First, he describes his life in wet images: he is poured out like water, his bones are out of joint, and his heart is like wax and melts (v. 14). Second, he describes his life in dry images: his mouth is dried up like a potsherd, his tongue sticks to his jaw, and he is lying in the dust of death (v. 15). It is very typical to use this kind of dual imagery to make the point that the whole person from wet to dry, from top to bottom, from inside to outside, is dying. Then the speaker returns to a description of the enemies as wild animals: a pack of dogs (v. 16a). The speaker again describes himself, this time as a skeleton whose bones can be numbered (vv. 16b–17a). Finally, in vv. 17b–18, the speaker concludes the description by returning to the mockery described in the first Predicament. In v. 7 when describing the enemies, the speaker says, "All who see me mock at me." Here he says, "They stare and gloat over me." Seeing and mocking are in both the first and last descriptions of the enemies. Taking the two Predicaments together, the first and last descriptions of the enemies are more literal in describing the real taunt that the enemies make against the speaker and in describing a real human act of casting lots for his clothing (vv. 7–8; vv. 17b–18). The middle two descriptions of the enemies are metaphorical in describing them like wild animals ready to eat him (vv. 12–13; v. 16a).

At the end of the second Predicament, the speaker includes a second Petition (vv. 19–21). In the Petition, he repeats the three kinds of animals used to describe the enemies: dog, lion, and oxen (bull). Notice that in the Petition the animals are in reverse order from their use in the Predicament descriptions. Also, in the descriptions of the condition of the speaker, the speaker's strength was a major issue. In the Petition, the speaker calls on God to provide strength.

The Command to Praise at the end of the psalm is also divided into two sections. The first section of the Command to Praise has two parts. The speaker promises to proclaim God's name in the assembly and then rehearses that speech. The promise addresses God directly using the second person (v. 22). The speech itself speaks of God in the third person but addresses the assembly in the second person (vv. 23–26). The second section of the Command to Praise (vv. 27–31) is a separate hymn of praise to Yahweh, speaking of God in the third person. This hymn is universal and is not directed only to the assembly as the first section was. Notice the repeated use of "all."

> Knowing the elements of a lament psalm helps us to understand the way this psalm progresses. Paying careful attention to the structure helps us to appreciate the connections between the separate parts.

The Poetry of Psalm 22

To get a feel for the poetry of the Psalms it might help to look more closely at a section of Psalm 22. Verses 12–21 constitute a unit of the poem. This unit begins with bulls and lions (12–13) and ends with oxen and lions (21). This is called an inclusion or brackets, for this section. Verse 12 is a good example of synonymous parallelism. The two measures of this line say exactly the same thing. Verse 15 is an example of a line with three measures. The first two measures are synonymous parallelism but the third measure could be considered synthetic parallelism because it takes the image of dryness further and equates it with death. Verse 16a is an example of emblematic parallelism—where one measure is a metaphor and the second measure is the reality. The first measure of v. 16a describes the dogs that surround the psalmist, whereas the second measure explains that these are evildoers. The dogs are a metaphor for the evildoers. Verses 16b–17a constitute an example of synonymous parallelism. To say that you can count all his bones is another way of saying that his hands and feet are shriveled. Both point to the emaciated state of the psalmist.

World in front of the Text

Suffering One

This psalm is used by all the canonical gospels to describe Jesus' passion and crucifixion. All four gospels allude to Psalm 22:18 in which the psalmist's persecutors divide his garments and throw lots for his cloak or tunic. Mark (followed by Matthew and Luke) also alludes to v. 7 by having the passersby shake their heads and the chief priests and scribes mock. Matthew takes the allusion even farther by having the chief priests mock Jesus with the words, "He trusts in God; let God deliver him now, if he wants to" (Matt 27:43), which are taken from Psalm 22:8. Mark (15:34) followed by Matthew has Jesus cry out with the opening words of Psalm 22: "My God, my God, why have you forsaken me?" The placing of these words in the mouth of Jesus by Mark and John's directly quoting Psalm 22 in his reference to the dividing of Jesus' clothing inform the gospel readers that Psalm 22 is an interpretive key to Jesus' passion and death. He is the suffering righteous one who trusts in God, who will be vindicated by God, and who will proclaim God's praise in the sanctuary.

> An appreciation of the formal and liturgical character of this psalm can help us to appreciate the religious picture of Jesus that the gospel writers are painting for us at the crucifixion.

Proverbs

INTRODUCTION

World behind the Text

Solomon as Author of Proverbs

Just as the Book of Psalms is associated with David, the Book of Proverbs is associated with Solomon. He is not the author of the proverbs, but many of the proverbs are quite old and may even go back to the time of Solomon or before. Proverbs 25:1 ascribes the second collection of proverbs to Solomon and notes that they are transmitted (collected and written down) by the men of Hezekiah, king of Judah. It is entirely possible that the great reputation of Solomon for wisdom and for being the author of Proverbs and other of the Wisdom Books comes from the time of Hezekiah (715–687 B.C.E.). This may be when the compiling of collections of proverbs and the attributing of them to Solomon was begun. Some of the proverbs are probably taken from, or dependent on, collections of proverbs from other nations (Egypt, Babylon, Canaan). The original setting for the proverbs would probably be first the home and later the school. They were used for training young men how to be successful in life.

World of the Text

The Genre of the Proverb

Proverbs, like many of the Wisdom Books, is a collection of wisdom sayings. Like Psalms, it is a collection of collections, but unlike Psalms it is not arranged into five books. Proverbs would seem to include between seven and nine collections, some of which are attributed to Solomon (chapters 10—22 and 25—29) and some to other authors (chapter 30 is attributed to Agur, son of Jakeh, and chapter 31 is attributed to King Lemuel).

The Hebrew word for proverb is *mashal*. It is the word used both in 10:1 and 25:1 to introduce a collection of proverbs. The word *mashal* can be used for a great variety of literary forms, but in its root meaning it refers to a comparison. Usually some human behavior or event is compared to something in nature. The simplest form of a proverb and a clear example of the root meaning of *mashal* is seen in Proverbs 25:25: "Like cold water to a thirsty soul, so is good news from a far country." Proverbs come in two basic types: wisdom sentences and admonitions. Wisdom sentences are simple statements of fact that make a statement about the way things are. Admonitions are commands to act in a certain way. Although both are built on parallelism and are aphoristic, the wisdom sentence is the purest form of an aphorism.

An *aphorism* is a short and concise statement that makes a connection between two things. It does not pose a question, offer an explanation, or give advice. The connection the aphorism makes is meant to lead the hearer to understand human behavior in a new way, to make a lightbulb go off in a person's head. The connection contains a paradox that challenges the hearer to come to new insight. Proverbs 25:20 says, "Like a moth in clothing or a worm in wood, sorrow gnaws at the human heart." This is a simple assertion of the way things are. However, because it is built on a metaphorical comparison, there is a paradox contained in it. Sorrow is not exactly like a maggot or a moth. Sorrow is an emotion and not a living being. The proverb challenges the hearer to gain insight into the connection between these disparate objects. Proverbs 6:20 is a good example of an admonition: "My child, keep your father's commandment, and do not forsake your mother's teaching." An admonition offers advice that is not specific but based more on the nature of learning itself. Often admonitions are coupled with more traditional wisdom sentences. Proverbs 6:23 continues the thought and language of 6:20 but as a simple wisdom sentence: "For the commandment is a lamp and the teaching a light, and the reproofs of discipline are the way of life." The admonitions point to the setting of the proverbs as instructions for life (they often speak directly to "my child"), but their being coupled with wisdom sentences show that they are very different from law.

Each proverb was originally intended to stand independently. The original proverbs were not written as part of a collection, but invented spontaneously to influence an audience. In fact, a proverb can often lose its powerful impact when read as a part of a collection. A proverb is meant to come out of nowhere and surprise the hearer with its simplicity, lucidity, and paradox. As part of a collection the proverbs often seem not to be surprising new ways of looking at the world, but old-fashioned, traditional ways. They can seem archaic and worn out by overuse.

Yet the proverbs as we have them come as part of collections. They should be interpreted in light of the collection they are part of and as part of the whole book of collections. The proverbs teach the way a person should live, but they are not at all a simple "how to" manual. They are not "ten easy steps to successful living." One proverb cannot be taken by itself as a guide to life. Rather the proverbs repeat similar material but in different contexts and often with different conclusions. Studying the proverbs is more like being trained in lateral or nonlinear thinking. However, they should not simply be reduced to a training of the imagination; they are fundamentally theistic, maintaining that God is the foundation and source of all wisdom.

World in front of the Text

Hearing the Proverbs Today

It is a shame that the Book of Proverbs is not read more today. Even though the proverbs contain many things that are archaic, dated, chauvinistic, patriarchal, and silly, they contain many more pearls of wisdom and gems of human psychology. It would be worth our while to spend time sifting through them, laughing at what is silly and taking to heart what is still very wise. It is probably not the best idea to start at the beginning and plod your way through all thirty-one chapters of Proverbs. The proverbs can be experienced more powerfully by opening the book and picking out proverbs at random. This will allow the proverb to regain its unique and surprising character. In some ways, a proverb is like a Buddhist koan—it is meant to be savored. It should be heard as a surprising zinger and not as a piece of pious advice.

PROVERBS 9

World behind the Text

Wisdom as Royalty or Goddess

The image of Wisdom as a woman presents a very intriguing problem. Where did the image come from? Is this just a case of an attribute of God (like justice, kindness, and truth) being personified? Personification is frequent in the Old Testament, where the floods clap their hands (Ps 98:8), gates lift up their heads (Ps 24:7), and righteousness looks down from skies (Ps 85:11). Some suggest that Wisdom is simply an attribute of God that is portrayed as a female because wisdom in Hebrew *(hokmah)* is a feminine noun. However, in Proverbs 8:22 Woman Wisdom is portrayed as a being separate from God. Therefore, some see Woman Wisdom as a personification of the order of creation more than as an attribute of God. Although there is some truth to this, Woman Wisdom cannot simply be reduced to the order of creation. Rather, Woman Wisdom is God's way of relating to creation. In Proverbs 8—9 Woman Wisdom is a female figure who is a creation of God, but was created by God before everything else. Woman Wisdom was present with God at creation and was the plan and order of creation. Because of this, Woman Wisdom offers, to those who partake of it, insight into and understanding of the true nature and order of all of creation. Others have suggested that Woman Wisdom was originally a goddess of wisdom who over time has been changed into an attribute of God but still has a certain amount of independence. It is not uncommon to find mythological elements in the Old Testament. Woman Wisdom is pictured as having built a house with seven columns, which might indicate a temple or a palace. She is throwing a sumptuous banquet and inviting all. It was very typical for a king to provide a huge banquet on the completion of a palace, or for a banquet to be held in the honor of a god at the completion of a temple. Israelites would never have thought of Woman Wisdom as a goddess in competition with Yahweh, but they would have recognized the goddesslike attributes given to her. She would have been entirely obedient to and dependent on Yahweh, but still pictured in her own right as a type of goddess or heavenly queen who brings about creation and leads humans to knowledge of God.

World of the Text

Chapters 1—9 as an Introduction to the Book of Proverbs

Chapters 1—9 of Proverbs constitute a description of the value of Wisdom, and stand out as different from the unrelated proverbs that make up the rest of the collection. Chapters 1—9 have a sustained argument and image that connects them together. These chapters also tend to have more admonitions than the rest of the collections.

Wisdom's Invitation

The poem in Proverbs 9 has three sections: the description and invitation of Woman Wisdom (1–6), advice to one seeking wisdom (7–12), and the description and invitation of Woman Folly (13–18). The way the poem stands in its present form, the advice to one seeking wisdom should be read as a continuation of the invitation of Woman Wisdom. Verses 1–3 are the narrative introduction to chapter 9. They describe Woman Wisdom as a female figure who has prepared a banquet. In verses 4–6, Woman Wisdom speaks directly to her audience inviting the hearer to come to the banquet. Verses 7–12 continue the direct speech of Wisdom, although these verses are more conventional proverbs about living a wise life (they are wisdom sentences). Verses 11–12, though, return to second person direct address. The direct second person address in verses 11–12 indicates that all of verses 7–12 should be read as a speech of Woman Wisdom. This allows the author to incorporate some standard proverbs into Woman Wisdom's invitation to come to her banquet. Verses 4–6 and 11–12 serve as brackets around the standard proverbs. In verses 13–18, a counterimage to Woman Wisdom is presented. Woman Folly sits at the door of her house inviting guests to leave the straight path and come into her house. Folly, like Wisdom, speaks in proverbs, but her proverbs are antiwisdom: "Stolen water is sweet."

The Way of Wisdom

An important image in the wisdom literature and in all of the Old Testament is the correct path. Wisdom speaks of a way of insight (9:6), and Folly calls to those who are going straight on their way to turn in at her door (9:15–16). Being on the correct path is a frequent image for following the law and being faithful to God. In fact, the path is an image for one's life. To turn aside is to sin; to return or turn back is to repent of sin. All throughout wisdom literature, you will find this image of a way or a path as a description of the correct life.

World in front of the Text

Jesus as Wisdom

The image of Wisdom from the Hebrew scriptures is developed and expanded in later Judaism and Christianity. In Hellenistic philosophy, especially in Stoicism, the concept of the *Logos* (the Word) was used to explain the order of creation. The *Logos* was the rational concept behind creation. Hellenistic Judaism, especially Philo, related the *Logos* of the Greeks to Wisdom of the Old Testament. However, the *Logos* for the Stoics is the only divinity. It is not a personal being but is the divine principle of reason and meaning. For Jews and Christians, Wisdom/*Logos* is always related to and subservient to God. But this Greek-influenced understanding of Wisdom as *Logos* was probably an important ingredient in the early Christian reflection on Jesus Christ. Jesus is portrayed as Wisdom who will be vindicated by her deeds (Matt 11:19). He is the Logos through whom the world came into being (John 1:1–18). Recently scholars have argued that early Christianity was more influenced by these ideas and images than was formerly thought. What is important here is the use of a feminine image to describe Jesus.

Learning Achievements

After studying this chapter, students should be able to:

- Read and appreciate an English translation of Hebrew poetry and identify the different kinds of parallelism and the structure of chiasm.

- Outline the structure of Job.

- Discuss Job's critique of the Deuteronomistic theology.

- Describe the process of collecting psalms and proverbs into larger collections.

- Define the different kinds of psalms, especially the lament.

- Explain how the genre of proverb works.

- Describe the importance of the figure of Woman Wisdom for the New Testament.

Recommended Reading

Brenner, Athalaya. *A Feminist Companion to Wisdom Literature.* Sheffield: Sheffield Academic Press, 1995.

Crenshaw, James L. *Old Testament Wisdom: An Introduction.* Louisville, Ky.: Westminster John Knox, 1981.

Gutierrez, Gustavo. *On Job: God-Talk and the Suffering of the Innocent.* Maryknoll, N.Y.: Orbis, 1987.

Murphy, Roland E. *Tree of Life: An Exploration of Biblical Wisdom Literature.* New York: Doubleday, 1992.

Rohr, Richard. *Job and the Mystery of Suffering: Spiritual Reflections.* New York: Crossroad, 1996.

Zuck, Roy B. *Learning from the Sages: Selected Studies on the Book of Proverbs.* Grand Rapids, Mich.: Baker Books, 1995.

Chapter 6
THE PROPHETS

Introduction

World behind the Text

Who Are the Prophets?

Professional prophets were a recognized social group in the ancient Near East and often belonged to guilds. Theirs was an inherited occupation that was performed for life. They served the administration, either in the palace or in the Temple, as part of the status quo. Besides the professional prophets there were also other individuals (charismatics or seers) who were inspired by the spirit of God to speak out. These persons would not have been of the professional prophetic class but would have belonged to some other class and simply been moved by God to prophesy. There is evidence in Israel for both kinds of prophets; however, the distinctions between the two groups are not always clearly defined. Elijah and Elisha belong to a guild of prophets, and are recognized as such by the king, and yet they get into quite a bit of trouble from the administration and seem not to be court-sponsored prophets. Isaiah is not a prophet in the sense of a member of the prophetic guild, but he has access to the king and the king's respect. He is a member of the status quo. Jeremiah is a Levite and does not belong to any prophetic guild, and yet he is recognized as a seer by the king. However, he is also considered subversive and a traitor and is persecuted severely. Finally, Amos tells the priest at Bethel that he is not a prophet of the prophetic guild, but is a sheepherder who has been called by God to prophesy. His credentials are rejected by the chief priest of Bethel. As a general rule we can say that the prophets, whose writings have been collected in the Bible, based the credibility of their words on the call of God and not on belonging to a guild of prophets or on being sanctioned by king or priest. The written prophets in the Bible were most often critical of the kingly and priestly administration. Still they did garner respect and fear from the administrations that they criticized. Mostly they were not dismissed out of hand as "crazies," although at times they were accused of treason.

The Prophet behind the Book

After having read the Pentateuch and the Historical Books what must strike a first-time reader of the Bible is how different the Prophetic Books are. They do not contain a historical narrative or lists of laws. They are also not anonymous. These books are the collections of the sayings of one particular person. The Historical Books have an anonymous narrator. The narrator in the Pentateuch is anonymous, in spite of the tradition that Moses is the author. The only exception to this is the Book of Deuteronomy, which has some narration by the narrator, but is mostly composed of Moses speaking directly to the people reminding them of the words of God that he had spoken to them earlier. In fact, many feel that the closest parallel to the prophets both in genre and in theology is the Book of Deuteronomy. In that book, Moses is understood as the greatest of the prophets (18:15).

The books of the prophets, in the form that we have them in the Bible, are introduced as the sayings of a particular person at a particular time and place. Even if in some cases the attribution is fictional (as in the additions to the books of Isaiah and Zechariah), it is still important for the interpretation of the genre to recognize that the books of the prophets are oracles of a particular person called by God to speak in God's name. In contrast, the Pentateuch is a narrative of the history of God and God's people by an anonymous and omniscient narrator. This makes a difference both in how we read the text and with what background we will be concerned. In the Prophetic Books, the speaker is brought to the foreground. For the reader of the Book of Jeremiah, the person Jeremiah matters. He does not claim to have omniscient knowledge of God's work in history. He must make claims about being called by God and about being told by God when to speak. Therefore Jeremiah's interaction with God is as much the story as are the oracles. Jeremiah as a person in history, his background, his motives, his reaction, his life history are important for the reading of the text because the text tells us they are. We are told who Jeremiah is, where he comes from, some of what he thinks and feels, and what happens to him. Although we might be very curious about who the narrator of the Pentateuch is, that text never leads us to consider the narrator as an object of our focus like the texts of the prophets do.

The History of Prophecy in Israel

Prophecy has a long history in Israel. Samuel, the last of the judges, is also identified as a prophet and performed prophetic tasks. Nathan is perhaps the most famous of the professional court prophets. We encountered him in the story of David's adultery with Bathsheba (2 Sam 11). However, the tradition of the biblical prophet who is inspired by God to criticize the king and challenge the idolatry endemic to the monarchy first appeared in Israel's history with Elijah and Elisha. Nearly sixteen chapters of 1 and 2 Kings are devoted to the preaching and miracles of these two great prophets who were active in the northern kingdom of Israel during the period of 860–820 B.C.E. They confronted the royal house for its idolatry in making accommodations to the religion of Baal. Even though the Deuteronomistic historian emphasizes Elijah and Elisha's deeds more than their words, it presents these two as the paradigm for the biblical prophet who stands up to the unfaithful monarchy and proclaims an uncompromising fidelity to Yahweh. The written prophets began about 760 B.C.E. and are tied to the major crises in Israel and Judah. The early prophets (Amos, Hosea, Isaiah, and Micah) prophesied during the Assyrian crisis, when Assyrian imperialism threatened the kingdoms of Israel and Judah (760–700). The middle prophets (especially Jeremiah and Ezekiel) were active during the Babylonian crisis, when Babylonia put down a rebellion in Judah and then eliminated the nation entirely (600–580). The later prophets (Second Isaiah, Haggai, Zechariah, and Malachi) preached during what can be called the Persian crisis (540–480). This was the time when the exiles return to Judah under the authority of the Persians. The crisis involved the ongoing problem of establishing any kind of successful new state in Judah.

What Do the Prophets Do?

In common usage *prophecy* means foretelling the future, and most people think that is what the prophets in the Old Testament did. Often Christians think that the prophets primarily foretold the coming of Jesus Christ. To understand the prophets in their own context and even to appreciate the fulfillment their words find in Jesus Christ, it is important to understand their true function in Israel.

First, there is a long history of "prophets" before the time of the biblical prophets. It seems that the earliest prophets were associated with warfare and the cult. They would intercede with the gods on the behalf of the people. They would speak in God's name to encourage and direct the war. A good example of this can be seen in the Book of Judges with the prophetess (and judge) Deborah. She tells Barak, the general, that God has spoken that it is time to attack the enemy position. Barak wants her to accompany the troops to intercede for them and keep them apprised of God's word.

As we pointed out earlier, there were two kinds of prophets—the professionals and the interlopers. The written biblical prophets were mostly of the latter kind. For the sake of simplicity (though it is an oversimplification) we will make the distinction between the regular prophets (mainly the professional prophets) and the biblical prophets (meaning those whose writings are recorded in the Bible). The primary function of either kind of prophet was to speak in the name of God and to announce God's plan. Although both kinds of prophets made the claim to speak of God's plan and will, there were some differences between regular prophets and biblical prophets that might help us to understand how and why the biblical prophets were so important. First, the prophecies of the regular prophets were mostly given on a specific occasion for which they were asked to prophesy. If the king needed an opinion about some matter of state or if the people needed some word of God about their lives, the prophet would be asked to inquire of God, and the prophet would perform a divination. The prophet then would pronounce in staid and formal language what God intended for this specific occasion. In contrast, the biblical prophets were not usually asked questions by the king or by the people. They were not giving an answer to a particular question. One could say that instead of answering the questions of the king or the people the biblical prophets questioned their answers. Uninvited, the prophets, in the name of God, interposed themselves in the affairs of state and made pronouncements about God's will that were at odds with the direction of the state. They called into question the assumptions that were the foundations of the state—powerful armies and war instruments, alliances, and national pride—and challenged the king and the people to see the foundations of a true people of God: trust in God, rejection of idolatry, and humility.

There were also differences in how the prophets understood their role in relation to the future. The regular prophets had a role in society that had as much to do with intercession as with proclaiming God's will. The prophet spoke in God's name and announced what God planned to do but was also the messenger who brought the concerns of the people to God. The prophet was the negotiator between God and the people. It is striking that the biblical prophets often left no room for any response of the people, and in several instances God explicitly told the prophets that they must not intercede for the people. The biblical prophets announced to the people what God had decided to do (punish or save), no matter what the response of the people. There were messages of the prophets that called for repentance and asked the people to respond to God's plan, but many more were statements that God had reached the limit and there was no more hope. The words of the prophets that are contained in the Bible are the result of a long dialogue. The prophetic word was God's last response to a people who had failed to repent.

The language of the regular prophets was not collected and handed down, but it was probably a very formal and official language. In contrast, the language of the biblical prophets was shocking, unseemly, and innovative. One of the main purposes of their language was to shock the people and wake them up to the reality of their rejection of God. It is not difficult to find sexually oriented images that are shocking. Hosea spoke of Israel as a whore (2:4–7). Jeremiah used an obscene word to describe the whorish activity of Israel with the pagan gods (3:2). Ezekiel was pornographic in his description of Israel and Judah as sisters who prostitute themselves with the neighboring nations (23:1–23). One prophet described God as a maggot feeding on the rotten flesh of Israel (Hos 5:12). Israel was described as dirty rotted underwear that God would never put on again (Jer 13:10). Israel was pictured as a vessel of clay that God was not happy with and so would crush back into a lump and make over again (Jer 18:1–12). Although some of these images were shocking in their own right, some would have been shocking in their traitorous implications. Israel regarded herself as God's chosen people, and to claim that God would destroy or exile Israel would have been considered treason by the state.

The task of a prophet was divination—to find out what God wanted or had to say about a situation. Divination in the ancient world was most often inductive. The prophet performed some act or considered some natural event that could be read to indicate God's will. Throwing dice, observing the stars, or doing an augury on a live animal were all means of determining the will of God for the future. In contrast to the regular prophets who obtained their answers from inductive divination, the biblical prophets received their oracles from intuitive divination. By intuitive divination, the word of God came directly to their minds in a vision or a word. In contrast to the auguries, dreams, and spirit possessions of regular prophets, the biblical prophets stand out as having direct, unaided, and conscious exchanges with God.

Production of the Prophetic Books

It is not enough to simply describe the cultural and social phenomenon of prophecy and place the biblical prophets in their social and historical context in Israel. The history of biblical prophets must also take into account the history of the production of the books of the prophets. This includes the history of a community that over many generations received, preserved, collected, compiled, added to, and edited the words and deeds of the prophets.

The books of the prophets that we have now were not written down by the prophets themselves but are collections of their words, edited by later generations. It is important to look at some of the prehistory of the text before examining the text itself. First, there are several of the prophetic books that are a compilation of several different prophets. Isaiah is probably the most famous and complex of the compilations, given that there are at least three Isaiahs. Not that there were three people whose names were Isaiah who contributed to this work. Rather, there were three prophets from three different times whose prophecies were collected into one book, but only the first prophet is identified: Isaiah of Jerusalem. Second, even those books that are not a compilation of the work of several prophets do include sayings, or even chapters, that come from the hand of a later editor. Third, there is the likelihood that the compilations of the words of the prophets were made using sources. For this reason, sometimes there are duplicates of the same speech or event, which was recorded in two different sources. In Jeremiah, we find two versions of his Temple speech (7:1—8:3; 26:1–19). At a late stage (postexilic) the books of the prophets were collected together and edited (perhaps by Deuteronomistic editors) to put the books into a uniform form.

The collection of prophets in the Old Testament includes sixteen books. The first three are the Major Prophets: Isaiah, Jeremiah, and Ezekiel. Then there is the book of Daniel, which is included among the prophets in the Christian Old Testament, but is found in the collection of the Writings *(ketubim)* in the Jewish Bible. Then follows the twelve Minor Prophets: Hosea, Joel, Amos, Obadiah, Jonah, Micah, Nahum, Habakkuk, Zephaniah, Haggai, Zechariah, and Malachi. In the Jewish Bible, the twelve Minor Prophets were collected all in one scroll; thus, in the Jewish Bible there were only four books of prophets: Isaiah, Jeremiah, Ezekiel, and the Twelve.

World of the Text

Composition of the Prophetic Books

The material we find in the Books of the Prophets is of three kinds: shorter poetic oracles (which are divided into oracles of judgment and oracles of salvation), longer prosaic speeches attributed to the prophets, and narrative accounts about the life and work of the prophets. Although many scholars try to reconstruct the original historical context of each of these three kinds of writings (for example, the shorter poetic oracles may be the words of the original prophet, the longer prosaic sayings are compilations and summaries of his sayings by his disciples, and the prose narrative of his life would be the work of later editors who compiled the material in written form), for the ordinary reader of the Bible the original situation is not as important as how the three kinds of writings work together to form a picture of the prophet and his message.

As we noted earlier, later editors are probably responsible for compiling the books of the prophets. The material is organized in a regular pattern. The oracles of judgment against Israel are usually collected together at the beginning of the book, followed by the oracles of judgment against the nations. The oracles of salvation are next, and the book concludes with narratives about the life of the prophet. We find this structure especially in the longer books. Beyond this larger structure, the oracles themselves are often collected together by theme, image, or catchword. In the Book of Ezekiel, however, the collections seem ruled by chronology because most of his prophecies are dated.

The Form of a Judgment Oracle

It is not necessary to enter into a discussion of the literary form of each kind of writing, but it might be helpful to look briefly at the form of the judgment oracle. The judgment oracle is made up of five parts. An oracle is a statement given by a messenger on behalf of someone else. The first element in an oracle is an identification of the one who is sending this message. The form is often "Thus says the LORD." Next, the recipient of the message is identified. This is often, simply, "Hear, O Israel."

146

Then comes a statement that summarizes the history of the sender and the recipient (what God has done for the people): "I led you out of Egypt." Then there is a statement of the sin or failure of the people: "You have forgotten me and worshiped other gods." The prophetic formula statement follows this: "Therefore thus says the LORD." Finally, there is the statement of the punishment: "I will hand you over to your enemies." This is a relatively fixed form for the oracles, but not every oracle has every element or in this order. If you remember the form of the covenant discussed in the chapter on the Pentateuch, you will notice that this outline of the judgment oracle follows the form of the covenant quite closely. The covenant form is made up of four parts: the names of the parties, the historical background, the requirements of the covenant, and the curses and blessings. The oracle of judgment, so characteristic of the prophets, has much the same form because it is a judgment on failing to live up to the covenant.

A simpler form of the oracle contains just two parts: the reason and the punishment. Sometimes we find oracles that consist of only the announcement of the punishment, which in the final analysis is the main point of the oracle. In this truncated form, the oracles do seem to be foretelling the future. However, an oracle that contains only an announcement of punishment should still be interpreted in light of the complete judgment oracle form.

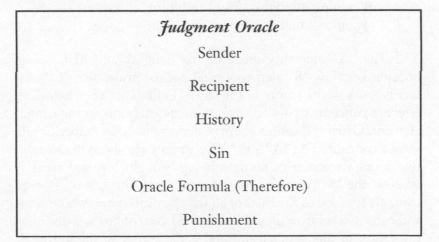

Judgment Oracle

Sender

Recipient

History

Sin

Oracle Formula (Therefore)

Punishment

Hebrew Poetry

We noted that the bulk of the material in the prophets, and the material that is considered by many to be the most original, is the poetic oracle. Because we have already examined Hebrew poetry in some depth in the chapter on the Wisdom Books, we will add just a few words here about the poetry of the prophets. The poetry of the prophets is perhaps more complex and complicated than that found in the Wisdom Books. The proverbs are the simplest kind of Hebrew poetry, often with just one line of two parallel measures. The poems of the prophets will include more diverse images and poetic forms than is normal in a psalm or a proverb.

Most of the parallelism in the prophets is synonymous parallelism, but antithetical and synthetic parallelisms are also common, as is chiastic parallelism. An expanded version of chiastic parallelism is called **concentric parallelism.** This form of parallelism adds more elements in the center: ABCC'B'A.' A good example of this form of parallelism is found in Isaiah 2:11–12:

> **A** The haughty eyes of people shall be brought low,
>   **B** and the pride of everyone shall be humbled;
>   **C** and the LORD alone will be exalted in that day.
>   **C'** For the LORD of hosts has a day
>   **B'** against all that is proud and lofty,
> **A'** against all that is lifted up and high;

The **"A"** elements speak of the haughty and high being brought low. The **"B"** elements speak against pride. The **"C"** elements speak of the LORD on the day of exaltation. The rhetorical effect of concentric parallelism is to focus attention on the center element. Often the center element and the outside elements will form a contrast. The **"A"** and **"B"** elements are about the haughtiness and arrogance of humans being brought low and abased, whereas the **"C"** element contrasts this with the LORD of hosts (the title for God as the ruler of all the cosmic powers) whose time will come for being exalted. God, as the LORD of hosts, is not only the center of this parallelism, God is the center of the universe. The form of this poetry helps to make the theological point.

The Language of the Prophets

As we said earlier the shocking language of the prophets distinguishes them from the regular prophets. Here I would just like to make a comment on the rhetorical strategy of that language. Walter Brueggemann says that the prophet as a poet must shatter the old world of the people's idolatry and form and evoke a new world of trust and faith in God. The language of the prophets is, first of all, attention grabbing. Second, it is world (or thought) altering. It is often shocking and new and always subversive of the conventional and easy way of thinking. An appreciation of the power of the language is central to reading the text.

Themes of the Prophets

As advocates of God's covenant with God's people, the prophets focus much of their attention on the theme of covenant, even when the word is not used. The Hebrew word for covenant is *berith* and means an agreement entered into between two parties. The prophets treat the theme of covenant under many different images. Marriage is a very frequent and controversial image of the covenant. Israel is pictured as the unfaithful wife who whores around with other gods/nations. God is the faithful but outraged husband. This image is powerful in portraying the intimacy between God and God's people as well as the love and affection God has for the people. However, the image also perpetuates a very destructive stereotype of women as sexually dangerous and unfaithful and men as needing to control women's sexuality. This adds to the already problematic portrayal of women in the Old Testament. (We will investigate this issue further in the world in front of the text.) Another image frequently used for covenant is parent (both father and mother) and child. Other images, such as field and farmer, or pot and potter, picture God as the creator and owner of Israel who can and does expect some result or accomplishment from what belongs to God.

Under the theme of covenant, the prophets focus on two primary failings of the people: **injustice** and **idolatry.** These are the two main areas where the people fail in keeping the covenant. The people are prone to worship other gods or at least to put their trust in things other than Yahweh, whether these are horses and chariots, military alliances, or treaties. Worshiping other gods and trusting in other things are the actions most often referred to as whoring. However, the nation is also faulted for hoarding and centralizing wealth, mistreating the lowly and powerless, stealing the livelihood of the poor, and shedding innocent blood. These are just as severe crimes against the covenant relationship with God. For the prophets, there is no separation between idolatry and injustice because all injustice is really a matter of trusting and respecting a god other than Yahweh.

World in front of the Text

Christological Fulfillment of the Prophets

As we pointed out in our introduction to the whole Bible, the Books of the Prophets are the last books in the Christian Old Testament and thus immediately precede the beginning of the story of Jesus in the gospels. The placement of the prophets contains a theological message for the Christian community because it makes a clear connection between the prophets and the gospels. The prophets prophesy the coming of the Messiah, and the gospels recount the prophecies' fulfillment in Jesus. From the gospel accounts it appears that Jesus himself used the prophets to interpret God's work in his life and in the world at that time. Certainly the gospel writers portray him that way. The Jesus of the gospels uses Isaiah, Jeremiah, Ezekiel, and many of the minor prophets to interpret his work on behalf of God's kingdom. The rejection that Jesus experiences from his fellow countrymen is explained in light of the experience of the prophets (Mark 6:4). Jesus' critique of the Temple system of sacrifices is made in terms of the prophetic critique of that same system in Hosea 6:6 (Matt 9:13; 12:7). The gospel writers interpret the death of Jesus in light of the suffering servant in Second Isaiah (Matt 26:63 = Isa 53:7; Matt 26:28 and 1 Cor 15:3 = Isa 53:10) and in light of the lament in Psalm 22 (Mark 15:29 and 31 = Ps 22:7; Matt 27:43 = Ps 22:8; John 19:24 = Ps 22:18). The hoped-for return of the risen Jesus is described as the coming of the Son of man on the clouds as described in Daniel 7:13–14 (Mark 13:26; 14:62). The best preparation for reading the gospels is a careful study of the prophets.

We can see that the world in front of the prophetic text has always been a vibrant and resourceful one for Christianity, beginning with Jesus. Although the author of chapter 7 of Daniel was not describing the return of Jesus as Son of man, this is a legitimate reading of this text in a new historical situation using the lens of Jesus the Christ. In a similar way, Matthew found in the Book of Jeremiah an explanation for the catastrophic destruction of Jerusalem in Matthew's own day. He read Jeremiah 19, which speaks of the violence and shedding of innocent blood in Jerusalem as the reason why God will destroy the city (in 586 B.C.E.) and send the people into exile. Matthew reinterprets this to apply to the violence against Jesus and the shedding of his innocent blood as the reason why God allowed the Romans to destroy Jerusalem in 70 C.E. (Matt 27:3–10). The prophets by their use of startling and revolutionary images provided a fertile ground for Christians to interpret the epoch-shaking revolution inaugurated by Jesus. Also, the prophets' words of hope for God's coming intervention provided a language for the Christians' hope for God's future intervention in the return of Jesus.

Issues of the prophets' language still challenge us as readers in the present. The prophetic indictment of the religious establishment with its reliance on rituals still challenges the Christian churches to repentance and renewal. The prophets' descriptions of the wealthy Israelites' abuse of the poor and powerless stands today as a powerful indictment of the developed nations' oppression of the world's poor. Perhaps the most problematic issue that the prophetic books raise for the modern reader is how to understand the imagery of Israel as the whoring wife, unfaithful to God. There are basically three possible ways of dealing with this image: uncritical acceptance, critical evaluation, and rejection. There are readers of the Bible who do not find the images in the prophets in any way problematic, but given the recent documents of the American bishops about domestic violence and about women in the church, that is not a position that can be called Catholic. The challenges of feminism to the church have been in the other two positions. The second position, critical evaluation, would hold that the images of the prophets must be understood within their original historical context and must be explained or even rephrased as necessary for a new and more gender-sensitive world. This position does not advocate rejecting the imagery out of hand, but rather contextualizing, revising, and reinterpreting it for a new age. The third position holds that this imagery is fundamentally patriarchal and even misogynist and must be rejected as word of God. Catholic biblical scholars do not normally take this third position.

Isaiah

INTRODUCTION

World behind the Text

The Three Isaiahs

The sixty-six chapters of the Book of Isaiah were not written by one author in one historical situation. Rather, we have essentially three different works by three authors from three very different historical situations. We need, therefore, to look at each of the three texts separately. First Isaiah consists of chapters 1—39. Although not all of this material came directly from Isaiah of Jerusalem and although this is not a unified document set down by the prophet in this form and in this order, for the sake of our study we will refer to this document as the work of First Isaiah. Chapters 40—55 make up Second Isaiah. This author was writing at the end of the time of exile in Babylon (540 B.C.E.) and focused much of his attention on the change in fortunes for Babylon and for the Jews because of the advances of Cyrus king of Persia. This is a much more unified text. Chapters 56—66 are known as Third Isaiah and are the work of a postexilic prophet concerned about the Temple and the priesthood.

Who Was First Isaiah?

We know very little about the prophet Isaiah except for his name, his father's and sons' names, and the fact that his wife was a prophetess. 2 Kings 19—20 recounts Isaiah's role as prophet to the king during Assyria's siege of Jerusalem and during Hezekiah's illness. We know that Isaiah had access to the king and was working as a prophet in Jerusalem during the reigns of Ahaz and Hezekiah from the prophet's own words and from the biographical chapters in Isaiah. The Book of Isaiah makes it clear that Isaiah lived in Jerusalem. He seems to have been a respected insider in the court, occupying a position that gave him access to the king. One conjecture is that he was in charge of the court schools because there are references to his being mocked along the lines of a schoolhouse ditty. He is also concerned about knowledge and learning, sobriety, right order, and hierarchy. None of this proves that he was a teacher, but it would fit with his thought. Isaiah was active (though not continuously) from about 740 to 680 B.C.E. The material we have from him is directed to a small number of important crises: the Syro-Ehpraimite war in 743 B.C.E., the Assyrian invasion of Ashdod in 713–711 B.C.E., and the Assyrian invasion of Jerusalem in 701 B.C.E.

From hints in the text of Book of Isaiah, we can offer a tentative description of the prophet's profession.

World of the Text

The Structure of the Book of Isaiah

As we noted earlier the Book of Isaiah can be divided into three different books: chapters 1—39 are First Isaiah, chapters 40–55 are Second Isaiah, and chapters 56—66 are Third Isaiah. First Isaiah is the only section of Isaiah that we will examine in this book. It can be outlined as follows:

Judgment Oracles	Chapters 1—12
Oracles against the Nations	Chapters 13—23
Isaian Apocalypse	Chapters 24—27
Salvation Oracles	Chapters 28—35
Historical Review	Chapters 36—39

It is clear from the outline that some editing of the material has been done to place similar material together: all the oracles of judgment, all the oracles against the pagan nations, and so forth. As the book now stands, the salvation oracles lead nicely into the consolations offered by Second Isaiah in chapters 40–55.

Themes of the Book of Isaiah

Of all the prophets, Isaiah is the most concerned about the king and the royal city of Jerusalem. Isaiah is also the most consistent and developed in his philosophy of history. For Isaiah, God is the power behind all other powers, and the king and the people owe allegiance to God. Isaiah calls God the LORD of hosts and frequently speaks of God's holiness and power. The fundamental attitude required of the people is trust in God. However, because Isaiah has a hierarchical view of society, it is the king's trust in God that determines the well-being of the nation. With the king at the top of the social order and in closest contact with God, everything depends on whether the king is humble, trusts in God, dispenses justice and judgment, and brings about peace. If the king relies on God, then the whole social order will be stable and strong from the king down to the orphans and widows. If the king does not rely on God but relies on his own power or alliances and armies, the whole nation will suffer. The princes will plot, the priests will steal, the judges will be bribed, and the widows and orphans will be oppressed. There will be no justice, judgment, or peace in the land. The right rule of the king is discussed in two primary areas in Isaiah. First, Isaiah is concerned about the role of the king (and the nation) in international politics. The king must trust in the international policies of God and not make his own alliances with foreign nations or trust in his own military strength. Second, Isaiah is concerned about the administration of justice within the nation of Judah. The king is responsible for making sure that justice, right judgment, and peace are extended to all citizens. In the first twelve chapters, Isaiah laments the lack of proper government in Judah and looks forward to a future perfect king. He tells Ahaz that even if he, Ahaz, does not act as a proper king, God will raise up after him a king (his son?) who will be God's instrument, will trust, be just, and bring about peace.

World in front of the Text

The Fifth Gospel

The Book of Isaiah has been called the fifth gospel because of its importance for the New Testament portrait of Jesus. Two images are especially important in the New Testament use of Isaiah. The first is the image of the coming Messiah, the future perfect king of Israel, described by First Isaiah in chapters 7—11. The famous quote that a virgin will bear a son and call him Emmanuel is taken from Isaiah 7 and applied by Matthew to Jesus not only to defend the virginal conception of Jesus but even more to show that Jesus is the fulfillment of Isaiah's prophecies for the coming Messiah. The second image is the suffering servant described by Second Isaiah. The ignominious death of Jesus was a major stumbling block to claiming he was the Messiah. The suffering servant songs of Second Isaiah gave the Christian community a theological foundation on which to make this unlikely claim. These texts were very important for the earliest Christians and continued to be important for later generations as evidenced by Handel's *Messiah* in which the texts of Isaiah figure most prominently. Even today, in the Common Sunday Lectionary the Book of Isaiah is used for the first reading more than any other Old Testament book.

ISAIAH 6

World behind the Text

The Kingdom of Judah in 742 B.C.E.

Some historical background is necessary if we are to read Isaiah 6 with understanding. The text mentions that this vision of Isaiah took place in the year of the death of Uzziah, which scholars date to 742 B.C.E. In 745 Tiglath-pileser III became king of

155

Assyria and brought about a resurgence of Assyria as the foremost power in the Near East after fifty years of weakness. During the time of Assyria's weakness, the kingdoms of Israel and Judah had become wealthy and quite powerful, especially the northern kingdom of Israel. During the reign of Uzziah, Israel and Judah were in alliance, although in 742, Assyria gained power and extended its territory. The rich and complacent nations of Israel and Judah were confronted with a powerful and ruthless Assyria intent on extending its dominion and collecting tribute monies. It seems that Isaiah shared with Amos and Hosea a concern about the worldliness and pride of the two nations.

Call or Memoir?

If the vision found in Isaiah 6:1–7 had been placed in chapter 1, there would be little doubt about what its purpose was. However, because what looks like a call to be a prophet is not placed in the opening chapter, scholars have argued over how to understand this text. Many scholars treat chapter 6 as if it were in chapter 1 and read it as the inaugural vision of Isaiah when he was called by God to be a prophet. Others, noting that it is not at the beginning of the book and seeking to explain its negative attitude toward the possibility of repentance, speculate that the vision of God and the commission to preach constitute a summary of Isaiah's mission rather than an inaugural call. At the end of his career, Isaiah looked back over what had not been accomplished and realized that the failure of his message had actually been the will of God. A third possibility is to see chapter 6 as an inaugural vision only for the mission during the Syro-Ephraimite war. It would then be a call to preach the message found in chapters 7 and 8 only.

Seraphim in the Courtroom

The location of the vision is the heavenly courtroom of the LORD. It seems to be a combination of a royal throne room and a temple. The LORD is seated on a throne and wearing a magnificent robe, but there is also an altar of incense (from the Temple) in the throne room. The court of the LORD is composed of Seraphim (in Hebrew the suffix "im" indicates a plural. This then is a group of

Seraphs). We are not sure what these beings were. In Numbers, the snakes that bite and kill the Hebrews in the desert are called poisonous (*seraph* in Hebrew) serpents (21:6), and some have suggested that these beings are serpent or dragonlike. Actually, we know that there was a bronze serpent called the Nehushtan that was in the Temple and was venerated with incense (2 Kgs 18:4). It is possible that Isaiah used this sacred object as the model for God's attendants. However, the word *seraph* means fiery, and it is likely that the serpents of Numbers were called seraph simply because of their fiery (poisonous) bite. The seraphs in Isaiah 6 might not be related to those poisonous snakes of Numbers, but might simply be fiery beings that attend to the LORD.

World of the Text

The Structure of Isaiah 6

Chapter 6 can be divided into three parts. It consists of a description of the setting, a dialogue between Isaiah and a Seraph, and a dialogue between Yahweh and Isaiah. Each of the three sections contains a statement followed by a response. In the first section (vv. 1–4) there is a statement describing the LORD in the Temple seated on a throne. The description focuses on what surrounds Yahweh (his train and the Seraphim) not on God's own person. The response to this sight is made by the Seraphim who cry out God's holiness. The threefold repetition of "holy" is the Hebrew form of a superlative—God is the most holy. The second section (vv. 5–7) begins with a statement by Isaiah that he and the people to whom he belongs are unclean and unworthy of being in the presence of the holy God. The response to this comes from a Seraph who brings a coal from the altar of incense and touches his lips to cleanse him of sin. The final section (vv. 8–13) begins with a question by God about whom to send (as his prophet), followed by Isaiah's response that he will go. Yahweh tells Isaiah to give the people a harsh message predicting their failure. Isaiah questions how long this terrible failure on their part can last. God's response is that it will last until the whole earth is desolate, until all the cities and houses that the people have built lie deserted.

The structure reveals the text's meaning. First, the structure shows the contrast between scenes one and two. God's superlative holiness contrasts with the uncleanness of Isaiah and the people, although the contrast is not complete. In scene one, the Seraphim recognize the awesome holiness of God and show reverence and respect by covering their faces and their feet. In scene two Isaiah recognizes the holiness of God and his own unclean state. This unclean state is remedied when the burning coal is placed to his mouth. He is then able to have a conversation with God. Scene three must be understood in relation to scenes one and two. Isaiah sees the vision of God's glory and recognizes his own uncleanness. Because of a cleansing, he is able to stand in conversation with God. The people in scene three have eyes that do not see, ears that do not hear, and hearts that are closed. They refuse to look on the vision of God's glory, and they close their hearts to any recognition of their own sin. They are unable to hear the word of God. So while Isaiah is purged of sin and wickedness, the people will not turn (repent) and be healed. The contrast between the holiness of God in scene one and the uncleanness of Isaiah in scene two shows how humans must stand before God. The contrast between the way Isaiah acts in scene two and the way the people are going to respond in scene three shows the fundamental problem in Judah. The people do not have a vision of the holiness of God that is able to lead them to adequate repentance.

The Poetry of Isaiah 6

The most difficult and controversial verses of this chapter are the words of God to Isaiah in 6:9–10. What God tells Isaiah to say to the people is contained in three lines of poetry. The first line contains two measures. These first two measures are addressed to the people and are in synonymous parallelism. Together they represent the two means of human perception: seeing and hearing. Each of the measures has two parts that are antithetical: listen but not comprehend, look but not understand. The antithesis is heightened in the Hebrew by the repetition of the verbs "to listen" and "to look." The Hebrew says, "Looking, look" and "Listening, listen." This is accurately translated into English as "keep listening" and "keep looking." The exaggeration of the attempts to listen and look is contrasted with the total lack of results. The reader wonders how someone could keep listening and not comprehend, could keep looking and not understand.

The next line (v. 10a) is also in synonymous parallelism, although this line (and the next line) is directed to the prophet who is commanded to make the heart of this people dull. In this line, the measure that speaks of the mind (literally "heart" in Hebrew) is in parallel with the measure that speaks of the eyes and ears. The eyes and ears, which are in parallelism with each other in the two measures of the first line, are joined into one measure in this line and placed in parallelism with the mind. The poet has added another element to the equation. The concern that the eyes and ears do not look or listen is really a concern about the mind. For the Israelites, the mind/heart was the seat of knowing, judging, and reasoning. The poem is saying that the Israelites have closed their minds. The eyes and ears were the portals of knowledge and learning that fed the mind/heart. So God is saying the same thing twice: they have closed their minds. The reader is left to wonder how is the prophet to make this happen and why?

The next line of poetry (v. 10b) continues God's command to Isaiah and contains a loose synonymous parallelism. The prophet is commanded to close the people's minds else their eyes will see, their ears hear, and their mind/heart comprehend (these are the three elements that were in parallelism earlier) and they will turn and be healed. Now the prophet has created a parallel between the eyes, ears, and mind/heart, on the one hand, and the ability to turn and be healed, on the other. This leads the reader deeper into the real concern. It is not the eyes, the ears, or even the mind/heart that concerns God as much as it is the people's ability to turn and be healed. The word *turn* is a very important theological word in the Old Testament. The Hebrew word *shub* can mean simply to turn physically in another direction, but often it comes much closer to our English word *repent*. It can be used both of God and of humans. Humans beg God not to turn away from them, or they plead with God to turn back toward them. Humans who sin against God are said to turn away from God. They turn away from following God. They turn away from standing before

God in obedience and humility. They turn away to do their own thing or to follow other gods. In contrast, humans who recognize their sin are said to have turned back, or returned, to God. The same word is used for all of these meanings.

These first words of God proceed in three steps—three lines of poetry. In the first line, hearing and seeing are placed in parallel. In the second, the mind/heart is parallel with ears and eyes. Then in the third, eyes, ears, and mind/heart are in parallel with repentance. Each time the author has added a new element that brings the reader deeper into the real issue—the people have turned away from God. The author has also cleverly placed the elements in a chiastic parallelism. In the second line, the elements are mind/heart, ears, and eyes. In the third line, the elements are eyes, ears, and mind/heart.

God's next words, and the next piece of poetry, are an answer to Isaiah's plea/question: "How long, O LORD?" This is a common plea often associated with God's being turned away from God's people. How long will God turn away from the people to punish them? The answer is shocking. God will turn away until nothing is left, until every city, every house, even the stump of the royal nation is chopped down.

What does the study of the text tell us about its meaning? If we follow the text step by step, we are led to the real concern, which is that the people turn back to God. It is not a matter of God turning to the people anymore. God can do nothing more for them if they do not turn toward God. In their poetic form, these words of God are ironic and supremely challenging. This poem should not be read as a statement of fact expressing God's intention to confuse the people to condemn them. Rather, the people are the ones who have eyes and ears but refuse to understand and know anything of God. Their lack of seeing and hearing is really a malady of the mind/heart. They are closed-minded and hard-hearted, which is a matter of choosing to turn away from God. The genius of this poem is to make God's command to the prophet ironically the very thing the people have chosen for themselves. The point of the poem is to emphasize the inevitability of the consequences because of the decision of the people. The question/plea of Isaiah reinforces this. He asks, how long? When will this end? The answer is that there will be no end to the destruction of the people until they turn from their ways. They have it in their power to see and hear and turn to God, but they refuse. The poem shows the fatal choice of the people in the face of a God who is their only hope.

World in front of the Text

Parables and the Hard-Hearted

Jesus quotes Isaiah 6:9–10 (loosely) in Mark 4:12 to describe how some who hear the parables will not understand the mystery of the kingdom. This text has caused a great deal of controversy because it sounds as if Jesus is saying that he teaches in parables so that his hearers will not understand and therefore will not be converted and forgiven. Mark (and Jesus) saw a parallel between God's message to Israel through Isaiah and Jesus' message to Israel. Using this quotation from Isaiah, Mark draws a parallel between Isaiah and Jesus and reveals Jesus as a prophet. The text in Mark keeps the irony of the original text of Isaiah. Jesus tells the disciples that they have been given the mystery of the kingdom and that those outside hear the parables so that they might not see and hear, although as the narrative of Mark's Gospel progresses, we find that the disciples begin to act like those who are outside. In Mark 8:17–18 Jesus says to the disciples, "Do you still not perceive or understand? Are your hearts hardened? Do you have eyes, and fail to see? Do you have ears, and fail to hear?" This is exactly the language of Isaiah: eyes, ears, mind/heart. These are the problems humans have in their response to God. The irony in Mark is that the disciples who are supposed to see, hear, and understand are pictured as outsiders who do not see, hear, and understand. Mark's irony, like that in Isaiah, emphasizes the importance of the human response to God's call. None is exempt from having to turn to God and open his/her eyes, ears, and heart.

The challenge of this passage for us today may be in a literal reading. Are our eyes, our ears, and our hearts open to God's words, deeds, and will that are made visible around us by the poor, the weak, the outcast, in politics, nature, and society? Too often, our spiritual journey can be cut off from the real world. The words of Isaiah challenge us to pay attention in the world to a God who is seen and heard and felt.

Jeremiah

INTRODUCTION

World behind the Text

Who Was Jeremiah?

Jeremiah was a Levite from the village of Anathoth about six miles north of Jerusalem. It has often been suggested that he was descended from the high priest Abiathar who was sent back to his home in Anathoth after being relieved of his priestly duties by Solomon. Jeremiah lived in Jerusalem and was active as a prophet off and on during the period of 627–587 B.C.E. However, scholars are divided on whether the date 627 refers to the beginning of Jeremiah's prophetic ministry or to his birth. Because there is nothing in the book that must be attributed to the time of Josiah, the date of 627 is probably too early for the beginning of Jeremiah's ministry. It is also possible that the date of 627 was a later addition by the Deuteronomistic historians to make the career of Jeremiah last forty years, like that of Moses.

Deuteronomic Reform

In 620 B.C.E. after spending the early years of his reign under the authority of regents, Josiah inaugurated a nationalistic reform based on the book of the law that was "discovered" in the Temple. Most scholars believe that the discovered book was the core of what is now the Book of Deuteronomy. The core of the book dates perhaps to about 650. This book was a compilation of the laws found in Exodus and showed the stamp of northern theology (prophetic, moralistic, concern for the land). This book was the foundation for a nationalistic reform that not only called for an end to idolatry but also called for a centralization of all worship in Jerusalem and rejected associations with outsiders. This kind of reform would have been possible and expedient during the reign of Josiah. With little interference and pressure from the major empires of the time (Assyria, Babylonia, and Egypt), Josiah was able to pursue nationalistic policies, creating a strong central government in Judah and expanding its borders.

The Decline and Fall of the Southern Kingdom

Most of the prophetic career of Jeremiah takes place under kings Jehoiakim and Zedekiah. King Josiah was killed in 609 when he tried to prevent the Egyptian army from advancing to the north to come to the aid of Assyria against Babylonia. The Egyptians took control of Palestine by placing Josiah's son, Jehoiakim, on the throne; but when they lost the war against the Babylonians in Carchemish in 605, control of the whole area passed to the Babylonians. Jehoiakim vacillated throughout his reign between loyalty to Babylonia or siding with Egypt in various attempts to overthrow Babylonian control. In the end, Jehoiakim revolted against Nebuchadnezzar, king of Babylonia, who sent an army and laid siege to the city of Jerusalem. Jehoiakim was killed in a battle; and his son, Jehoiachin, was taken prisoner. Together with the royal family, prominent officials, artisans, and the treasures of the Temple, he was taken into exile in Babylon. Jehoiakim's brother, Zedekiah, was placed on the throne after promising loyalty to Babylonia. In the end, he followed the path of Jehoiakim and, backed by Egypt, revolted against Babylonia. The results were even more disastrous this time. After a painful and strife-ridden year-and-a-half siege, the Babylonians captured and razed the city of Jerusalem in 586. The Temple was burnt, and all of Jerusalem's prominent or useful inhabitants were taken into exile. Jeremiah was the thorn in the side of Jehoiakim and Zedekiah during these crises. He consistently exhorted them to trust in God by accepting the rule of Babylonia.

The Deuteronomistic Editor of Jeremiah

Scholars generally agree that the Deuteronomistic historians have edited the Book of Jeremiah. These editors recognized Jeremiah as the last and greatest of God's "servants the prophets" who followed Moses. Jeremiah is pictured as receiving his call from God even in the womb. He objects to this call because he does not know how to speak, and God assures him that he will give him the words. In Exodus 2:1–10, God intervenes in the birth of Moses. When God calls Moses to lead God's people, Moses objects to his mission because he is not eloquent (Exod 4:10). He is told that God, the LORD, will teach him what to speak (Exod 4:11–12). The Deuteronomistic editing of the Book of Jeremiah is a clear attempt to portray Jeremiah as a type of Moses.

World of the Text

Structure of the Book of Jeremiah

The structure of the Book of Jeremiah is as follows:

Call of Jeremiah	Chapter 1
Judgment Oracles	Chapters 2—25
Biographical Narratives	Chapters 26—29 and 34—45
Salvation Oracles (The Book of Consolation)	Chapters 30—33
Oracles against the Nations	Chapters 46—51
Historical Appendix	Chapter 52

Even though the order of the elements is not the same as in Isaiah, the elements (Judgment Oracles, Salvation Oracles, Oracles against the Nations, and Biographical/Historical Narratives) are the same. The Judgment Oracles are also arranged chronologically, with the first oracles being the earliest in Jeremiah's career.

Characteristic Genres and Styles of Jeremiah

Jeremiah's rhetoric and style are perhaps the most striking and unique of all the prophets, and yet in some ways his style is also the paradigm for later writings. More than any of the other prophets, Jeremiah's writings are dramas. They usually have three actors: God, Israel, and Jeremiah. What is most powerful about the writings of Jeremiah is the extent to which the feelings, frustrations, and concerns of each of the actors are expressed. Another of Jeremiah's genres is the symbolic action. Earlier prophets, such as Hosea and Isaiah, performed symbolic actions, but Jeremiah uses this strategy the most frequently and memorably. The actions not only dramatize the message but also give to the message a reality that makes the fulfillment of the prophecy more certain. A third genre characteristic of Jeremiah's style is the confession. In several notable texts, Jeremiah engages in a private harangue against God, complaining about his role as a prophet, the way God treats him, and the way the people have received his message. These harangues, called "the Confessions of Jeremiah," are similar to the psalms of personal lament found in the Book of Psalms. The fourth characteristic genre of Jeremiah is the dirge lamenting the death of Israel (e.g., Jer 9:17–22). The dirge is a funeral song and is characterized by wailing and lamenting for loss. In fact, an overall characteristic of Jeremiah is his pessimism. A later apocryphal book, the Book of Lamentations, is attributed to him for just this reason.

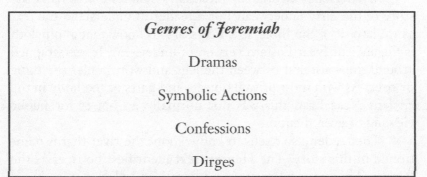

Genres of Jeremiah

Dramas

Symbolic Actions

Confessions

Dirges

World in front of the Text

The Suffering Prophet

Jeremiah is perhaps the greatest of the prophets and is most revered for his suffering (some have even suggested that the suffering servant in Second Isaiah referred originally to Jeremiah). For Matthew, Jeremiah is the epitome of a prophet, especially in his suffering. In numerous places, Matthew likens Jesus to Jeremiah and uses the words of Jeremiah to reflect on Jesus' passion (see Matt

2:17–18; 16:14; 27:9–10). What today's readers need to recognize is that the sufferings of Jeremiah and Jesus were the result of their unrelenting criticism of the political and religious structures and policies of their time. Jeremiah becomes a model even for Jesus because he advocates for God's will above all else but is at the same time passionately concerned for the well-being of his fellow Israelites. He is one who loved God above all else and his neighbor as himself. It is in being faithful to God and his calling that makes Jeremiah such a vulnerable target to the rulers of his time.

JEREMIAH 13:1–11

World behind the Text

Some Underwear and a River

My personal favorite of Jeremiah's symbolic actions is the story of the dirty underwear. For a reader to understand the text as we have it in the Bible, it is necessary to know that a loincloth is the ancient Near Eastern version of underwear. It was wrapped around the waist and between the legs and worn under the tunic or robe. As with most private objects and parts of the body in the ancient Near East, this was not normally an object for public viewing or even mention.

The reader also needs to know about the river that is mentioned in this story. The Hebrew text identifies the river as the Parath. There was no river called Parath in Judah that we know of. It is possible that the river is the Euphrates (that is the way the NRSV translates it). However, it is unlikely that Jeremiah traveled that great a distance to make his point. A more likely possibility is that the "river" is a spring called the Parath that is located near Jeremiah's hometown of Anathoth. By calling it the "river" Parath, though, Jeremiah is making an allusion to the Euphrates River. Taking the underwear (which represents Israel) to the "river" Parath (alluding to the Euphrates River, which runs through Babylonia) would be Jeremiah's way of demonstrating the Exile.

World of the Text

You Want Me to Do What?

The plot of this symbolic action is clear and straightforward. Yahweh tells Jeremiah to buy a loincloth, wear it, not wash it, hide it under a rock by the river Parath/Euphrates, and then retrieve it after a long interval. After it is retrieved, the loincloth, of course, is rotted and good for nothing. On the simplest level, the point is that Judah has become rotten and disgusting to God. This message could of course just be spoken simply without the need for the symbolic action, although what the action allows for is the engagement of the viewers and readers on a level not possible with discursive language. To engage the audience in this game of hide and seek is much more powerful than just to give them a message. For Jeremiah and his audience, it also seemed to have an almost magic effect. By acting out the rottenness of Judah and its exile, Jeremiah intensifies the authority of the word and makes it more certain to happen in this way.

That the item of clothing is a loincloth is significant. The message is not simply that Judah has become rotten, but that Judah was meant to be God's underwear. God intended Judah to be that most clean, pure, and comfortable article of clothing that God places next to God's most intimate self. Instead, Judah is so rotten and disgusting that God would not want it anywhere near God's person, much less next to God's most intimate parts. It is even more powerful for Jeremiah to act this out. To put on a drama about a loincloth would not have been the most seemly spectacle, but to have that drama be about God's underwear would have been considered supremely inappropriate. The spectators (and the readers who are identifying with the spectators) would be embarrassed and uncomfortable by the sight of the rotted loincloth and by the thought of a person putting it on. Experiencing this for themselves makes real to them how God feels. The ability to express what God is feeling toward God's people is a major characteristic of the prophets, and none is better at it than Jeremiah. His use of symbolic actions allows his audience (the original spectators and the readers of the story) to experience firsthand, as their own experience, the disgust, outrage, shame, and revulsion that God feels toward a people who have rejected God and deceived themselves. Once this is experienced as a real event, there is no way to stop its fulfillment.

World in front of the Text

Spiritual Shock Therapy

This story and many other sayings in Jeremiah challenge us when we get comfortable and set in our relationship to God. We come to expect things to be nice, edifying, and appropriate. God is our God and will always be tame and proper. So much of contemporary, first-world Christianity is tied to the status quo and fixated on social propriety. For most Americans it is socially advantageous to belong to a church. The God of Jeremiah is sick of the vacuous, false, and hypocritical worship and prayers of the people. The God of Jeremiah feels that those who call on God's name are two-timing and false. They go to the Temple and worship Yahweh but all the time are really worshiping false gods (money, military hardware, political alliances). Yahweh even accuses the people of being whores to the other gods and asks the people if there is any place they have not been lain with (Jer 3:2). (A famous commentary on the prophets even uses the "f-word" here. In the Hebrew the word that Jeremiah uses is not the normal word for sexual intercourse but is an obscene word.) Jeremiah's contemporaries would have found it just as shocking as we do. This is not the way God speaks! This is no way to talk about God! However, the point of the symbolic action in chapter 13 and the point of God's question to Israel in chapter 3 is that when the intimate committed relationship between God and God's people is broken by the people's faithlessness and their addiction to other gods (power, money, prestige, war, sensuality), God, out of the immense love God has for the people, will do anything to wake them out of their blindness and addiction. If it takes shocking them with inappropriate language, so be it. The point of the language of the prophets is always to wake the people up, to destroy their false world, and to create the possibility for the people to see the world as it really is, as God sees it. That is something that is needed in every age.

JEREMIAH 20:7–18

World behind the Text

The First Modern Person

To appreciate this "confession" of Jeremiah, it is important to understand that this harangue against God, which Jeremiah engaged in, was unique at that time in history. The will of the gods was inscrutable and unquestioned. No human would have even thought to challenge or question the gods. Yet, no human saw him/herself as separate from the group to which they belonged. Jeremiah questioned God and God's plan. Jeremiah claimed that he has been faithful and true to what God called him to do, but God had not been fair and responsible to Jeremiah in return. Also, Jeremiah separated himself from the people, and was able to see himself as distinct and alone. Never before had there been such an individualist who set himself over against God and over against his fellow countrymen as Jeremiah did. This for the first time in history was a truly modern individual.

The historical situation presumed in the text is that Jeremiah had spoken the condemnation of the nation of Judah and the coming punishment at the hands of Babylon in the name of God. He had gained a reputation for announcing terror and destruction, but nothing had happened. He was denounced by his countrymen and abandoned by God. Even his own clan from Anathoth tried to have him put to death. Besides, he did not feel he had any choice in the matter. Jeremiah felt that God had taken over his insides. Even if he tried not to speak in God's name his insides rebelled and tore him apart. He was an unwilling agent of God's word—and yet, Jeremiah recognized a center of individuality that could even criticize that experience of possession.

World of the Text

"Enticed" by God

This text, which is one of the "Confessions of Jeremiah," shares much with the selection we have already studied. Jeremiah's message is of destruction and punishment. He is not an optimistic or hopeful guy. His language tends to be quite rough. In chapter 13 (and 3) we saw God's use of some pretty harsh language to condemn Judah, but here Jeremiah uses some equally harsh language to accuse God. The word that is translated as "enticed" is a word for force and can have sexual connotations. Using it would come close to accusing God of rape.

The structure of the text is a source of debate. The text begins with an accusation against God, gives reasons for the accusation, then shifts to a very positive praise of God's care for Jeremiah, then abruptly shifts back to harsh words cursing (God for) Jeremiah's birth. The reader of Jeremiah must make sense of this confusing text. One could suppose that Jeremiah is greatly upset (or mentally unstable), and his moods swing wildly as he writes. Some scholars propose that a later redactor, who was perhaps uncomfortable with Jeremiah's unmitigated negativity, added the positive words in vv. 11–13. Some have conjectured that a positive prophecy of Jeremiah was inserted here by mistake in the process of copying. Other scholars suggest that perhaps the positive verses, which seem to interrupt the flow of the text, are actually ironic. They are the words that a prophet would be expected to say at this point, and so Jeremiah says them sarcastically but then launches in to his scathing condemnation of God's plan for him by wishing that he had never been born, but had been aborted. Whereas I normally think that scholars too easily reject difficult texts by claiming that they are the additions of later redactors, in this case I can see no other explanation for the text as we have it. Either vv. 10–13 or vv. 14–18 must be a later addition. I will argue that vv. 14–18 are the addition. (But remember that a good rule of thumb in being trained as a reader is to opt for emending the text only as a last resort. Often what seems like inconsistency or incongruity in the biblical text would have made perfect sense to the original audience who was trained in a different kind of thinking than we are.)

All of the arguments against including vv. 11–13 are psychological or thematic. Jeremiah could not have said all this in one piece. He could not have moved from a complaint to praise and back to a curse. However, if we look carefully at the text we can see that vv. 7–13 reflect the structure of an individual lament psalm.

> Invocation (v. 7a, which in this case is something of an
> accusation)
> Description of the Predicament of the speaker (vv. 7b–10)
> Confession of Confidence (v. 11)
> Petition (v. 12)
> Command to Praise (v. 13)

This is the normal form of the psalms of lament. The movement from vv. 7–10 to vv.11–13 is not unnatural. Verses 11–13 do not need to be considered a separate literary unit added by a later editor.

The focus of the lament is on the predicament of the speaker, not only because of the amount of text devoted to it (three-and-a-half verses) but also because of its powerful language. These verses are constructed in concentric parallelism. The first element of Jeremiah's predicament (v. 7b) says that he is mocked. The last element (v. 10b) is much longer but is in the same line of thought: all are looking for any stumble to entice him and take revenge on him. The second element of Jeremiah's predicament (v. 8) states that his message is always violence and destruction. The second to last element (v. 10a) describes how many accuse him (rightly) of only saying, "Terror is all around!" In the middle of the predicament (v. 9) is Jeremiah's wrenching description of how he tries not to mention God's word, but it becomes a fire burning his insides. Jeremiah is unable to hold it in. The center of the predicament matches the opening invocation/accusation: God is too powerful for Jeremiah. There is no way to have one's say or to object to God.

Given this structure for the text, vv. 14–18 would seem to be a later addition. Although these verses fit the mood of vv. 7–10, they do not fit with the structure of the lament. They were probably added at this point in Jeremiah because they do build on the themes of vv. 1–10. However, they would have been added at the end of the text because the editors recognized that vv. 7–13 were a distinct unit in the form of a lament and, therefore, not to be tampered with.

> It is sometimes necessary to make decisions about the form and structure of a text to understand the meaning of the text.

World in front of the Text

Job the Copy Cat

Jeremiah's curse of the day he was born, his complaint against God for being too strong, and his anguish over being mocked and despised are all picked up in the Book of Job and made into the central themes of Job's arguments with his friends. The Book of Job uses the language of the Confessions of Jeremiah to make Job's complaint against God. In Job 3:3 Job cries out, "Let the day perish in which I was born, and the night that said, 'A man-child is conceived.'" In 3:11 Job asks, "Why did I not die at birth, come forth from the womb and expire?" and in 3:16, "Or why was I not buried like a stillborn child, like an infant that never sees the light?" All of these texts reflect Jeremiah's curse of the day of his birth and his desire that he should have been killed at birth. In Job 9:3 Job says, "If one wished to contend with him, one could not answer him once in a thousand." And in Job 9:12 Job says, "He snatches away; who can stop him? Who will say to him, 'What are you doing?'" These quotes match Jeremiah's complaint about God being too powerful for him. Finally, in Job 6:15 Job complains, "My companions are treacherous like a torrent-bed, like freshets that pass away"; and in 16:9–10 he says, "my adversary sharpens his eyes against me. They have gaped at me with their mouths; they have struck me insolently on the cheek; they mass themselves together against me." These texts parallel Jeremiah's complaint that his friends are on the watch for any misstep.

These texts show how the powerful and moving words of a prophet can be taken over by a later biblical writer. Out of Jeremiah's confessions, the author of the Book of Job creates a book that makes its central issue the problem of the holy man who is faithful to God but whose situation in life does not bring to him the rewards of the covenant. This is a good example of how the Bible constantly reflects on the Bible, interpreting and developing it. As the author of Job used Jeremiah's words to confront the issues of his or her own day, so should we.

The reader of the Bible should pay close attention to the cross-references given in the text of the Bible. Reading these cross-referenced texts will help the reader see how the Bible constantly reflects on itself. The reader's appreciation of both texts will thereby be increased.

Daniel

INTRODUCTION

World behind the Text

Historical Context

The Book of Daniel contains two different types of stories that come from two distinct social and historical settings. The first six chapters contain stories of Daniel and his friends as they confront the situation of living a life faithful to Yahweh in exile in Babylon. These historical novellas are often called "tales of the successful courtier." Similar stories tell of the successes of Joseph, Esther, and Tobit in foreign courts. These stories reflect a situation that is not completely hostile to the government under which the authors live. A certain amount of assimilation and cooperation is presupposed. These stories probably came out of the Persian period. The next six chapters of Daniel are apocalypses (visions in which supernatural realities are revealed to Daniel). They came from the later

Hellenistic period. After the death of Alexander the Great, his empire was divided among four of his generals. Rule over the area of Palestine alternated between the Ptolemies in Egypt and the Seleucids in Syria. In the mid–second century B.C.E. the Seleucid ruler was Antiochus IV Epiphanes. The Jews nick-named him Epimanes, which means "crazy" because of his repressive policies. He required them to eat pork and not be circumcised, but his major crime was to defile the Temple by placing an idolatrous statue or altar in the Holy of Holies. In response the Jews staged a revolt led by Judas Maccabeus and his brothers. The stories of Antiochus's reign and the Maccabean revolt are recounted in 1 and 2 Maccabees (a deute-rocanonical [for Roman Catholics] or apocryphal [for Protestants] book). The revolt was successful, and in 164 B.C.E. the Temple was rededicated, an event celebrated by the Jewish feast of Hanukkah. The Book of Daniel was probably written before the final victory of the Maccabeans and before the death of Antiochus IV in 163 B.C.E. Scholars believe that the author of the apocalyptic chapters of Daniel was not opposed to the revolt of the Maccabees, but considered it ineffective in the end. For this author, the victory would be won by God and in God's own way. The author apparently took an older collection of stories about the ancient wise man Daniel and then added new chapters using Daniel as the seer of these new apocalyptic visions. As with most apocalyptic writing, the apocalyptic chap-ters of Daniel came from a disenfranchised minority. The visions were meant to inspire hope for a future unattainable by ordinary human means, a future made possible only by the direct intervention of God.

Another oddity about the Book of Daniel is the fact that half of it is in Aramaic and half is in Hebrew. The first chapter and then chapters 8—12 are in Hebrew, whereas chapters 2—7 are in Aramaic. Scholars believe that the original novellas about Daniel were in Aramaic. The author added another story in Hebrew at the beginning of the collection (this story links not only in lan-guage but also in themes and images with chapters 7—12) and then wrote his first vision (chapter 7) in Aramaic to link the two parts together into a whole.

World of the Text

Visions of Empires

As we noted earlier, the Book of Daniel can be divided into two parts based on the literary type of its contents. The first six chapters are historical novellas, and the next six chapters are apocalyptic visions. In the Roman Catholic canon, there are two other chapters added at the end of the book. These contain the stories of Susannah and Bel and the Dragon and are similar in style to the first six chapters. Our concern is with the six apocalyptic chapters. These chapters contain four visions (chapters 7, 8, 9, and 10—12) which are dated during the times of three different empires, starting with the reign of Belshazzar of Babylonia and ending with the reign of Cyrus of Persia. (In a similar way the first of the six novellas occurs during the reign of Nebuchadnezzar of Babylonia and the last novella occurs during the reign of Darius the Mede.)

Apocalyptic Genre

Chapters 7—12 of Daniel are the first sustained work of apocalyptic writing in the Bible. This genre, or type of literature, developed later in Judaism. It contains a description of a revelation of heavenly knowledge (knowledge not available normally to humans) given to a seer who has been taken up into the heavens, has had the symbolic visions interpreted by an angel, and has been told to keep this revelation secret until the appointed time. Usually, these texts are ascribed to some ancient hero who is supposed to have had the vision a long time ago and who prophesied all the events of history up until the present time. This feature is called "prophecy after the fact," meaning that the story line pretends that an ancient figure "prophesied" all that would happen up to the present time of the author, who is actually writing the story after the events have occurred. The visions are often quite bizarre with strange combinations of animal figures, symbolic numbers, and terrible natural and supernatural disasters. The meanings of these visions are symbolic and need to be explained by an angel interpreter. A prediction of the future end of the world (or the end of the present time of persecution) in specific terms is often a feature of apocalyptic literature. In Daniel we find a prediction that the end (of the persecution) will come in 1,150 days, then in 1,290 days, and finally in 1,335 days.

World in front of the Text

The Two Minds of Daniel

One of the most interesting features of the Book of Daniel is its juxtapositioning of two different kinds of literature. Not only are the novellas and the apocalyptic visions very different genres; they represent almost opposing views of the world. The novellas as we noted are stories about the success of the Jewish courtier. Although there is persecution in these stories, their conclusion is that a faithful Jew who trusts in God not only can succeed in a foreign land but can even become very powerful. Often the king of the nation is portrayed sympathetically, with his advisors being the more aggressive opponents of the Jews and their religion. These stories offer hope for Jews being able to live a normal and faithful life under foreign rule. The apocalyptic visions, however, do not see a possibility for a normal and faithful life for Jews under foreign rule. They portray foreign rulers as preordained enemies of God who must be destroyed by God before God's people can live and worship in peace. The fact that these two kinds of stories and these two worldviews are placed together in one book, challenges us not to be too hasty in choosing one worldview over the other. The view that Christians can live successfully and faithfully in the world ruled by the forces of power, money, violence, and oppression needs the challenge of the apocalyptic visions. The view that Christians are an oppressed minor-

A historical critical approach to the Bible tells us that the two parts of Daniel come from very different situations and should be studied accordingly. Armed with this knowledge, readers might never place these two parts in dialogue with each other. The value of **canonical criticism** is that it allows texts from different times, genres, and even books of the Bible to speak to each other because they are placed together in the canon of the Bible.

ity besieged by the enemies of God on every side, likewise, needs the challenge of the successful courtiers in the novellas.

DANIEL 7

World behind the Text

The Four Kingdoms

The text dates this vision of Daniel during the reign of Belshazzar, king of Babylon. However, we know that Belshazzar was never king of Babylon, but served only as regent in Babylon while his father, Nabonidus, was away in his temporary capital in the desert. The actual setting of the vision, though, is seen in the description of history that it gives. Daniel sees four animals that represent four great empires in Israel's history, as the interpreting angel explains in 7:17. The interpreting angel does not tell us which empires they are; however, the four apocalyptic visions date visions to the reigns of kings, beginning with the king of Babylon, moving to the king of Media, and ending with the king of Persia. Given that the author clearly intends the fourth kingdom to be the Hellenistic kingdom of the Seleucids, it seems clear that the first three kingdoms are meant to be Babylonia, Media, and Persia. This does not exactly square with history as we now know it. Media was never really a world empire, at least not one that had much influence on the history of Israel. We would expect Assyria to be included in the list because it destroyed the northern kingdom and took its people into exile, although this does not seem to be the intention of the author of Daniel. The seer describes the first empire as a lion. This corresponds to Babylon, given that the lion was often used as a symbol for that nation or its king. The bear is a symbol for Media. The leopard could be appropriate for Persia because Cyrus moved with such speed and stealth to capture Babylon. However, none of these nations is the real concern of the seer.

In the vision, the four winds of heaven stir up the great sea from which the four beasts emerge. This tells us a great deal about the author's understanding of the beasts/kingdoms. The primordial ocean was, according to ancient cosmological myths, the chaos out of which the order of the universe was created. The ocean/chaos constantly threatened to destroy the order of the universe, and the ruling god or gods kept the chaotic destruction of the ocean at bay. We find evidence of this myth in the Old Testament (Isa 27:1; 51:9; Job 7:12), where it describes Yahweh as vanquishing the sea or the monster of the sea (Rahab or the dragon). By describing these kingdoms as coming out of the sea, the author of Daniel declares them to be destructive and chaotic realities opposed to the orderly rule of God.

The Little Horn

The fourth beast is not even identified with a known animal. It is different from the rest and is horrible, terrifying, and extraordinarily strong. This beast has ten horns, but a little horn springs out of the midst of the ten horns and displaces three of them. This little horn is Antiochus IV, but the exact identification of the three horns that he replaced (perhaps his father and two brothers) is not known. The little horn has eyes and a mouth that speaks arrogantly. Antiochus used the title Epiphanes (meaning the manifestation of God on earth) and made a statue or altar to himself as Jupiter. To the Jews, this idolatrous claim to divinity would have been the ultimate in arrogance. In v. 21, the small horn makes war against the holy ones (faithful Jews) and is victorious until the Ancient One arrives. For the author of Daniel, it will not be the efforts of the Maccabees that will spell victory for the Jews, but only the direct intervention of God. In v. 25 the little horn speaks against the Most High and oppresses the holy ones, thinking of changing the feast days and the law. This is a description of the policies of Antiochus IV, who attempted to impose Hellenistic culture and customs on the Jews.

The Ancient One and the Son of Man

The picture of God as the Ancient One is drawn from the Book of Ezekiel. In chapter 1 (and again in chapter 10), Ezekiel describes the cherubim who are holding up the throne of God. The cherubim are accompanied by (or standing on) wheels. There is also fire for incense in the middle of the four cherubim.

Finally in 1:26, Ezekiel gets around to describing what is above the cherubim. There is a throne of sapphire and the one sitting on the throne has the appearance of a human. His appearance was half of electrum and half of fire. He is surrounded with splendor. The author of the vision of Daniel uses the material of Ezekiel for his own purposes. The one like a human becomes the Ancient One with hair white as wool, indicating his great wisdom. His throne is made up of fire, and there are wheels of fire connected with it. The Ancient One in Daniel is surrounded by thousands ministering to him and not by only four cherubim as in Ezekiel.

The "one like a human being" (traditionally translated as "one like a son of man") also comes from Ezekiel. There are two traditions in Ezekiel. On the one hand in Ezekiel 1, God is portrayed as having the appearance of human form. On the other hand, when God addresses Ezekiel in his visions, God refers to him as "mortal" (literally in Hebrew, "son of man"), a title that seems only to emphasize Ezekiel's humanity over against God's divine powers and glory. In that case "son of man" means simply a human being. In the text of Daniel, a figure is described as "one like a human being." In later tradition, this figure is simply called the "Son of man." What is this figure? Is it human, angelic, or divine? Scholars think that the figure is either a corporate image for the "holy ones," or the archangel Michael, who is the guardian and protector of Israel (Dan 10:21—11:1). If the title refers to the holy ones, then the figure would be human and more in keeping with the use of son of man to refer to Ezekiel as a human being. If the title refers to Michael, then the figure would be angelic/divine and more in keeping with Ezekiel's use of human likeness to describe divine and angelic beings. There is ample precedent for making a single figure stand for a group. Often the prophets speak to Israel as to one person (a good example is Hos 11:1 where God calls Israel, "my son"). However, given that the Book of Daniel describes angels as being in human likeness, and describes Michael as being "your prince" (10:21), it is probably best to understand the "one like a human being" of Daniel 7:13 as the archangel Michael.

179

A Year, Two Years, and a Half-Year

In Daniel 7:25 the interpreting angel tells Daniel that the holy ones of the Most High will be handed over to the little horn for "for a time, two times, and half a time." This statement must be understood in the context of the author's understanding of the time since the Exile. Jeremiah had predicted that the Exile would last seventy years, and then the people would return, and there would be a new age of God reigning over the people of Judea. Although the actual exile in Babylon did last approximately seventy years, later prophets and visionaries did not see the new age envisioned by Jeremiah as having materialized. The author of the apocalypses of Daniel sees in a vision that the seventy years to which Jeremiah referred were actually seventy weeks of years, or 490 years (Dan 9:24–27). For the author of this vision the Jews are in the final week of years, and half-finished even with that. There are only three-and-a-half years left until the new age comes, although this last half-week of years (three-and-a-half years) will bring with it the abolition of the Temple sacrifices and the setting up of the abomination (altar or idol) that desecrates (9:27). This is being written after the altar/idol has been placed in the Temple, and the author of Daniel is encouraging patience because God has set a limit to this abomination. In Daniel 8:14, the angel tells Daniel that this situation will last for 2,300 evenings and mornings before the Temple is purified. This is only 1,150 days and a good bit less than three-and-a-half years. At the end of chapter 12, the angel tells Daniel that the time from when the sacrifice is abolished and when the abomination is set up until the time of the purification of the temple is 1,290 days (somewhat more than three-and-a-half years). Immediately after this is a blessing for those who have the patience to persevere for 1,335 days. It is clear that the author kept adjusting the time period before the purification of the Temple because it was taking longer than he first expected.

The inconsistencies in the dates given in Daniel give us a window into its composition. We can see the author constantly updating the text because of changed historical circumstances. In this way, we can date the final version quite precisely to 164 B.C.E.

World of the Text

Narrative Repetition

In the vision/dream, there are essentially three main actors: the Ancient One, the Son of Man/Holy Ones, and the Little Horn. The descriptions of the four kingdoms are meant to emphasize how much more terrible this present ruler is than any corrupt and oppressive empire that has gone before. The appearance of the little horn causes the heavenly court to be convened with God enthroned and judging. The beast with the little horn is slain and only then does "one like a human being" (son of man) appear. He is given dominion and kingship. Then in v. 18, and again in v. 22, it is said that the holy ones receive the kingship and dominion. It is generally agreed that one like a son of man in some ways represents the holy and faithful Jews (the author of Daniel probably does not think that all the Jews will be judged worthy to receive this kingship). If we are correct to understand that the one like a human being is Michael, his dominion, as the prince of Israel, would mean the kingship and dominion of all the holy people of God. Therefore, we need not make a sharp distinction between Michael receiving dominion and the holy people of God (faithful Jews) receiving dominion.

This narrative (the actions of the little horn, his judgment by God, and the kingship being given to the holy people) is repeated two more times when Daniel asks the angel the meaning of the vision (vv. 15–22) and when the angel explains the vision to Daniel (vv. 23–27). The emphasis in both of these reviews is on the terrible actions of the little horn. This is the most important rhetorical feature of this story. It tells the same events three times: the vision, Daniel's questioning the meaning of the vision, and the angel's interpretation of the vision. It is also noteworthy that the angel's interpretation is in poetry. Each of these repetitions has three parts: the description of the terrible actions of the little horn, the judgment by God against the horn by taking away his power and destroying him, and the giving of the kingship to the son of man/holy ones. In each successive repetition, the description of the little horn gets more specific and condemnatory. The repetition drives home the point that God is aware of the terrible nature of Antiochus and has already judged him as idolatrous and destined for destruction. The judgment against Antiochus will take effect soon, and the holy ones will reign forever in peace.

World in front of the Text

Jesus as Son of Man

One could argue that the point of Daniel 7 is political independence for Judea, although that is not how Jesus and the gospels writers interpret it. The element that they focus on in this text is the figure, the Son of man. After considering both Ezekiel and Daniel, we can see that this image is fluid and multivalent. By New Testament times this figure has probably been developed in popular Jewish thinking into a supernatural, end-time figure who would bring about God's reign on earth. Jesus describes the Son of man coming on the clouds as the coming of the final judgment of God and the end of time. However, Jesus in the gospels also uses the term Son of man to refer to himself as a human destined for suffering and death. This represents a subversion of the meaning of this image. In Daniel, the Son of man represents victory and dominion, not suffering and death. By taking over this image as both suffering one and victorious one, Jesus makes a strong point about the nature of his mission.

A Time Table for the End of the World?

Although a feature of apocalyptic is the prediction of future events, we can see in the apocalypses of Daniel that this was not a very successful endeavor. The Book of Daniel is wrong about the time that the Temple will remain defiled. It is wrong about how and when Antiochus IV will die. It is even wrong about the kingship and dominion of the holy ones after the victory (the reign of the Hasmoneans in Judea can hardly be understood as "their kingdom shall be an everlasting kingdom, and all dominions shall serve and obey them" [7:27]). We saw earlier how the author of the apocalypses of Daniel had to go back and give new dates for the end of the oppression of Antiochus. This should warn us about ever thinking that the end of an era or the end of the world can be predicted. In Mark 13, Jesus speaks of the day when the Son of man will come in the clouds and gather the elect into God's kingdom, although he says that "about that day or hour no one knows, neither the angels in heaven, nor the Son, but only the Father" (13:32).

The predictions of Daniel offer us hope for the future and a methodology of reinterpretation. The primary message of the apocalypses of Daniel is not the date when the Temple will be purified, but the fact that God can be trusted to defeat the powers of oppression and idolatry and to bring about the reign of God. Also, we see enshrined in the Bible the willingness to reinterpret sayings to keep the message of hope alive. If the new age envisioned by Jeremiah had been fulfilled in seventy years, that vision would have been an impoverished one. God's reign would not be very exciting or liberating. However, if Jeremiah could be reinterpreted so that the reign of God was still to come, then hope could still motivate people to faithfulness to God. The Bible is always discovering that there is more to be discovered in its flawed images and interpretations. The Bible itself teaches us that we can never fix one event, one statement, or one time as definitive and final. Hope always presses onward and upward.

Learning Achievements

After studying this chapter, students should be able to:

- Explain the difference between regular prophets and biblical prophets.

- Outline the form of the judgment oracle and discuss its relationship to the covenant form.

- Describe the three divisions of the book of Isaiah.

- Discuss the meaning of God's command to Isaiah in Isaiah 6 to close the ears and eyes of the people.

- Describe the historical and political situation leading up to and following the Exile when Jeremiah was writing.

- Discuss Jeremiah's use of "confessions," dirges, and symbolic actions in his preaching.

- Describe the historical and political situation at the time of the Maccabean revolt.

- Explain what makes Daniel 7—12 an apocalyptic text.

Recommended Reading

Blenkinsopp, Joseph. *A History of Prophecy in Israel.* Louisville, Ky.: Westminster John Knox, 1996.

Heschel, Abraham. *The Prophets (Perennial Classics).* New York: Harper Perennial, 2001.

Koch, Klaus. *The Prophets.* Translated by Margaret Kohl. Vol. 1, *The Assyrian Period* and Vol. 2, *The Babylonian and Persian Periods.* Philadelphia: Fortress, 1982.

Mays, James Luther, and Paul J. Achtemeier. *Interpreting the Prophets.* Philadelphia: Fortress, 1987.

Chapter 7
NEW TESTAMENT INTRODUCTION

World behind the Text

History

In 539 B.C.E. Cyrus of Persia allowed the Jews to return to their homeland of Judea. Over the next four hundred years, there were numerous migrations of Jews from the former Babylonian Empire to Judea. However, many Jews remained in the east in Babylon and Persia. In 519 the Temple of Jerusalem was rededicated. This period from 519 B.C.E. to 70 C.E. is known as the Second Temple period of Judaism. The historical events of the Second Temple period are the backdrop for the founding of Christianity and form the world out of which Jesus and the New Testament grew. In 330 Alexander the Great conquered the Persian Empire, bringing Greek rule to the whole of the Near Eastern world even as far as India. With his death in 323 the empire was divided into four parts and taken over by four prominent generals. The two dynasties that controlled the land of Judea were Ptolemy, who ruled in Egypt, and Seleucus, who ruled in Babylon and Syria. For the first one hundred years, Ptolemy ruled over Judea, and there was relative political and religious calm, although after about 200 B.C.E., the Seleucid dynasty in Syria began to make inroads into the Ptolemaic Empire and eventually took over the area of Judea. One of the later Seleucid kings, Antiochus IV, was not sympathetic to the religious and social customs of the Jews and wanted to Hellenize Judea. In 167, because of the repressive measures taken against the Jews, their religion, and their Temple (Antiochus went so far as to set up a statue of Zeus in the Temple), a group of revolutionaries in Galilee began

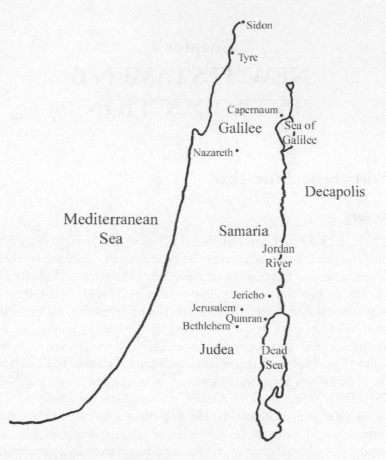

Figure 2. Palestine at the Time of Jesus

a revolt. The revolt was initiated by Mattathias, an elderly priest, and continued by his three sons: Judas, nicknamed the Maccabee (the hammer), Jonathan, and Simon. The Maccabean revolt eventually gained some autonomy and religious freedom for Judea. In 164 Judas rededicated the Temple, and the yearly celebration of that glorious event is the feast of Hanukkah. The Maccabeans became the leaders of an independent Judea (Simon took the titles of both king and high priest) and inaugurated the Hasmonean dynasty. Although the original revolt was meant to relieve Judea from the pressure of Hellenization, under the Hasmonean dynasty that pressure continued. In 63 B.C.E. during a struggle for power between two of the Hasmonean princes, both princes called on the Roman general Pompey for aid. Pompey intervened by capturing Jerusalem, and from that time on Judea was subject in some fashion to the authority of Rome.

In 40 B.C.E. Herod, son of Antipater of Edom, was named the king of the Jews by Rome. He married into the Hasmonean family, but was not himself a Hasmonean. He was a Jew by rabbinic law—his mother was Jewish, although his father was an Edomite. He was a tenacious and ruthless political operator, switching his allegiance to whomever was in power at the time. He built great cities to flatter the Roman emperor, Augustus, filling them with pagan temples. At the same time, he rebuilt the Temple of Jerusalem to its former Solomonic splendor. However, the Jews resented him for being a ruthless despot who played both sides— Roman and Jewish—at once. His strategy was effective to the extent that he was able to stay in power until his death in 4 B.C.E.

After Herod's death, the area that he ruled was divided among his three remaining sons. Herod Antipas was in control of the north—Galilee. Archelaus was given charge of Judea in the south, and Philip was put over the region east of the Jordan—the Decapolis. Archelaus was quickly removed by Rome for incompetence and replaced by a governor. This was the situation at the time of Jesus' ministry: Roman governors ruled in Judea, Herod Antipas ruled Galilee, and Philip ruled in the Decapolis. After a succession of many Roman governors in Judea, the governor during the ministry of Jesus was Pontius Pilate. All during the life of Jesus and up until the revolt in 66 C.E. there were tensions between the common people of Judea and Galilee and the Roman overlords. For the most part, the Jewish landlords, priests, and ruling classes tried to play both sides, but were considered by the revolutionaries as part of Roman oppression.

In 49 C.E. during the reign of Claudius, there was a disturbance in Rome that caused Claudius to expel some (or maybe even all) of the Jews from Rome. Later writers indicate that the disturbance was caused by one called Chrestus. It is possible that there was a conflict between Jews who believed in Jesus and Jews who did not. In 64 C.E. a terrible fire destroyed much of Rome. Nero was suspected of having started the fire so that he could rebuild Rome according to his design. To steer the blame away from himself, Nero blamed the Christians. There followed a persecution of the Christians of Rome but not a general persecution of Christians throughout the empire. However, it should be noted that at this time, Christians were generally considered "haters of humanity" because of their refusal to participate in many of the social functions of the empire.

In 66 C.E. the Jews of Palestine revolted against their Roman overlords. The Roman general Vespasian was sent to put down the revolt. After three years the revolt was all but ended and Vespasian returned to Rome to become emperor. His son Titus finished the war against the Jews, destroyed the Temple, and wiped out the last pockets of resistance (most notably Masada). The war against the Jews was a calamity for the Christian community of Jerusalem, who had to flee to the Syrian city of Pella, although for the most part, the Jewish war did not greatly affect the situation of Christians throughout the Roman Empire.

Geography of the New Testament World

The world of the New Testament was not confined to Palestine. Palestine (as described in the geography of the Old Testament) was the location of the ministry of Jesus and some of his earliest disciples, but most of the ministry of early Christianity took place outside of Palestine. Jesus himself was from Galilee and spent much of his time around the Sea of Galilee. His ministry ended with his execution in Jerusalem. Jerusalem was built on an easily defended hill that was surrounded by valleys. The northern wall of the city was the most accessible. The Temple Mount was at the northeastern edge of the city. To the east of the city was the Kidron Valley and on the hill across the valley and opposite Jerusalem was the Mount of Olives. The eastern and southern edges of the city had the steepest inclines to the valleys below. To the south of Jerusalem was the Valley of Hinnom, which was also called Gehenna. It contained Jerusalem's trash dump.

Apart from the gospels, the rest of the New Testament refers mostly to places outside of Palestine. To the north in Syria, the cities of Antioch on the coast and Damascus in the Transjordan plateau were important centers of Christian missionary activity. To the south and east of Palestine was the kingdom of Nabatea. Early in his career Paul did missionary work in this area. Much further south in Egypt, Christians were active early. Alexandria had a large Jewish population that would have provided a natural place for missionaries to begin to spread the message about Jesus. Acts describes the missionary Apollos as being from Alexandria. However, the bulk of the New Testament material refers to Asia Minor, Greece, and Rome. Many of the cities addressed by Paul, the cities addressed in the Book of Revelation, probably the cities addressed by the letters of John and some of the other Catholic letters were all in Asia Minor (modern-day Turkey). Ephesus, Philadelphia, Colossae, and Smyrna were in the western part of Asia Minor. Paul's home of Tarsus and the cities of Lystra and Derbe were in the eastern end of Asia Minor. Others of Paul's letters refer to cities in Greece: Philippi, Thessalonica, and Corinth. Besides Paul's letter to the Romans, Rome is the subject of the Book of Revelation, which constantly refers to Rome under the symbolic name of Babylon. In the letter to the Romans Paul even speaks of wanting to undertake a missionary journey to Spain (it is possible that he was able to accomplish this). Thus, the New Testament world surrounds the Mediterranean Sea. To the east were Palestine and Syria, to the south Egypt and Libya, to the north Asia Minor, Greece, and Italy, and to the west was Spain. These were the lands from which the New Testament texts originated and to which they were sent.

Greco-Roman Culture and Religion

Hellenistic culture was pervasive throughout the Roman Empire. In any major city in the empire, one would find a temple to one of the Greco-Roman gods, a gymnasium, a forum, and a theater. Anywhere one went in the empire, Greek was spoken. A major innovation accomplished by the Romans was the building of roads. This allowed for the swift movement of news, troops, and supplies to all corners of the empire in a very short time. In the first century C.E. travel by boat on the Mediterranean was neither swift nor safe, and was impossible during the winter months. Walking on roads was the fastest and safest way to travel. This innovation was essential for the spread of Christianity. Because of the relative safety and speed of Roman roads Christianity was able to spread quickly, and communities far from each other could keep in contact.

The religious situation of the Roman Empire was one of syncretism. Most people in the empire would have believed in many gods. They would have worshiped in a special way certain gods and goddesses who were related to their city, their nation, and their work. There was no "separation of church and state" in the Roman Empire. The worship of gods and goddesses was intimately tied to all aspects of life. The carpenter's union had a patron god, and union meetings involved sacrifices and prayers to that god. The city had a patron god, and any civic festival involved worship of a deity. Worship of the emperor was common, especially in the eastern half of the empire. Because of this religious syncretism, religious tolerance was the order of the day. People were not persecuted if they chose to worship Demeter instead of Apollo or Bacchus. No one was persecuted for belonging to one of the mystery religions of foreign origin such as the cults of Isis or Mithra. However, it was considered unpatriotic and even heretical to reject the worship of the gods and goddesses in normal everyday life and to condemn these gods and their worship as evil and demonic. Christians were called "haters of humanity" for just such beliefs. Their intolerance of religious syncretism was not tolerated in the empire.

Socioeconomic Situation of Palestine

At the time of Jesus Palestine had an agricultural economy. The majority of the people were peasants. They were small landholders, tenant farmers, or slaves involved in agriculture. Absentee landlords, both Jewish and Gentile, owned much of the land. Artisans, urban slaves, and fishermen made up the rest of the lower class. The upper class was small and concentrated in the urban centers. In Jerusalem the upper classes were mainly the priests. In Galilee the upper classes were mostly Gentiles. The economy worked by means of taxation. Landowners demanded a fairly large percentage of the produce from their land, leaving the tenant farmers with barely a subsistence living. The empire required a fixed tax from each of its subject rulers or governors. These rulers in turn needed to tax the cities and the people. Tax collectors paid a fixed amount to the ruler for the right to collect the taxes in a given area. Surplus taxes were theirs to keep. There was a tax or toll on transporting any property, and a tax on all Jews for the support of the Temple. Taxes were the way the empire ran, and a burden that constantly inspired revolt and sedition.

Jewish Religion

At the time of Jesus, there were three sects of Judaism. The **Sadducees** were the traditional party of priests, and its members included most of the ruling aristocracy. The Sadducees were conservative in their interpretations of scripture and in their beliefs. They did not accept the more recent theological innovations of resurrection of the dead and oral law. Their attitude toward Rome was one of conciliation. As long as the Romans gave them control of the Temple and the right to administer the Law of Moses among the people, they were willing to support Roman rule. The **Pharisees** were a reform party of populist teachers of the law. They considered the study of the law, both the written law of Moses and the oral law passed down from rabbi to rabbi, as the most important occupation of a Jew. They felt that it was the obligation of every Jew to study and keep the law. Therefore, they developed a list of all the separate laws in the Law that every Jew was required to keep. This was not meant as legalism but as an aid for the ordinary people (the people of the land) who were unable to study the law themselves. The Sadducees, in contrast, were not as concerned for the spiritual development of the common person. The **Essenes** were apocalyptic monks living in the desert and preparing for the coming intervention of God. When the Dead Sea Scrolls were discovered in 1947, the remains of a monastery nearby (Qumran) were recognized to have been the center of the

Essenes. Although there seems to have been followers of the Essene movement who did not live in this monastery, the apocalyptic vision of the community is fixed to this place. The community had separated itself from Jerusalem and other Jews, considering them to be defiled by inappropriate worship (they celebrated the feasts on the wrong days). Led by the Teacher of Righteousness, the Essenes had gone into the desert to prepare the way of the Lord. (They used the same reference from Isaiah 40 to justify their mission as the gospels use to justify John the Baptist's mission.)

At the time of Jesus, the Temple was the center of Jewish life in Palestine. Even Jews living in Galilee would go to Jerusalem frequently to worship in the Temple. In chapter 2, we discussed the major feasts of Judaism. The feasts of Hanukkah and Purim would also have been celebrated during the time of Jesus, but the three main pilgrim feasts of Passover, Pentecost, and Booths were still the most important. A new feature at the time of Jesus was the synagogue. During the Exile and later in the Diaspora, Jews who did not have access to the Temple would gather to pray and discuss the Law of Moses. These gatherings were called synagogues. Later when special buildings were built for the purpose of these gatherings, the buildings came to be called synagogues. At the time of Jesus there were synagogue buildings in most of the towns and cities of Palestine and many of the major cities of the Roman Empire.

Apocalypticism

It has been said that an apocalyptic worldview is the mother of Christianity, and there is truth to that statement. Christianity began as an apocalyptic movement in Judaism. The first Christians were Jews who believed that God had begun the end time. All the gospels begin their story of Jesus with John the Baptist, an apocalyptic prophet who was characterized as Elijah returned. The Book of Malachi predicted Elijah's return at the end time to prepare the way for the coming of God. John the Baptist appeared at the end time and prepared the way for the coming (birth) of the Messiah Jesus, although this coming of the Messiah Jesus was not the end but only inaugurated the end time. The resurrection of Jesus was understood as the beginning of the end time when all the dead were to be raised. Early Christians expected Jesus Christ to return from heaven and finalize the end time with the resurrection of all the dead, the judgment of all, and the inauguration of God's kingdom ruled by the Messiah. This Jewish apocalyptic theology is at the heart of Christianity. Christianity would not exist without the theological foundation of apocalyptic thinking: end times, the coming of the Messiah, resurrection of the dead, and final judgment.

World of the Text

Parts of the New Testament

The New Testament consists of three main sections. The New Testament begins with the four gospels and the Acts of the Apostles (which is actually volume two of the Gospel of Luke). The second section of the New Testament is the Pauline corpus. Where the authentic letters of Paul end and the later letters of his followers begin is a matter of much contention. However, wherever one places the line of demarcation between Paul and his followers, all of these letters, from Romans to Titus, belong to the Pauline corpus and share a similar style and language. The letter to the Hebrews, although sometimes attributed to Paul and included in the canon at the end of Paul's letters, should be considered as belonging to the letters of the other apostles that follow. The Pauline corpus is followed by the third section, which contains other letters, attributed to other apostles—James, Peter, John, and Jude. The Book of Revelation, as an apocalyptic vision, really belongs in a class by itself, but because it begins with a letter to the seven churches of Asia Minor, we will include it in this last section of letters.

World in front of the Text

Formation of the Canon

The books of the New Testament were not written to be in the Bible. They were letters sent to real churches, or interpretations of the life, death, and resurrection of Jesus for use in the teaching and worship of different communities. Eventually, as the books were used, they were circulated among other communities and preserved. In the course of about one hundred years, a fixed collection of books developed that were considered authoritative. Their authority was first based on their acceptance and use, but eventually the reason for their authority was tied to their apostolic origins. They were either written by an apostle or contained the remembrances of the apostle written down by one of his followers. As early as 110 C.E. the early church fathers were quoting the gospels and the letters of Paul as authoritative scripture. It was not, however, until around 400 that several church councils defined the books that were considered apostolic and authoritative.

It is now clear that there were other writings circulating in the early Christian communities that were not preserved in the canon of the church. We even know of the controversies surrounding several of the books of the New Testament. There was considerable argument over whether to accept the Book of Revelation or the letter to the Hebrews into the canon. In recent years, archaeologists have discovered books used by early Christian communities that were previously unknown. In Nag Hammadi, they discovered gospels, apocalypses, and letters that contain Christian language and themes.

After the books were written and in final form there was still a process of interpretation, acceptance, and evaluation for the books. This process continues. Even though the Catholic Church made a definitive statement of the canon at the Council of Trent (1546) that will not change, she is still in the ongoing process of evaluating, accepting, and interpreting the books.

Learning Achievements

After studying this chapter, students should be able to:

- Outline the history of Palestine and the Jews from Alexander the Great to the destruction of the Temple by the Romans.

- Discuss the cultural and economic situation of the Roman Empire.

- List the different sects in Judaism and describe the religious practice of Judaism in the first century C.E.

- List the contents of the New Testament, with its three sections.

- Describe the process of forming the New Testament.

Recommended Reading

Blaiklock, E. M. *The Compact Handbook of New Testament Life.* Minneapolis: Bethany House, 1979.

Brown, Raymond. *Introduction to the New Testament.* New York: Doubleday, 1997.

Malina, Bruce. *The New Testament World: Insights from Cultural Anthropology,* 3d ed. Louisville, Ky.: Westminster John Knox, 2001.

Roetzel, Calvin. *The World that Shaped the New Testament.* Atlanta: John Knox, 1985.

Chapter 8

GOSPELS AND ACTS
OF THE APOSTLES

Introduction

World behind the Text

Historical Jesus

What do we know about the life of Jesus? Two important sources from the time of the gospels mention Jesus. Josephus, a Jewish military leader during the Jewish war against Rome (66–70 C.E.), was captured by the Romans and went on to write a history of the war (*Jewish War*). He also wrote a compendium of Jewish history, lore, and belief (*Jewish Antiquities*). One reference in *Jewish Antiquities* tells of Jesus' life, death, resurrection and how he fulfilled the prophets. Although some core of this may have been in Josephus's original text, most scholars believe that the text as we have it is the work of a Christian interpolator. Another reference in *Antiquities* mentions James of Jerusalem and calls him "the brother of Jesus, the alleged Christ." This text does not seem to be the work of a Christian interpolator and would lead us to suspect that the text about Jesus in the earlier volume of *Antiquities* has some core that does go back to Josephus.

Tacitus, a Roman senator who in his *Annals* writes about the great fire of Rome in 64 C.E., tells of Nero's attempt to shift the blame for starting the fire from himself to the Christians and his subsequent persecution of these Christians. Tacitus, who is neither pro-Christian nor pro-Nero, tells his readers that the Christians are named for *Chrestus*, who was put to death during the reign of Tiberius at the hands of Pontius Pilate, the Roman procurator. Tacitus was writing about 110 C.E., just after the gospels had taken their final form. There is evidence then that there was a tradition, already known to nonbelieving Jews and Gentiles about the life of a man Jesus, who was given the title of Christ (Messiah) by his followers, who lived in Palestine, and was put to death during the reign of Tiberius.

To reconstruct any life of Jesus the primary source material must be the gospels. There can be no biography of the historical Jesus by modern standards because our sources are too few and do not have our rigorous historical standards. The gospels, although they tell the life of Jesus in a narrative, chronological framework, are not interested in an accurate, chronological, and historical account of Jesus' words and actions. Nor are they to be considered novels or fictions. The gospels take history seriously, but just not in the same way we do. The history that concerns them is God's activity in the world, God's plan for the salvation of humans. The creators of the traditions about Jesus—in the earliest oral stories, in the first written compilations, and in the gospels—themselves came from a tradition that described God's activity in the context of a chronological narrative. The stories of the Patriarchs, the Exodus, the conquest, the judges, the life of David, and the history of the kingship were all historical, chronological narratives whose primary concern was to show God at work in the history of Israel. History, for the writers of these texts, was the means to the end of showing God's way with God's people. For moderns history is an end in itself. The truth of the biblical narratives is the truth of how God acts in history, whereas the truth of modern historical writings is the empirical truth of historical fact. Our modern historical mode of thinking would have been foreign to any of the biblical writers.

The Three Stages of Gospel Development

The Pontifical Biblical Commission, in its document "The Historical Truth of the Gospels," has offered a helpful way to approach the issue of the historical Jesus and the nature of the gospels. The document notes that the gospels in their final form are the result of three stages of growth. The first stage is the ministry of Jesus. Jesus lived and worked in a rural environment in Palestine, speaking Aramaic, and preaching the coming of God's kingdom. His followers remembered and repeated his words and deeds.

After his death his disciples experienced him as raised from the dead, and they continued the Jesus tradition in its second stage. The message in stage two was no longer simply the coming of God's kingdom but the presence of God's kingdom in the risen Christ Jesus. This message was being preached in both Greek and Aramaic to urban as well as rural audiences. Because of these changes, there was not a simple transmission of all the words and deeds of Jesus. Words and deeds were selected that would inspire and convince particular audiences. The words and deeds were translated into Greek. Words and deeds were altered to be understandable in a new social and economic context and were expanded or reapplied to make a new point about Jesus' own role in the kingdom.

After a number of years of evangelization, the third stage (the gospels) appeared. This too involved a new situation. This stage came out of established Christian churches. The message was no longer an attempt to convince hearers about Jesus' resurrection and his role in God's plan of salvation. The message was about how to live this new life in Christ in the ongoing life of the church in the world. Now all the gospels were in Greek. They reflected urban environments mostly outside of Palestine. They presumed knowledge of the life of Jesus and faith in him as the Christ. The words and deeds of Jesus and the apostolic preaching about Jesus as the Christ were again selected for their suitability as teachings in the church. They were revised, translated, and expanded to apply to the new situation of Christians living in established churches in the world, with the coming of Christ not as imminent as was first thought. New sayings of Jesus, received by Christian prophets, may have been added to the words of Jesus at this stage.

So, when we examine the gospels, we see the words and deeds of Jesus that have passed through these three stages of development. We cannot expect to find a historical account of Stage One in a Stage Three document. However, the document from the Pontifical Biblical Commission also asserts that the Stage Three documents (the gospels) were not creations of their authors, but were the result of an organic process of transmission and development of the words and deeds of Jesus in a Spirit-inspired community that applied these words and deeds in altered circumstances.

Synoptic Problem

An early tradition claimed that Matthew, one of the Twelve, wrote the first gospel. However, none of the gospels identifies its author, and there is nothing about the text of the Gospel of Matthew that suggests that a companion of Jesus wrote it. Modern scholarship has developed a theory about the order and development of the gospels that seeks to explain the great similarity between Matthew, Mark, and Luke. These three are known as the "Synoptic Gospels" because of their similarity ("synoptic" means "seeing with"). The books have a common view of the life of Jesus and can be placed side by side and easily compared. The synoptic problem became the concern of scholarship more than a century ago. Scholars recognized that the similarities between the Synoptic Gospels could not be explained by insisting that the writers were simply telling the same stories and words of Jesus in their own ways. Rather, it became clear that the gospel writers used each other as sources. They often have the exact same wording, the same comments of the narrator, and the same order of stories. This raised the question of which gospel was source and which gospels copied.

The theory that developed a century ago and that remains the best explanation for the relationship between these three gospels is known as the two-source hypothesis. According to this hypothesis (it will probably never be proved to everyone's satisfaction), Mark is the oldest of the gospels. Matthew and Luke both had copies of Mark and used Mark as the primary source for their gospels. This solves many of the questions of why Matthew, Mark, and Luke are so similar, although there remained another problem having to do with Matthew and Luke. There are sayings of Jesus that are not in Mark but that correspond exactly in Matthew and Luke. If Matthew and Luke did not get these sayings from Mark, did one of them have a copy of the other? If this were the case—if Matthew had a copy of Luke or Luke had a copy of Matthew—scholars believe that Matthew would have used other material in Luke or Luke used other material from

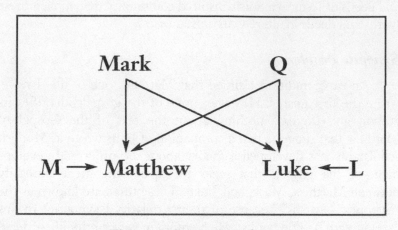

Figure 3. Synoptic Solution

Matthew. Because of this belief, scholars hypothesized that there must have been a second written source, which contained a collection of sayings of Jesus, that both Matthew and Luke had available to them. This source was known as "Q" (abbreviated from *Quelle*, the German word for "source"). In the two-source hypothesis, Mark and Q were the two sources used by Matthew and Luke. The hypothesis was expanded because scholars believed that there was other material that was unique to Matthew (scholars designate this material "M") and material unique to Luke (designated "L"). "M" and "L" are not sources in the same sense as Mark and Q, and so this theory is still referred to as the two-source hypothesis. It can be schematized as shown in Figure 3.

Sources of Mark and John

Scholars believe that both Mark and John also used sources in the writing of their gospels, although because we do not have these sources and do not know of any other work that used these sources, it is very difficult to reconstruct them. Scholars have sought to differentiate between what is source and what is the writing or editing of the gospel writer. In this way, scholars have been able to isolate one or two collections of miracle stories in Mark and a sign source in John. The parables of Mark seem also to come from a source, and the passion narratives of both John and Mark probably rely on a written source. Any discussion of sources for Mark and John, however, remains very tentative.

Redaction Criticism

The two-source hypothesis allows us to do redaction criticism as a method for interpreting the gospels. *Redaction criticism* involves the study of the changes an author makes to a source. When we examine a story in Matthew that also appears in Mark, then according to the two-source hypothesis we know that Matthew took the story from Mark. If we place the stories side by side and examine the differences between the two stories, we know that the differences are the result of changes made by Matthew to the original story in Mark. This allows us to develop theories about the kinds of changes Matthew made to Mark and why he made those changes. For example, the narrator in Mark 1:4 says, "John the baptizer appeared in the wilderness, proclaiming a baptism of repentance for the forgiveness of sins." Matthew changed this so that the narrator in Matthew 3:1–2 says, "In those days John the Baptist appeared in the wilderness of Judea, proclaiming, 'Repent, for the kingdom of heaven has come near.'" Matthew changed the focus of the preaching of John the Baptist from a baptism of repentance for the forgiveness of sins to simply repentance attributed to the nearness of the kingdom for two reasons. First, Matthew probably deleted the baptism of repentance for the forgiveness of sins because Jesus submitted to that baptism from John. Matthew believed that Jesus was sinless, and therefore the baptism had to have a different meaning. Also, Matthew believed that Jesus' death, not John's baptism, took away sin. Second, Matthew made John's message identical to the message that Jesus preached at the beginning of his ministry (4:17). Matthew also aligned the preaching of the disciples in 10:7 to this same message. Thus, the one who precedes Jesus, Jesus, and those who follow Jesus all preach the same message of the kingdom of God. By doing redaction criticism we begin to develop a picture of Matthew's interests, theological concerns, and style.

201

World of the Text

Gospel Genre

The gospel genre is unique. There is no literary form in the ancient world known as a gospel. The word *gospel* is used by Paul to designate the message about the world-transforming event that took place with Jesus' death and resurrection. The word means "good news" and most often refers to an announcement of what the emperor has done to bring about peace and prosperity. Pronouncements concerning the gospel of the emperor were common. Paul deliberately steals this word, used in imperial propaganda, to show that the good news that truly makes for peace and prosperity in the lives of the empire's citizens is not the deeds of the emperor but the deeds of one who was murdered by the empire. Paul uses the term, not to define a genre for the life story of Jesus, but to identify the announcement of what God has done for the world in the death and resurrection of Jesus. In time, however, the word *gospel* becomes a title for the message about Jesus. So by the time Mark decides to write a narrative of the life and death of Jesus, he summarizes the message by entitling his book "the good news [gospel] of Jesus Christ." The other gospel writers do not call their works gospels (Matthew calls his a genealogy, Luke calls his a narrative, and John calls his a genesis), but these works come to be called gospels on the model of Mark's Gospel.

The gospel genre, as it appears in the New Testament, is more than a biography of Jesus. The gospels share characteristics with ancient biographies. They also share many features with the historical narratives of the Old Testament. The gospels consciously present the words and deeds of Jesus as a historical narrative instead of as simply a collection of sayings (such as Q or the *Gospel of Thomas*). This does not mean that the gospels should be read as history according to modern standards. Rather, the story of Jesus for the early Christians was imbedded in a particular time and place in history and was part of God's plan of salvation worked out in history. The Jewish background of the gospels is most evident in the concern to present the plan of God as a salvation in historical events.

The Gospels and Acts

The four gospels are grouped together and placed first in the New Testament. Matthew's Gospel is placed first because it was considered to be the oldest and has the most to say about the church. Mark follows Matthew because it was considered a shortened form of Matthew. The Gospel of John is placed last because it is different from the others and is the most spiritual. The Acts of the Apostles follows the Gospel of John. It is right for Acts to be included with the gospels for several reasons. First, the Gospel of Luke and the Acts of the Apostles are both written by the same author and constitute two volumes of one work. Second, Acts is written to be a "gospel" (life story) of the early Church. The words, deeds, suffering, and death of the apostles are meant to imitate those of Jesus in the gospels.

Story Line of the Gospels and Acts

It is helpful to know the basic story line in the texts of the Bible. In the case of the gospels, there is a great deal of similarity in the story line of the Synoptic Gospels. The Gospel of John, however, diverges from the synoptic story line until the passion narrative. Here we will give only the barest bones of the story line, with emphasis on the synoptic account. (This is not a summary of the life of the historical Jesus but only a summary of the story line found in the gospels.) Jesus is born in Bethlehem and then moves with his parents to Nazareth where he grows up. At the age of thirty he leaves his family and his profession as a carpenter, and moves to the larger city of Capernaum, making it his center of operation. At the beginning of his ministry, he is associated with John the Baptist, who has a ministry of calling Israel to repentance and offering baptism in the Jordan River. Jesus' ministry consists of teaching about the kingdom of God and healing those in need. Some of his healings are exorcisms of demons. He gains attention and draws crowds because of his healings and teachings. Many follow him on his journeys and look after his needs (he is accompanied by some wealthier women who can afford to provide for him and his disciples). He gathers around himself a group of twelve who are being specially trained to do the work that he is doing. During his ministry, he makes enemies among the religious leaders because of his popularity—he is usurping their roles as teachers and mediators of healing and forgiveness. He also makes claims about his special relationship with God the Father, which anger the authorities. After only a short ministry (between one and three years) he meets his end in Jerusalem during the festival of the Passover. During Passover he celebrates a final supper with his closest disciples, and is betrayed by one of the Twelve, Judas. He is arrested as he spends the night in a garden outside of Jerusalem and is brought before the Sanhedrin and convicted of blasphemy. Because the Jewish leaders do not have the authority to assign the death penalty, he is taken before Pontius Pilate, who at first is unwilling to have Jesus executed. Pilate eventually gives in to the pressure of the leaders and sentences Jesus to death by crucifixion (a uniquely Roman form of execution). He is crucified with two others on the hill of Golgatha outside of Jerusalem. His crucifixion takes place on a Friday, and he dies before the sun goes down (when the Sabbath begins). He is buried in an adjacent garden by some wealthy sympathizers because his closest disciples have all fled. Nothing happens on the Sabbath, but on Sunday morning the women who followed him go to the tomb and find it empty. In the next few days, several of his disciples, both men and women, experience an appearance of the risen Jesus. Eventually these appearances cease, and the disciples, filled with the power of God's spirit that was the risen Jesus' gift to them, go about teaching and preaching as Jesus had. In a very short time, the followers of Jesus have spread this message to many different parts of the Roman Empire. Paul of Tarsus is especially singled out for his missionary work in Asia Minor and Greece.

World in front of the Text

Four Gospels

One of the significant features of the New Testament is that it includes four different accounts of the life of Jesus, four gospels. This fact tells us that there is not only one way to interpret the meaning of Jesus Christ for believers. Each of the gospels presents a different picture because of different concerns and circumstances in the communities for which they were written. The good news (gospel) of Jesus Christ must constantly be open to new interpretations for new circumstances and for new understandings of who we are as humans.

Matthew

INTRODUCTION

This section on Matthew will be more complete than other sections of this book because of the importance of the Synoptic Gospels for the New Testament and the Christian churches. In this section I examine three texts of the Gospel of Matthew. The first text is unique to Matthew and is taken from the Infancy Narrative. It shows how Matthew used the Old Testament to develop his picture of Jesus. The second text is a miracle story that Matthew has taken from Mark's Gospel. This study will show the value of doing redaction criticism and will give the reader an idea of the characteristics of Mark's Gospel. The final text is a parable that Matthew shares with Luke. This study will allow us to discuss how Matthew and Luke use the Q source and will give the reader a sketch of the characteristics of Luke's Gospel.

World behind the Text

Who Was Matthew?

None of the Synoptic Gospels gives any indication of who its author is. Unlike the letters of Paul, which announce in the opening verse who the sender and recipients are, the gospels are anonymous. Tradition attributes the gospel to Matthew. However, the author of the Gospel of Matthew was probably not one of the twelve apostles of Jesus. In Mark's list of the Twelve there is no apostle named Matthew. In Matthew's Gospel, the disciple who is named Levi in Mark becomes Matthew (Matt 9:9), although it is almost certain that whoever the author of this gospel was, he did not know Jesus firsthand but used the Gospel of Mark to write his gospel. The Gospel of Matthew has many character-istics that identify its author as a Jewish Christian, perhaps origi-nally a Pharisaic scribe. Some have suggested that the gospel came out of a school of Christian rabbis who studied the scriptures to come to a better understanding of Jesus. Because the author of the Gospel of Matthew used Mark (written around 70 C.E.) and has had ample time to reflect on the consequences of the fall of Jerusalem in 70 C.E., scholars generally date the gospel to about 85 C.E.

Jewish Christianity in Antioch

There is nothing in the Gospel of Matthew that explicitly names its place of origin. The community to which Matthew was writing seems to have been predominantly Jewish. The commu-nity was at one time closely linked to a Jewish community but later found itself in conflict with that community. Antioch is a likely candidate for the location of Matthew's community. It was a city with a large Jewish population and with a conservative Christian community that formed early and remained mostly Jewish for many years. We know a good bit about the early Christian community of Antioch through Paul's letter to the Galatians, the Acts of the Apostles, and the writings of Ignatius of Antioch (d. 107 C.E). These works allow us to reconstruct a com-munity whose profile fits that of the community reflected in Matthew's Gospel.

Sources of Matthew

Matthew used the Gospel of Mark as his main source. In fact, he used 90 percent of Mark's Gospel in his. He also used a source that scholars call "Q." This source consisted of sayings of Jesus and contained a number of parables, the beatitudes, and the Lord's Prayer. Beyond these two sources Matthew expanded the teaching of Jesus with sayings from his own source (M) and with his own editorial composition.

Reasons Matthew Wrote His Gospel

Four events had changed the world of Matthew's community since the time when the Gospel of Mark was written. From the changes that Matthew made to Mark's Gospel and from the themes that Matthew incorporated into his gospel, it is possible to get a glimpse of the events that caused him to write his gospel the way that he did. For Jews the most significant event to take place in the first century was the **destruction of the Temple** in Jerusalem by the Romans in 70 C.E. Even if the destruction had taken place by the time that Mark was written (and it is likely that it had not), Mark's Gospel was written early enough that there was not sufficient time to reflect yet on its implications. By the time of Matthew, however, Judaism was beginning to be transformed, and Matthew's Christian community was experiencing a parallel transformation. Before its destruction, the Temple was the center of Judaism. The Temple offered the way to be in relationship to God.

After the destruction of the Temple, the center of Judaism was the law. The study of the law and the keeping of the requirements of the law offered the way to be in relationship with God. Judaism became from this point on a religion of the book and not of the Temple. In parallel with this, Matthew portrayed Jesus as the New Law. Christianity in Matthew's Gospel also became a religion of the book—the teachings of Jesus the New Law.

After the destruction of the Temple, the Sadducees were no longer the ruling party in Judaism. Their party was either destroyed or marginalized. Judaism from this point on was not led by priests but by rabbis, the Pharisaic teachers of the law. The place of Judaism would now be the synagogue. Before this transformation, early Christianity was merely a sect within Judaism. Christians, especially in Jewish communities such as Matthew's, would have attended the local synagogue and been accepted there. After the fall of Jerusalem and the move of Judaism to the synagogue with its focus on the law, however, there was also a move toward greater unity and orthodoxy. After about 80 C.E. Christian Jews were considered part of a heretical sect of Judaism and not welcomed in the synagogues. In his gospel Matthew blamed the Pharisees for his community's

exclusion from the synagogue. Matthew's anti-Pharisee theme, which describes an intense conflict between Jesus and the Pharisees, reflects this post-70 situation.

The imminent Second Coming of Jesus is a primary theme in Mark's Gospel and was a feature of early Christianity (see Paul's letters). Matthew wrote his gospel about fifty years after the death of Jesus and fifteen years after the fall of Jerusalem. The Second Coming (*"parousia"* in Greek) no longer seemed imminent. This **delay of the parousia** had a major effect on Matthew's Gospel as well as on the other New Testament writings from this period. Matthew added to his gospel several parables whose main point was that the Second Coming was delayed (see the parables of the Faithful and Unfaithful Servants [Matt 24:45–51] and the Ten Virgins [Matt 25:1–13]). Matthew also presented the church's relationship to Christ in a different way. In Mark's Gospel followers of Jesus were to wait in hope for the parousia when they would share in the kingdom with Christ. The Christian life in the meantime was to be one of perseverance and patient hope. With the delay of the parousia, Matthew's community realized that their experience of Christ was not confined to hope in his future coming. For Matthew's community, Christ was present as Lord in the life of the community—in the Eucharist, in prophecies, in authoritative decisions, and in their shared life. Matthew is the only gospel to have Jesus tell his disciples, "For where two or three are gathered in my name, I am there among them" (Matt 18:20). Related to this is the greater emphasis Matthew placed on a correct life in the church. For Mark, Christians were to take up their cross and follow in the footsteps of Jesus. They were to persevere until Christ came again. Any who responded to this difficult and dangerous calling belonged to Christ. By the time of Matthew, times had changed, and the Christian calling was not quite as difficult and dangerous as it was for Mark's community. Matthew placed a much greater emphasis on those in the community who did not belong there or who did not live up to the requirements of the Christian calling. The parables of the Ten Virgins (25:1–13), the Faithful and Unfaithful Servants (24:45–51), the Talents (25:14–30), the Man without a Wedding

Garment (22:11—14) and the Judgment of the Nations (25:31–46) are all parables about persons who claim to be followers of Jesus but who do not make the cut, who are excluded from the kingdom at the final judgment. Perhaps the best statement of this theme of **mixed church** is found in the Sermon on the Mount, "Not everyone who says to me, 'Lord, Lord,' will enter the kingdom of heaven, but only the one who does the will of my Father in heaven" (7:21). This theme reflects a different community situation than the one behind the Gospel of Mark.

Finally, Matthew's Gospel also reflects an important change in the ethnic composition of the community. Originally a very conservative Jewish community, the Matthean community seems to have recently experienced an **influx of Gentile members.** Matthew's Gospel reflects the need to justify this. The two places in which Matthew dealt with this issue are the Infancy Narrative (1:1—2:23) and the Great Commission (28:16—20). The Magi were Gentiles who came to worship the Christ. Their gifts of gold, frankincense, and myrrh allude to Isaiah 60:6, which describes the Gentiles coming with gifts to worship the God of Israel in Jerusalem. In the Great Commission speech when the risen Jesus appears to the disciples, Jesus commands his disciples to go and "make disciples of all nations" (28:19). For Matthew, the ministry of the earthly Jesus was only to the house of Israel (Jews), but the ministry of the disciples of the risen Lord is to include all the nations (Gentiles) as was prophesied in Isaiah.

Reasons for Matthew's Gospel	
Event	**Theme**
Destruction of Temple	Jesus as New Law
Exclusion from Synagogue	Anti-Pharisee Theme
Delay of Parousia	Delay Parables
	Lord present in Church
	Mixed Church
Influx of Gentiles	Postresurrection ministry to Gentiles

World of the Text

Structure of Matthew's Gospel

Matthew has given his gospel a distinct structure by collecting the teachings of Jesus into five major discourses that are marked off with a statement at the beginning indicating that Jesus began to teach and a statement at the end noting that Jesus finished his teaching. Between the discourses, there are narrative sections. Some commentators think that the narratives preceding the discourse are to be coupled with the discourse, whereas others think that the narratives that follow the discourse are meant to be paired with the discourse. When the narrative section is thought to precede the discourse, the Infancy Narrative and the Passion Narrative are usually considered an introduction and a conclusion. This does not do justice to the centrality of either narrative. For that reason, it is best to have narrative sections that both precede and follow the discourses and not form pairs of discourse and narrative. The structure of Matthew's Gospel can be outlined as follows:

Infancy Narrative and John the Baptist (1:1—3:12)
　　Narrative Section (3:13—4:25)
First Discourse: Sermon on the Mount (5:3—7:27)
　　Narrative Section (8:1—9:38)
Second Discourse: Missionary Discourse (10:5—42)
　　Narrative Section (11:2—12:50)
Third Discourse: Parable Discourse (13:3—52)
　　Narrative Section (13:54—17:27)
Fourth Discourse: Community Discourse (18:1—35)
　　Narrative Section (19:1—23:39)
Fifth Discourse: End Time Discourse　　(24:1—25:46)
　　Narrative Section (26:1—28:15)
Great Commission (28:16—20)

This five-discourse structure is meant to imitate the five books of the Law. Matthew is presenting Jesus as a new lawgiver in the type of Moses, but greater than Moses.

Themes in Matthew

An aspect of Matthew's presentation of Jesus as the New Law is his use of *Moses typology*. In addition to modeling the gospel structure after the five books of the Law, Matthew characterizes Jesus as like Moses. Jesus' infancy recalls the infancy of Moses. Jesus gives his great discourse on the law on top of a mountain like Moses who gets the Law on Mount Sinai—but Jesus is greater than Moses. Moses received the law only from God, whereas Jesus claims the authority to promulgate the law himself.

No other gospel concerns itself with the **works of the law** to the extent that Matthew does. Matthew not only pictures Jesus as the Law and as the one who teaches the correct interpretation of the law; he also makes the law a central part of the Christian life. In Matthew 5:17 Jesus says that he did not come to abolish the law or the prophets but to fulfill them. He continues by saying that "whoever breaks one of the least of these commandments, and teaches others to do the same, will be called least in the kingdom of heaven" (5:19). In chapter 7, Jesus notes that one is known by one's fruits (actions) and that it is not the person who confesses him as Lord who will be saved but the one who does God's will. Finally, in a passage on the Conditions of Discipleship that Matthew takes from Mark, Matthew adds that when the Son of man comes with his angels "he will repay everyone for what has been done" (16:27). For Matthew it is not faith alone that matters in the kingdom of God, but also works. The best example of this is the parable of the Judgment of the Nations (25:31–46). In that parable, the criteria for being admitted to the kingdom of heaven are the corporal works of mercy (feeding the hungry, clothing the naked, visiting the imprisoned, and so forth).

One of the main areas in which Matthew has changed and expanded the Gospel of Mark is in his treatment of Christology (who Jesus is). The Gospel of Matthew has a more developed treatment of Jesus that points to his divinity. This is often referred to as a **higher Christology.** First, there are a number of places in Mark where Jesus is pictured as feeling pity or anger or being indignant. Matthew for the most part deletes the emotions of Jesus and has Jesus act with assurance and confidence. Second, in

Mark's Gospel Jesus is unable to work any mighty deeds in Nazareth (6:1–6) and must make two attempts to correct the blindness of the man of Bethsaida (8:22–26). In Matthew's Gospel, Jesus simply refuses to work mighty deeds in Nazareth because of their lack of faith (13:54–58), and Matthew deletes Mark's story of the blind man. Third, Matthew portrays Jesus as much more knowledgeable about the future and more in charge of what is happening. Jesus tells John the Baptist that he should baptize him, although John the Baptist thinks it would be improper. Jesus knows what Judas is going to do and even tells him to go ahead and do it. Fourth, Matthew adds an Infancy Narrative and resurrection appearances, all of which reveal Jesus' exalted role in God's plan of salvation.

Redaction criticism enables us to get a clear picture of the themes that Matthew wants to emphasize. When Matthew takes the time to change or add to a story from Mark, we know that the change represents an important theme.

World in front of the Text

Anti-Semitism and Matthew's Gospel

Many sections of Matthew's Gospel have been read as anti-Jewish. Chapter 23 contains a whole series of scathing condemnations of the Pharisees and other Jewish leaders. In the parable of the Tenants Jesus tells the chief priests and the Pharisees that "the kingdom of God will be taken away from you and given to a people that produces the fruits of the kingdom" (21:43). Finally, at the trial before Pilate, Matthew has the "people as a whole" reply to Pilate, "His blood be on us and on our children!" (27:25). Matthew believes that the destruction of Jerusalem and the Temple by the Romans in 70 C.E. was a punishment for the execution of Jesus (see 23:37—24:2). This language in Matthew was used by later Christians to blame all Jews for the death of Jesus and to inflict their own punishment on the Jews for that supposed crime. This has been one of the darkest chapters of Christian history. It must be remembered that Matthew and his community were ethnically Jewish and still considered themselves to be Jews by religion. Matthew and his community believed that Jesus was the fulfillment of Judaism. They did not believe that Jesus had founded a new religion to supplant Judaism. The Messiah Jesus movement (Christianity) was simply a reform movement within Judaism. As with any reform movement, the Messiah Jesus movement met with stiff opposition from many within the parent group (especially the leaders). The animosity between Jesus and the Pharisees in Matthew's Gospel reflects the animosity between Matthew and the Jewish leaders of the synagogue in his home city (probably Antioch). The inner-Jewish conflict in Antioch is no justification for considering Jews the murderers of Jesus. In fact, Matthew reminds us how indebted we are to Jews for our faith. We need to recognize how much we share and how much Jews and Christians can learn from each other. Our faith in Jesus does not make us enemies of the Jews, but their brothers and sisters.

> Reading the Gospel of Matthew in its original historical context is essential if Christians are ever to throw off the centuries-old disease of anti-Semitism.

MATTHEW 2:13–23

World behind the Text

Joseph the Dreamer

To read this text fruitfully, the reader must know something about its allusions to the Old Testament, which is a major source for Matthew's story. The husband of Mary, Jesus' mother, is named Joseph. In chapter 1, when Joseph finds out that Mary is pregnant, he is ready to divorce her quietly. An angel appears to him in a dream and tells him that the conception is by the power of the Holy Spirit. (Note that in Matthew's version the angel appears to Joseph, whereas in Luke's version [Luke 1:26–38] the angel appears to Mary.) Then in chapter 2 Joseph is warned in a dream about Herod's intention to kill Jesus and is told to take his family to Egypt. This Joseph is meant to remind the reader of another Joseph, the Joseph of Genesis 37–45 who becomes vizier of Egypt. Both Josephs have fathers named Jacob, both have a penchant for dreams, and both bring their families to Egypt. Matthew makes the connection to the Joseph story in Genesis even more explicit by the quotation from Hosea. It was through the Joseph of Genesis that the Hebrews came to dwell in Egypt and were later delivered from slavery by God. Hosea referred to the rescue of the Hebrews from slavery as God calling his son Israel out of Egypt. Matthew wants us to understand that Jesus represents the whole nation of Israel. His father is Joseph son of Jacob who will take the new Israel into Egypt for God to deliver them and bring them to the Promised Land in a recapitulation of the Exodus that fulfills the words of Hosea, "Out of Egypt I have called my son." A final connection to the Old Testament Joseph is found in another fulfillment quotation used by Matthew. Herod's massacre of all the infant boys in Bethlehem fulfills the words of Jeremiah the prophet who spoke of Rachel weeping for her children. (In Jeremiah this weeping is for the northern kingdom of Israel, which was destroyed by the Assyrians.) Rachel was the favorite wife of Jacob, and her eldest son was Joseph. Joseph's two sons, Ephraim and Manasseh, formed the core of the northern kingdom.

Moses the Law Giver

The other great Old Testament figure with a connection to Egypt is Moses. It is through Moses that God calls Israel out of Egypt. This section of Matthew's story contains direct allusions to Moses. Before Moses was born, the Hebrews had multiplied greatly in slavery in Egypt and the Pharaoh had ordered that all the male babies be killed (Exod 1:16). Moses, however, was saved from this fate. Herod, like Pharaoh, orders the murder of all the baby boys; and Jesus, like Moses, escapes from this massacre. In Matthew, after Herod dies, Joseph has another dream in which he is told to take his family back to the land of Israel. The angel informs Joseph that "those who were seeking the child's life are dead" (Matt 2:20). In Exodus, when Moses is a young man, he kills an Egyptian overseer who is abusing some Hebrew slaves and is forced to flee the country. Later, the Lord tells Moses to go back to Egypt, "for all those who were seeking your life are dead" (Exod 4:19). There can be no doubt that Matthew intended his readers to see the connection between the life of Jesus and the life of Moses. Several extrabiblical Jewish writings expand on the life of Moses in ways that are similar to Matthew's story of Jesus. It is likely that Matthew not only drew on the Book of Exodus for comparing Jesus to Moses, but also used these Jewish writings and traditions. Beyond our passage, Matthew makes even more connections between Jesus and Moses. We have already pointed out that the five discourses of Jesus in the gospel's structure match the five books of the Law of Moses. In the first discourse, the Sermon on the Mount, Jesus goes up on a mountain and teaches a law that surpasses the Law of Moses. In chapter 5 Jesus cites the Law of Moses ("you have heard that it was said") and then gives his version of the law that contradicts or surpasses the Law of Moses ("but I say to you"). Matthew wants us to see that Jesus is like Moses, but also greater than Moses.

The gospel writers' use of the Old Testament (intertextuality) and especially their use of Old Testament heroes (typology) constituted an important element in their portrayal of Jesus as the new hero in God's plan of salvation. God's Old Testament interventions (Exodus, Exile, return from Exile) were the paradigms for God's intervention in Jesus.

Herod the Great

The antagonist in this part of Matthew's story is Herod the king of Judea, often called Herod the Great to distinguish him from his sons who were also called Herod. At the beginning of chapter 2 he tries to convince the Magi (the wise men from the east who follow a star to come worship the newborn king) to come back after their visit to the new king and tell him where Jesus is. When the Magi, led by a dream, do not return to Herod with information about the location of Jesus, Herod must resort to the mass murder that is recounted in our passage. A reader may wonder whether this account is historical. We know a good deal about Herod from Josephus, the Jewish general-turned-historian. He was no fan of Herod and details Herod's cruelty, greed, deceptions, and murders. If Herod had killed all the young boys of Bethlehem, Josephus would, almost certainly, have put it in his book as another example of Herod's evil character. However, we do know for certain that there were any number of persons, many from Herod's own family, put to death because they were a threat to Herod's absolute power. Any contender for the throne, even in the distant future, was eliminated. So from this point of view, the account has historical verisimilitude, although in the exact form that we have it, this story is probably more the creation of Matthew than it is an account of an historical event.

In order not to judge Matthew as dishonest and deceptive, it is necessary to understand that Matthew is not writing history, as we would define it. He is writing hagiography, telling the life story of a holy figure to edify his audience. Matthew may have had several motives for writing this story in this way. He wants to portray Jesus as like Moses. Just as Moses was saved from a cruel ruler's mass murder of Jewish boys, so was Jesus. Beyond this, Matthew may have wished to foreshadow the coming persecution of Jesus. Already in his infancy Jesus' role as suffering, persecuted Messiah is clear. Finally, Matthew wishes to connect Jesus to the suffering, persecution, and murder of the people Israel in all of history (during the time of Moses, during the time when Assyria destroyed the northern kingdom, during the time when Babylonia destroyed the southern kingdom and sent the people into exile, during the persecutions of Antiochus IV, during the destruction of Jerusalem by the Romans, as well as during the reign of Herod the Great). Herod represents all the totalitarian rulers who have persecuted the people of Israel throughout their history. Jesus, as the hope and salvation of Israel, is delivered from this persecution to deliver Israel from it. The mother of the people (Rachel) weeps for all her dead children. Jesus will be the one who brings consolation.

> Historical documents from the time of the gospels can help us assess the historicity of the gospel stories.

Called a Nazorean

At the very end of this passage Matthew tells how Joseph and his family moved to Galilee and dwelt in Nazareth. (In Luke's Gospel, Joseph and his family are from Nazareth, but in Matthew's Gospel they are from Bethlehem and move to Nazareth only out of fear of Herod's son.) Matthew tells us that this was to fulfill what was spoken through the prophets. Then he cites a text that reads, "He will be called a Nazorean." This is one instance in Matthew when he cites a text that modern scholars have no idea what text he is referring to. There is no text in any of the prophets that mentions a Nazorean. However, the introduction to this fulfillment quotation is different from Matthew's usual introduction to a direct quotation from one prophet. It may be that Matthew was letting the reader know that this was an indirect quotation and that it did not refer to just one text but to many. Scholars suggest that Matthew may have been playing with the sounds of words. There are two important words in the Old Testament that could be taken as a play on the word *Nazorean.* The Old Testament tells of a group of religious persons, known as Nazirites, who dedicated their lives to God in a special way. They were restricted from cutting their hair, drinking any alcohol, or coming into contact with a corpse (Num 6:2–8). Another possible association is to the word *neser,* which in Hebrew means "shoot." In the Old Testament it is the word used to denote the new heir of the royal dynasty (that is, the Messiah). Isaiah 11:1 speaks of the shoot that will sprout from the stump of Jesse (the royal house of David). It is possible that Matthew used the word *Nazorean* (in Greek) to refer to Jesus as an inhabitant of the village of Nazareth, but also wanted his readers to hear the sounds of Hebrew words that portray him as a holy man dedicated to God in a special way (a Nazirite) and as the messianic offspring of David (*neser* = shoot). Matthew asks us to make these connections by telling us that Jesus' being a Nazorean was foretold in the prophets.

World of the Text

Structure

The passage that we are studying is made up of three scenes. They form a unity because the first and last scenes are related. In the first scene, Joseph takes his family to Egypt to escape Herod the Great, and in the last scene, Joseph is able to return his family to the land of Israel because Herod has died. In the middle of these two journey scenes is the story of the massacre of the baby boys of Bethlehem. In the first and last scenes, there is a fulfillment citation about Jesus. In scene one the citation is from Hosea and calls Jesus the Son of God. In the last scene, the fulfillment citation identifies Jesus as a Nazorean. The fulfillment citation in the middle scene refers to the baby boys who are massacred.

Midrash

A form of Jewish writing at this time is called *midrash*, which begins with a text from the scriptures and develops it in creative ways to answer questions and give meaning to the text for the contemporary reader. Many scholars believe that Matthew's and Luke's Infancy Narratives are midrash. They take stories from the Old Testament and develop them in new ways to make them relevant for their Christian readers. This story of Jesus' flight to Egypt and his return is often considered a midrash on the story of Moses. The problem with such an analysis is that true midrash uses the scriptural text as its starting point. Midrash is an attempt to find the meaning in the scriptural text. In the case of this story, the motivation for Matthew is not to find the meaning of the story of Moses' birth, flight from Egypt, and return. Matthew's concern is to tell the story of Jesus in such a way that his readers will understand the great significance of Jesus' birth and calling. This is not an interpretation of the story of Moses, but a typological use of the Moses story to interpret the story of Jesus. Therefore, it is probably more accurate to say that this story is midrashic but not actually a midrash.

The New Israel

Matthew does not stick to one Old Testament story but actually creates an intertextual collage of images and texts from the Old Testament. He thus creates a midrashic account of the entire history of the people Israel in Jesus. The allusions to the story of Moses point to the life of Jesus as a new Exodus. The weeping of Rachel refers to the time of Exile. These are the two determinative events in the history of God's people. In the next chapter, Matthew will describe the work of John the Baptist in the words of Second Isaiah. John is "the voice of one crying out in the wilderness: 'Prepare the way of the Lord, make his paths straight'" (Matt 3:3 from Isa 40:3). In that citation, the coming of Jesus is seen as a return from Exile. His teaching is the giving of a new law from Sinai. Jesus' life is a recapitulation of the history of Israel. However, the exile and return of Jesus, while ultimately bringing about the salvation of God's people, have at their heart a terrible and violent death. The weeping of Rachel for the northern tribes, for the baby boys of Bethlehem, and ultimately for Jesus himself, is real and painful. Matthew never lets his readers forget that the salvation of God's people comes through the terrible death of the one who is God's Son.

World in front of the Text

The Rulers of the World

Two thousand years of reading and interpreting Matthew's and Luke's Infancy Narratives (especially in liturgies) have resulted in their being combined to form one Christmas story. Although there can be value in this for popular piety, the amalgamation of the two stories into one has meant that most Christians do not appreciate the distinct messages of Matthew and Luke about the birth of Jesus. Each story contains its own rich theological message, which gets lost when the two stories are combined, with the Magi sharing a stable with shepherds and the star that led the Magi sharing the heavens with the angels who announce the good news to the shepherds.

219

When viewed on its own, Matthew's story in chapter 2 focuses our attention on Herod. Matthew's story of the birth of Jesus asks the reader to reflect on the power and tactics of the rulers of this world (be they Herod, Pharaoh, Caesar, Nebuchadnezzar, and Antiochus IV or Stalin and Hitler). The enemies of God's plan for history and for God's people are the rulers of this world. The power of God is found in an infant who flees to a foreign country; the voice of God is heard in a mother's weeping for the children killed by armies of the empire. The scion of the royal dynasty in God's plan is a peasant boy who lives in a small, out of the way village in a backwater of the empire. The contrast between Herod (and all rulers of this world) and Jesus (and all those who follow the crucified Messiah) could not be greater.

MATTHEW 9:18–26

World behind the Text

The Gospel of Mark

The story of the Official's Daughter and the Woman with a Hemorrhage is also found in the Gospel of Mark, and, according to the synoptic two-source hypothesis, this means that Matthew has edited Mark's version of the story to create his own. It is therefore imperative that we understand the Gospel of Mark and its version of the story.

Traditionally, the Gospel of Mark has been attributed to John Mark, the cousin of Barnabas who accompanied Barnabas and Paul on a missionary journey (Acts 12:25; 13:3; 15:36–39), but scholars are not convinced of that identification. In short, the author of this gospel is unknown. However, we are fairly certain that the gospel was written to a mainly Gentile audience and may have been written for the community in Rome. Mark is not familiar with the geography of Palestine; he presumes some customs that are principally associated with Rome; and he has a theme of persecution, which fits with the persecution of Christians by Nero in Rome at about 64–65 C.E.

The Gospel of Mark is characterized by two important themes. The theme of the **Messianic secret** includes Jesus' commands to demons to be quiet about his identity (1:25), his commands to those healed not to tell anyone (1:44), and his commands to the disciples not to tell anyone about the revelation of who he is (8:30). It can also include his words about the "secret of the kingdom of God" (4:11), his speaking in parables (4:11, 33–34), and the misunderstanding of his deeds and his person by the disciples themselves (8:17–18). This secret of who Jesus is builds throughout the gospel. Eventually it becomes clear to the reader that the truth of Jesus' identity can be understood only after his death and resurrection. The second theme of Mark is known as the **failure of the disciples.** Jesus makes a concerted effort to gather a group of specially chosen disciples (the twelve apostles) to accompany him (3:13–19). He instructs them and takes them with him apart from the crowd. As the gospel progresses, however, so does the lack of understanding of these disciples. When examined closely, Mark's portrayal of the disciples is amazingly harsh. The disciples of Jesus in Mark's Gospel grow increasingly resistant to what Jesus is trying to teach them, until at his arrest and trial they all flee and desert him (14:50, 66–72)— in spite of the fact that Jesus gives them so much special attention. The women who remain for the crucifixion flee from the tomb and seem to fail in what they have been told to do by the young man at the tomb (16:8). The apparent cause of all this failure is the disciples' inability to understand the importance of Jesus' death. Jesus constantly confronts the disciples' desire for power, glory, and victory with lowliness, suffering, and death. Taking the two themes together, Mark's Gospel makes a clear statement: To be a disciple of Jesus one must be willing to be lowly, suffer, and die just as Jesus, the Son of God, did. The only way to recognize Jesus as the Messiah, Son of God, and returning glorious Son of man, is by the path of lowliness, suffering, and death.

Besides these major themes, a reader should be aware of another literary characteristic of Mark. Mark frequently places one story within the context of another story, a technique called "sandwiching" (or "intercalation"). Mark will also arrange material in concentric parallelism, having the first element be parallel to the last element, the second element parallel to the second-to-the-last element, and so on.

Purity Rules

One of the most distinctive features of Judaism at the time of Jesus was its concern with purity laws. These laws developed especially during and after the Exile. The understanding was that as God's holy people, the Jews needed to set themselves apart from the ordinary world, from the pagan world, and from the world of death, disease, and uncleanness. For this reason, there were strict laws about marriage, about skin diseases, and about washing food and utensils. There were laws about menstruation that required women to be sequestered for seven days during their period and laws that forbade contact with corpses. When a relative was required to touch a corpse in preparing it for burial, that person was unclean and was to avoid contact with others for a time. Purity rules were important for keeping intact the boundaries between the sacred and the profane, the Jew and the Gentile, men and women, the righteous and the sinner. In this story, Jesus breaks two very important purity rules. The woman's hemorrhage was probably a "female" condition and, like menstruation, would have made her unclean. Jesus would have been made unclean by her touch. Although it is the woman who actually breaks the law, she does it because of Jesus, and Jesus commends her for it. The second purity rule that Jesus breaks is the rule about corpses. Jesus does not hesitate to take the hand of the dead girl and raise her to life.

Healing in the New Testament

It is natural for a modern reader of the gospels to try to diagnose the medical conditions of the persons involved and consider how they were cured of their diseases. Anthropologists have taught us to distinguish between disease and illness when examining stories from different cultures. Disease is a medical condition identified by modern science. It is understood as a malfunction of an organism in the body and can be treated biomedically. An illness is a social condition in which one's place in society has been disrupted. The causes for an illness are also social, such as sin or demons. Healing an illness involves reintegration into society. By touching the woman with the hemorrhage and by calling her "daughter" Jesus reintegrates the woman back into her place in society.

> Social science criticism can help us understand the cultural context in which to interpret the words and deeds of Jesus. We cannot appreciate the significance of what Jesus did unless we know about the purity rules in Judaism at that time and about the first century's understanding of illness and healing.

Redaction Criticism

If you simply do a cursory comparison of Matthew 9 and Mark 5 you will notice that Matthew's version is only half as long as Mark's. It is very typical of Matthew to shorten a miracle story in Mark by deleting extraneous or embarrassing details to focus more on Jesus. (You may also know that Matthew's Gospel is nearly twice as long as Mark in spite of his tendency to condense the stories of Mark. This is the result of the large amount of material from "Q" and "M" that Matthew adds.)

There are numerous changes that Matthew makes to Mark's version of the story, but for this redaction criticism we will focus only on the changes that are motivated by Matthew's theology. In Mark's version of the story, the man asks Jesus to heal his daughter who is near death. As Jesus goes off with the man, he encounters the woman with a hemorrhage. After curing this woman, messengers arrive to tell the man that the daughter has died and there is no need to trouble Jesus any further, but Jesus challenges the man to have faith and then continues on the journey to the man's house. In Matthew's version of the story, the man tells Jesus right from the outset that his daughter has died. Jesus goes with the man to touch the daughter and raise her to life from the very beginning. This is an example of Matthew seeking to simplify the story of Mark. The changes Matthew has made reveal a higher Christology. From the very beginning the synagogue official has faith that Jesus has power over death. Jesus is shown as one confident in such power.

Mark's version of the story emphasizes the press of the crowd (5:24) and the woman touching Jesus surreptitiously. In Mark's Gospel the woman is healed as soon as she touches Jesus and Jesus feels power go out from him but does not know who has touched him. Mark spends three verses (30–33) describing the situation of Jesus trying to find out who it is who touched him. In Matthew's Gospel this is all deleted. Matthew describes how the woman touches Jesus and Jesus turns around and speaks to her. After he speaks to her, telling her that her faith has saved her, she is then cured. Matthew's redactional tendency is to simplify a miracle story so as to focus on the personal interaction between Jesus and the one being healed. He will delete superfluous details about the illness and any description of the process of healing that might seem magical. In this section of Mark's story the woman is healed without Jesus even knowing who it is. In Mark's story it could seem as if touching Jesus was some kind of magic cure, although Matthew changes the story to make it very clear that the healing is an encounter between the woman who has faith and Jesus who has the power of God. Only when these two elements meet is there a cure.

In Mark's story the disciples have a role. When Jesus asks who has touched him, they respond, "You see the crowd pressing in on you; how can you say, 'Who touched me?'" (5:31). As we noted earlier, Mark's Gospel stresses the "failure of the disciples." The disciples' response to Jesus here seems peevish and uncomprehending of his power or mission. Matthew will frequently delete or tone down this theme of "failure of the disciples." Here Matthew removes the disciples from this part of the story. He is not interested in making a point about their failure to understand Jesus. His only point is about the power of Jesus as it meets the need of a believer.

In the third part of Mark's story, the messengers arrive with the news that the daughter has died; Jesus then goes into the house with his disciples. Jesus takes the girl by the hand and says (in Aramaic), *"Talitha cum,"* which Mark translates as "Little girl, get up!" (5:41). In Matthew's version of the story, Jesus simply takes the girl by the hand and she rises. Again, Matthew was probably uncomfortable with the words of Jesus that might have sounded a bit like magic. For Matthew it is not any specific word of Jesus that brings the healing but Jesus' presence and power. Mark continues the story by having Jesus give strict orders that no one should know about the healing. This is a good example of the Markan theme of "Messianic secret." Matthew will often delete or tone down this theme also. In this case Matthew deletes it altogether. For Matthew Jesus is to be recognized during his lifetime as Son of God with power. The overall effect of the changes Matthew has made is to show Jesus as one possessing great powers of life and healing. He leads his disciples and those who have faith in him with assurance and knowledge. The focus of Jesus' miracles is on his power and the faith of those in need.

World of the Text

Miracle Stories

The miracle story is one of a number of specific genres of stories in the gospels, and it can be defined by its elements. A miracle story begins with a description of the situation of the person who is in need of healing. In this case the woman was "suffering from hemorrhages for twelve years" (9:20). Second, there is a request for healing on the part of the person. The case of the woman is something of an anomaly because she merely says to herself, "If I only touch his cloak, I will be made well" (9:21). In the story of the synagogue official's daughter, the man kneels down before Jesus and says, "My daughter has just died; but come and lay your hand on her, and she will live" (9:18). Third, there is a description of a word and/or deed that Jesus does to perform the cure. With the woman, Jesus says, "Take heart, daughter; your faith has made you well" (9:22). In the story of the official's daughter, Jesus takes the girl by the hand. Fourth, there is a statement that the person is healed. Often the narrator emphasizes the miraculous nature of the healing by noting that it happened immediately. In the case of the woman, the narrator tells us that "instantly the woman was made well" (9:22). In the case of the official's daughter, we are told that "the girl got up" (9:25). Finally, there is usually a statement of the effect of the cure on the crowd. In the case of the woman, because the story is in the middle of another miracle story, this element is not included. In the story of the official's daughter, the narrator notes that "the report of this spread throughout that district" (9:26).

Miracle Story Form

1. Description of ailment

2. Request for healing

3. Words and/or action of healing

4. Description that healing has occurred (often immediately)

5. Reaction of the crowd

The Unity of the Narrative

As we noted earlier, this narrative is made up of two stories, one sandwiched in the middle of the other. The technical term for this "sandwiching" is *intercalation*. It is one of Mark's favorite narrative techniques. Matthew keeps this structure in his version of these two stories. In other stories, such as the stories of the withering of the fig tree and the cleansing of the Temple, Matthew rearranges the structure to allow one story to follow the other. In the text we are considering here, the story of the woman with the hemorrhage who touches Jesus is placed in the middle of the story of Jesus raising the official's daughter from the dead. In Mark's version of these stories there are more connections made between the two stories. Mark has both characters fall on their knees. Mark uses the word *faith* for both the man and the woman. Mark also makes a connection between the twelve years that the woman suffers hemorrhages and the twelve years that the daughter of Jairus has lived, although Matthew does not make these connections between the characters. Instead for Matthew it is the character of Jesus and his power to heal and give life that provide the unity to the two stories become one.

Literary Context of the Story

An important change that Matthew has made to this text is his placement of it in the gospel. Notice the order of stories in Mark and Matthew.

Mark	Matthew
Calming of Storm at Sea	(Calming of Storm at Sea)
Gerasene Demoniac	(Gadarene Demoniacs)
	(Cure of Paralytic)
	(Call of Matthew)
	(Question of Fasting)
Jairus's Daughter and Woman	(Official's Daughter and Woman)
Rejection at Nazareth	
	(Cure of Two Blind Men)
	(Cure of Mute Person)
	(Compassion of Jesus)
Mission of Twelve	(Mission of Twelve)

The context of the story in Mark's Gospel gives it a particular slant. It immediately precedes the story of the Rejection at Nazareth. In Mark's story Jairus needs to be encouraged to believe, and the disciples chide Jesus for asking who touched him. The story fits into a context of Jesus confronting the obstacle of unbelief.

In Matthew's Gospel the story fits into an entirely different context. The stories that precede it are the Call of Matthew and the Question about Fasting, both of which point to a new age when the rules have changed. The story of the Synagogue Official is the first of three healing miracles that conclude with a summary of Jesus' words and deeds on behalf of those in need. The context in Matthew fits with his high Christology. Jesus is shown as one with power who uses that power for those in need who have faith. The attack of the Pharisees in Matthew 9:34, at the end of the healing of the mute person, only further emphasizes the real power that Jesus has from God and not from the prince of demons. Finally, these deeds of mercy and compassion lead Jesus to ask the disciples to pray for more laborers to minister to those in need (9:38). This is followed by the naming of the Twelve (10:1–4) to go and minister as Jesus does. The focus in this whole section is on the power of Jesus to bring healing and new life.

A close examination of the texts that precede and follow a story can help a reader understand the meaning of the story in the larger narrative of the gospel writer.

World in front of the Text

Overcoming a Culture of Death

One of the seemingly extraneous details of Mark's version of the story of Jairus's daughter—one that Matthew does not delete—is the encounter of Jesus with the mourners at the house of the synagogue official. Two verses (23–24) in Matthew are dedicated to these mourners, whom Jesus chastises and who in return ridicule Jesus. In Matthew's very short story there is a large segment devoted to the conflict between Jesus, as the power of life, and the mourners, as the purveyors of death. This is a fascinating scene in light of the words of Pope John Paul II about our contemporary world's "culture of death." It is not difficult to find the purveyors of death in American culture—abortion, capital punishment, wars, drugs, and so forth. The words of Jesus to the mourners could be our words to those who promote death in our time: "Go away! This person is not meant for death."

MATTHEW 18:10–14

World behind the Text

Q Source

The parable of the Lost Sheep is found in Matthew and in Luke (15:1–7) and comes from the Q source. Q is the hypothetical document that contains parables, the Sermon on the Mount (or Plain), and other sayings of Jesus. It was not a "gospel" in the narrative sense. It was not a "life of Jesus" but simply a collection of sayings of Jesus. Even though we do not have any copies of this document or even any references to it, we do have the recently discovered *Gospel of Thomas*, which is not a narrative gospel but more a collection of sayings of Jesus. The *Gospel of Thomas* is not Q, but it does point to the probability that there were other collections of sayings of Jesus that did not include the major narratives of Jesus' life such as the passion and crucifixion.

Because we do not have a copy of Q, it is much more difficult to do a redaction criticism of Matthew's version of the parable. We must first compare the versions of the parable in Luke and in Matthew and then make a decision as to what the original source contained. Only after reconstructing the Q source can we then compare Matthew's version to it. To make these decisions and reconstruct Q we must have a good idea of the redactional themes and tendencies of both Matthew and Luke.

The Gospel of Luke

The Gospel of Luke contains many unique characteristics. Perhaps the most important characteristic of Luke's Gospel is the fact that he divides salvation history into three ages: the time of Israel, the time of Jesus, and the time of the Church. Each age is characterized by the gift of the Holy Spirit. In the first two chapters of Luke, members of Israel (Zechariah, Elizabeth, John, Simeon, Anna) are given the Holy Spirit and proclaim God's work of salvation. At the baptism of Jesus in chapter 3, however, the Spirit descends on Jesus and then for the rest of Jesus' ministry, the Holy Spirit works in Jesus. After Jesus' death and resurrection, he promises that he will send the promise of his Father on them. Then in the Acts of the Apostles (also written by Luke) the Spirit descends on the disciples of Jesus (2:4). The rest of Acts chronicles the missionary work of the first disciples of Jesus as they are led by the Holy Spirit. The Spirit theology in Luke/Acts is very important.

Luke presents Jesus as a prophet and teacher. Following Jesus means going in the way that he leads. The Gospel of Luke describes the ministry of Jesus as a journey to Jerusalem, and Acts describes the ministry of Paul as a journey to Rome. Luke (in Acts) notes that the early Christians called their movement "the Way." On the way to Jerusalem, Jesus frequently teaches his disciples in the context of meals. Meals also figure prominently in many of his parables. A characteristic of Greco-Roman philosophy was the symposium, the discussion of philosophy and ethics in the context of a meal. Luke seems to be portraying Jesus as a great teacher of life. The meal theme also calls to mind the Jewish idea of the heavenly banquet.

Luke will often picture Jesus at prayer, and Jesus has numerous teachings on prayer in Luke's Gospel. The gospel begins with Zechariah in the Temple at prayer (1:8–9) and ends with the disciples in the Temple blessing God (24:53). This attitude of prayer in Luke's Gospel is related to the attitude of joy. For Luke what has happened in Jesus is good news of great joy (2:10). At the annunciation, Mary's spirit rejoices in God. The parables of the Lost Sheep, Lost Coin, and Lost Son all have a theme of rejoicing. Finally, the disciples return to Jerusalem after Jesus' ascension filled with great joy (24:52). Prayer, praise, and rejoicing mark the new age that has been inaugurated in Jesus.

Finally, Luke's Gospel has much more emphasis on the poor, the lowly, and outsiders than the other gospels. Luke's Beatitudes speak of the poor and not the poor in spirit (as in Matthew's version). Luke tells several parables about the poor, the parable of Lazarus and the Rich Man being the most notable. Luke also tells stories about Samaritans, women, sinners, and other marginal persons much more frequently than the other gospels.

Reconstructing Q

The first question confronting a reader who wishes to reconstruct Q is to whom is the parable addressed and why. In Matthew's version, the parable of the Lost Sheep is part of the Community Discourse (18:1–19) and is addressed to the disciples who are being taught a lesson about humility and service. In Luke's version the parable is addressed to the Pharisees and scribes who have complained to Jesus about his eating with tax collectors and sinners (observant Jews would not share a meal with these unclean persons). In Matthew the parable serves as a lesson on how disciples should act, whereas in Luke it is a defense of why Jesus acts as he does.

In v. 10 Matthew introduces the parable with the saying, "Take care that you [the disciples] do not despise one of these little ones."

The phrase "little ones" is unique to Matthew. Matthew seems to use it to refer to those new in Christian faith or vulnerable in their faith. The second saying Matthew uses to introduce the parable states that the angels of the little ones "see the face of my Father in heaven." This is a Jewish image and so seems more at home in Matthew than in Luke. Overall these two sayings, and especially the first, seem like Matthew's own editorial additions used to introduce the Q parable into the context of his gospel. Therefore, we can hypothesize that the original Q parable was directed to the scribes and Pharisees as a defense of why Jesus associated with sinners.

When we compare Matthew and Luke's versions of the opening of the parable itself we notice that both contain rhetorical questions directed to the audience. In Matthew, Jesus asks the audience to consider the actions of the man in the parable, "What do you think?" Jesus then tells the parable in the third person. "If a shepherd has a hundred sheep..." (18:12). In Luke's version the rhetorical question is part of the parable itself. The members of the audience are asked to consider how they would act if they were in this situation: "Which one of you, having a hundred sheep..." (15:4). Was the parable in Q in the third person or second person? Did Matthew make the change to suit his intentions or did Luke? In Matthew the parable is more of a teaching about leadership. Luke probably preserves the more original Q version of engaging the audience in the second person. The original Q version challenges the Pharisees to put themselves in Jesus' shoes.

The parable story itself is essentially the same in both versions. There is, however, one exception: in Matthew's version the finding of the lost sheep is conditional—"if he finds it"; in Luke the finding is only a matter of time—"when he has found it." Again we must ask, what was the original? The usual way to find an answer is to ask who would have had more of a reason to change Q if Q contained the other wording. If Matthew had read "when" in the Q original would he have been motivated to change it to "if" and why? Some commentators argue that Matthew's Gospel recognizes failure. The very next story describes a situation that ends with the possible failure of the community to reconcile a sinful brother. Thus Matthew could have been motivated to allow for the possibility of the disciples' failure to bring back the lost "little one" in the community. However, if Luke had read "if" in the original Q would he have been motivated to change it to "when"? Other commentators argue that Luke has a theme of God's mercy and the inevitable nature of God's love and forgiveness. The lost are found by Jesus in the gospel. Jesus does not fail! After considering both arguments, I would conclude that Matthew has a greater reason for making the change. Therefore, I assume that the original was "when" and Matthew changed it to "if" for the reasons stated above.

The conclusions of both parables are also quite different. Matthew notes that the shepherd rejoices more over the lost one who is found than over the ninety-nine others. Then Matthew concludes that in the same way it is not the will of the Father in heaven that a little one should be lost. Luke does not make the comparison about the amount of joy experienced by the shepherd but about the amount of joy experienced in heaven. However, he expands the description of the joy of the shepherd, describing him as laying the sheep on his shoulders, and gathering his friends and neighbors, and asking them to rejoice with him because he has found his lost sheep. Luke then notes that there is more joy in heaven over the sinner that repents that over the ninety-nine others who need no repentance. (Notice that Luke has left the world of the parable and gone into an interpretation.) Did Q contrast the joy for one lost with the joy for ninety-nine who were not lost in the reaction of the shepherd or in the reaction of heaven? Did Q describe the party to be held by the shepherd? Did Q speak of sinners and repentance?

It seems that v. 13 in Matthew probably more accurately represents the Q original than vv. 5 and 6 in Luke. There does not seem to be a good reason why Matthew would move the comparison from heaven to the shepherd. It does make perfect sense that Luke would expand the joy of the shepherd and his gathering his friends to rejoice with him (probably for a meal). The theme of meals shared in joy is frequent in Luke (chapter 14 of Luke is a whole discourse on sharing meals). Luke also emphasizes the theme of joy and rejoicing. The words *joy* and *rejoice*, from the root *chairein/chara*, occur nineteen times in Luke as compared to three times in Mark and twelve times in Matthew. Luke, in having Jesus use the story to defend this action, wants to place the worth of sinners who repent over those who do not need to repent as a value judgment made in heaven. Jesus is thus shown to his adversaries as in conformity with heaven. Q compares the joy of the shepherd over one lost sheep who is found to the joy of the shepherd over the ninety-nine who were not lost. Q does not mention the party or sinners and repentance.

Given what we have concluded about the original Q parable, what has Matthew done to make the parable his own? I would argue that the context and addressees of the parable in Matthew are quite different from its original context and addressees in Q. The Q saying was probably addressed to the Pharisees and explained why Jesus ministered among the sinners and the unclean. Matthew places the parable in his Community Discourse and transforms the parable into a lesson for the disciples about caring for all those in the Christian community.

The second important change Matthew has made is the change of the adverb "when" to "if." In the original context of Q, the lost are all those who are considered sinful and unclean. Jesus goes to them. There is not an issue of how hard it is to find them, but only an issue of the religious leaders' willingness to go out after them. Jesus will find those who are lost. When the context is changed in Matthew to the situation of those who have sinned or are contemplating leaving the community, the group under consideration is smaller and more specific. Some of those who are in the Christian community will be lost, will go astray, and will not be found. Matthew is concerned that everything be done to rehabilitate and retain these lapsing Christians, but he is also realistic in knowing that it will not be possible in every case. Thus, he uses the conditional clause: "if" the lost are found.

World of the Text

The Community Discourse

The meaning of this parable in Matthew's Gospel is significantly affected by its placement in the Community Discourse.

The discourse contains five stories focused on how the leaders of the community should protect the little ones.

> *The Greatest in the Kingdom*—"whoever welcomes one such child in my name"
> *Temptations to Sin*—"if any of you put a stumbling block before one of these little ones"
> *The Parable of the Lost Sheep*—"do not despise one of these little ones"
> *A Brother Who Sins*—"if the member listens to you, you have regained that one"
> *The Parable of the Unforgiving Servant*—"if another member of the church sins against me, how often should I forgive"

Notice all the family imagery in each of these stories or sayings. The Community Discourse in Matthew is concerned about making the family of the Christian community a place of safety, security, forgiveness, and support. It is the responsibility of the community to save and protect all its members. It is not its responsibility (like it was in the Qumran community) to punish and exclude members who do not live up to the standards.

Parables

There are numerous parables in the Synoptic Gospels from all of the sources—Mark, Q, M, and L. The parables of Jesus are related to Old Testament parables (like the story Nathan tells to David in 2 Sam 12:1–6) and to later parables told by the rabbis. Still the parables of Jesus have their own unique quality. There is no universal structure to the parables in the Synoptic Gospels like there is to the miracles stories. Essentially parables are metaphorical stories (often about the kingdom of God) about ordinary life that use exaggeration and plot twist to surprise the hearers/readers into seeing reality (again, often the kingdom of God) in a new way. The parables are often open-ended to force to hearers/readers to respond to this challenge to their way of thinking.

Structure of the Parable

There is a careful and neat structure to Matthew's version of the parable. This structure is much more evident in the Greek, especially in the center section. The parable begins with Jesus telling the disciples not to despise the little ones for their angels see the face of the Father in heaven (A). Jesus proposes the parable itself with the invitation to consider this situation. The parable is then composed of two conditional clauses. (In Greek both conditional clauses begin with *ean genetai*, which is literally translated as "if it happens.") First, "if it happens that a shepherd has a hundred sheep...does he not leave the ninety-nine" (B). Second, "if it happens that he finds it...then he rejoices over it more" (B'). Jesus concludes the parable by noting, "So it is not the will of your Father in heaven that one of these little ones should be lost" (A'). Notice the verbal connections between A and A.' The titles "little ones" and "Father in heaven" occur in both. B and B' are parallel because of the grammatical structure of the conditional clause used in each.

A Do not despise these **little ones** whose angels see the face of the **Father in heaven**
B If it happens that a shepherd has
B' If it happens that he finds it
A' It is not the will of the **Father in heaven** that one of these **little ones** be lost

World in front of the Text

Leadership in the Christian Community

This story in its context in Matthew has much to say to us today. The role of the leaders in Matthew's community is to protect those who are vulnerable, forgive those who fail, keep safe those at risk, and seek out those who are lost. Leadership in Matthew's community is in contrast to leadership in many other communities. Too often the role of leaders is to protect those in power, to reward those who succeed, keep safe those with a lot invested, and seek out new members who "fit" in with the group.

The power of the parable in Matthew comes at the conclusion. It is not the will of your heavenly Father that one of these be lost. God's will is human well-being. God's will is for all to have as many chances as possible to succeed, and to find a home in God's family.

John

INTRODUCTION

World behind the Text

The Author of John

The author of the Gospel of John is not identified in the text but only in later tradition. However, in contrast to the other gospels, the Gospel of John does speak of its author, although indirectly. In the crucifixion scene when the soldier lances Jesus' side, the narrator pauses the action to tell the reader, "He who saw this has testified so that you also may believe. His testimony is true, and he knows that he tells the truth" (John 19:35). At the conclusion of the epilogue, the narrator again speaks directly to the reader and says, "This is the disciple who is testifying to these things and has written them, and we know that his testimony is true" (John 21:24).

It is generally agreed now that the final version of the Gospel of John was not written by a disciple of Jesus who accompanied him during his life, but was written latter, perhaps even as late as 90 C.E. It is also agreed that the Gospel of John probably went through numerous versions before acquiring its final form. It is most likely that the earliest versions come from an original disciple of Jesus, a disciple who has the title "the Beloved Disciple" in his own community. (The Beloved Disciple is one of the disciples in the narrative.) Scholars are divided on the form of the tradition that goes back to the Beloved Disciple. It is possible that the version of the gospel from the Beloved Disciple was only in the form of homilies, although it is also possible that the Beloved Disciple wrote a version of the gospel. It is also a matter of debate whether the Beloved Disciple should be identified with John the son of Zebedee.

The Community of John

The Gospel of John, when read as a reflection of the community out of which it grew, gives us information about that community. The Johannine community was originally made up of Jewish Christians who remained part of the synagogue for a time. At some point in the history of the community, they were no longer welcome in the Jewish synagogue. We see this reflected in the way the gospel talks about "the Jews," "*their* synagogue," and about Jewish leaders. This attitude is not anti-Semitic, but reflects a Jewish community that is angry with another Jewish community for the way they have been treated. It reflects a dispute within the Jewish community.

For a long time, it was assumed that the Gospel of John was the spiritual gospel and so contained very little historical data. With recent archaeological discoveries and further study of Judaism and Palestine during that period, it is recognized that John contains accurate historical data not found in the Synoptic Gospels. With this recognition, it is now assumed that the Johannine community was originally from Palestine. Early in its history, the community opened itself to Hellenistic Jews and even to Samaritans. This led to the formation of the unique Johannine Christology—a Logos Christology—and to the separation of the community from the Jewish synagogue.

Sources and the Synoptic Gospels

The Gospel of John is different from the other gospels. It has its own literary style and theology. It contains a whole different set of stories and sayings of Jesus, and places the stories that it shares with the Synoptic Gospels in different parts of the narrative. For example, in John's Gospel the cleansing of the Temple occurs at the very beginning of the gospel, whereas in the Synoptic Gospels it occurs at the end immediately before Jesus' passion. There are seven miracles in John, which are presented not so much as miracles but as signs that point to a deeper theological meaning. There are no parables in John. There are also very few pithy sayings like those in the Synoptic Gospels. Instead, Jesus teaches in long discourses that are highly symbolic. The

Gospel of John does not depend on Mark or any of the other gospels. It does not seem to know Q, either its parables or its sayings. John was dependent primarily on traditions that were unique to his own community. However, in the passion narrative especially, there are a few places where John coincides with either Mark or Luke in a way that leads scholars to suggest that, for the passion narrative, they may have shared a common source. The Johannine community was isolated from and even looked down on the emerging great church that used the gospels of Mark, Matthew, and Luke and the letters of Paul. At some point early in the second century C.E., the Johannine community suffered internal conflict (as we see reflected in the first letter of John), and one part of the Johannine community joined itself to the great church and brought with it the gospel and letters of John.

World of the Text

The Structure of the Gospel

The Gospel of John is usually divided into two main parts: the Book of Signs (1:19—12:50) and the Book of Glory (13:1—20:31). The Book of Signs is made up of seven signs (John's miracles). The Book of Glory contains Jesus' Last Supper Discourse (chapters 14—17), his Passion, and the Resurrection appearance stories. Besides these two main parts, the gospel is introduced by the Prologue (1:1—18), the great hymn to the Logos (the Word of God who is Jesus Christ), and concludes with the Epilogue (21:1—25), a final Resurrection appearance story.

Themes and Style

The Gospel of John is unique in its themes and style. One of the favorite techniques used by John for telling a story is the technique of misunderstanding. In a **misunderstanding** story, Jesus does or says something, and the other character takes what he says literally and misunderstands its meaning. This gives Jesus the opportunity to teach about the deeper meaning of what he has said. In chapter 3 Jesus tells Nicodemus he must be born anew, and Nicodemus asks how a grown man can get back into his mother's womb. Jesus then teaches about rebirth in the Spirit. Jesus tells the Samaritan woman in chapter 4 that she should ask him for a drink of water. She says he does not have a bucket to draw the water. This leads to Jesus teaching her about the living water of the Holy Spirit. Examples like this can be found throughout the gospel. Connected to this technique is Jesus' use of symbolic language. The wine at Cana (chapter 2), the feeding with the bread (chapter 6), and the blindness of the Pharisees in contrast to the man born blind (chapter 9) are all symbolic of some deeper reality.

Another feature of John's Gospel is the **"I AM" sayings.** Jesus declares that he is "I AM," several times with no object (8:58; 13:19), and many more times with objects. The objects of the "I AM" are bread of life; living water; good shepherd; way, truth, and life; and the resurrection. It is possible that the "I AM" statements with an object are meant to make a different point than the "I AM" statements without an object, but most scholars see them both as giving Jesus the title of God, whose name is "I AM." This is an example of the high Christology in John's Gospel.

John's Gospel has the **highest Christology** of any of the gospels. By that, we mean that this gospel uses language that ascribes divinity to Jesus Christ in his very being (as opposed to just honorary titles). The first example of this is the title "Word of God" used of Jesus in the Prologue. God's Word is of the very essence of God. It is by God's Word that the world is created. To say that Jesus is the Word is to describe him in divine terms. The Prologue goes even further by saying that the Word was with God from the beginning and the Word was divine. The "I AM" sayings also imply Jesus' equality with God in a way that is not found in the other gospels. Finally, in several discourses Jesus describes his relationship with the Father in a way that is even more intimate than in the Synoptic Gospels. In answer to Philip's request that Jesus show them the Father, Jesus says, "Have I been with you all this time, Philip, and you still do not know me? Whoever has seen me has seen the Father. How can you say, 'Show us the Father'? Do you not believe that I am in the Father and the Father is in me?" (14:9–10). In 10:30 Jesus states clearly, "The Father and I are one." In no other gospel does Jesus speak so constantly of himself as "the Son" and so intimately of his relationship to the

Father. Everything the Father says and does has been given to the Son to do and say. Although he says that the Father and he are one, we should not interpret this to mean that there is no distinction or that it is the Father who has become flesh. In Johannine Christology, the Son is subservient to the Father, receives everything from him, and does only what the Father commands.

A part of John's high Christology is his belief in the **preexistence** of Christ. The prologue presents the Word with God before creation. At a particular point in time, the Word becomes flesh in the person of Jesus. *Preexistence* means that the Word/Son of God existed before the birth of Jesus. John describes the mission of the Word as a journey from the Father to the world in human flesh. It is in human flesh that the Word reveals the heavenly Father to humans. At his death/resurrection, the Word returns to the Father in heaven. By way of contrast, the journey of Christ in Mark's Gospel would be the inverse. Jesus, at his death/resurrection, is taken up to sit at the right hand of the Father in heaven. In the near future, he will return to the earth as the glorious Messiah to bring about the fullness of God's kingdom.

John describes the relationship of Jesus Christ to the Father as union. The Son is in the Father and the Father is in the Son. The Son remains in the Father and knows the Father. John is describing a mystical union between the Father and the Son. This same **mystical union** is the goal of discipleship. The disciple of Jesus is to become one with the Son and so also with the Father. The disciple is to remain in the Son as a branch remains connected to the vine. The Spirit is the means for this mystical union. The disciple's union with the Son means that all disciples are joined in union with each other.

In Mark and Paul, especially, there is a very pronounced expectation of a near future Second Coming of Christ. One of the features we saw in Matthew's Gospel was the delay in the parousia. Matthew's community came to believe that the Lord Jesus is already present in the life of the Church. John's Gospel has moved the furthest away from an expectation of the Second Coming of Christ in the near future. Scholars refer to this view as **"realized eschatology."** "Eschatology" is the study or discussion of the end times. For John the end times have come, and Christ has already returned in the Holy Spirit. Christians are already drawn into union with Christ and God. The realized eschatology of John's Gospel is intimately connected to his understanding of the Spirit. Because of his union with the Father, Jesus possesses the Spirit of God. When Jesus returns to the Father (at his death/resurrection), he passes on the Spirit to his disciples. The blood and water that pour from his side at his death (John 19:34) symbolize the giving of the **Holy Spirit.**

World in front of the Text

Logos Christology in the Early Church

The Logos Christology of John's Gospel, with its description of the Word with God at the beginning of time, was a main source of the early church's reflection on the divinity of Jesus. The Nicean Creed, which proclaims that Jesus Christ is "God from God, Light from Light, true God from true God, begotten not made, one in being with the Father," received its inspiration from the Christology expressed in John's Gospel.

The mystical/spiritual nature of John's Gospel makes it a rich source for modern reflection. John's Gospel does not focus on an imminent return of Christ, healing miracles, church regulations and hierarchy, or rules for living, all of which are difficult to translate into our modern experience. John's message of mystical union with the Father through the Son in human flesh is a message that remains appealing and intelligible in any age.

JOHN 10:1–18

World behind the Text

Shepherd Image in the Old Testament

There are two important texts in the Old Testament that affect the way we understand the image of the Shepherd in John's Gospel. In the parable of the shepherds (Ezekiel 34), Ezekiel is told by God to prophesy against the shepherds of the people (the

241

leaders). They are accused of pasturing themselves and not the sheep and of using the sheep for wool and food. The indictment against the leaders of Judah is that they have oppressed and exploited the people for financial gain. The shepherds are also guilty of letting the sheep stray and be lost (exile), so that they are also victims of foreign powers. The punishment for this is that God will remove the sheep from the shepherds and will shepherd the sheep himself. This means that God plans to put an end to the kingship and the ruling class and take over the care of the sheep himself. God then describes the care with which he will shepherd the sheep himself, bringing them back to their own country (out of exile) and giving them pasture. God will seek out the lost, bind up the injured, and heal the sick.

The second Old Testament text that uses the image of the shepherd is Zechariah 11, a text that uses Ezekiel as a source for its image. This allegory is the story of a shepherd hired by sheep merchants to shepherd a flock to be slaughtered. At the word of God, this shepherd ends his service as shepherd, and God announces that he will raise up a worthless shepherd who will not care for the sheep. In this allegory, which is probably to be assigned a late postexilic date, the religious leaders of the people (not the secular leaders as in Ezekiel) are condemned for not caring for the people. The shepherd image as Jesus uses it in John's Gospel is dependent on these two texts.

The Festivals of Booths and Dedication

The stories that precede our text, beginning in 7:1, take place during the festival of Booths ("Tabernacles" in some translations) when Jesus is in Jerusalem. The festival of Booths takes place during the fall wine and olive harvests and commemorates the time of wandering in the desert when the people lived in booths or tabernacles. The story that follows our text again takes place in Jerusalem but during the festival of the Dedication. The festival of the Dedication celebrates the rededication of the Temple by the Maccabees after its desecration by Antiochus IV. By the placement of the Good Shepherd Discourse, John connects it to both of the festivals. There are two connections to the festival of Booths. First, the time of wandering in the desert was a time before the institutions of kingship, Temple, land, or nation when God alone led the people. The Good Shepherd Discourse pictures a nomadic existence under the direct care of God's shepherd. Second, the Good Shepherd Discourse ends with some people asking, "Can a demon open the eyes of the blind?" (10:21). This connection makes the Pharisees of the story of the blind man the thieves of this discourse. The Good Shepherd Discourse is connected to the festival of the Dedication by the use of Ezekiel 34, which is the source for the Discourse in John and is one of the readings used for the festival of the Dedication.

World of the Text

Three-Part Structure of the Image of the Shepherd

The analogy that Jesus makes in chapter 10 of John seems confused and repetitive until we see that it is divided into three sections (1–5, 7–10 and 11–16) and both the first and third sections make two points. In the first section, the image of the shepherd is introduced by comparing how the thief enters the sheepfold with how the shepherd enters. Then the way the sheep relate to the shepherd (they recognize his voice and follow him) is compared to the way they relate to strangers (they run away).

Because the audience does not understand, Jesus changes the image in section two so that he is now the gate of the sheepfold. Those who come before him (other Jewish teachers) are thieves and bandits. They come to the sheepfold to steal and kill and destroy. In contrast to those who raid the sheep, Jesus is the gate by which the sheep go to and from pasture, having protection at night and food during the day. In this section, we have one of the "I AM" sayings—"I am the gate for the sheep."

In the third section, Jesus returns to the first image of the shepherd, and uses the "I AM" saying again—"I am the good shepherd." In this third section, he gives two interpretations of what it means that he is the good shepherd. In vv. 11–13 he shows himself to be the good shepherd because he is willing to die to protect the sheep in contrast to hired help who runs away at approaching danger.

In vv. 14–16 he shows himself to be the good shepherd because he and his sheep know each other intimately. This second part of the third section is very similar to the second part of the first section.

Outline of the Image of the Good Shepherd

Section One: Two ways of looking at the shepherd image.

a) 1–3: True shepherd's way of entering versus thief's way.

b) 3b–5: Shepherd's relationship to the sheep versus stranger's relationship.

Section Two: I AM the gate.

Those who came before steal and slaughter, while, as the gate, Jesus provides passage to safety and to food.

Section Three: I AM the good shepherd: Two interpretations.

a) 11–13: Good shepherd is willing to die to protect the sheep.

b) 14–16: Good shepherd knows his sheep and his sheep know him.

Meaning of the Image

The image of the shepherd in sections one and three brackets the image of the gate in section two. The two parts of section one match the two parts of section two. The "a" parts of sections one and three both describe the way the shepherd acts. In section one, he acts like a shepherd who is authorized by the gatekeeper (God) and not like a thief. In section three, he acts like a shepherd who risks his life to save the sheep and not like a hired hand who runs at the first sign of danger. The "b" parts of sections one and three describe the relationship between the shepherd and the sheep. In both, the sheep recognize the voice of the shepherd and the shepherd knows the sheep and calls them by name.

Against the background of Ezekiel 34 and Zechariah 11 and in the context of the story of the healing of the man born blind, there can be little doubt that the strangers, thieves, and hired hands who do such a poor job of shepherding the sheep are the Pharisees and other religious leaders. The central image of the gate deepens the role of the shepherd. Besides leading God's people through teaching and example, Jesus, as the gate, is the passage to salvation. The pasture, which those who pass through him will enter, is the heavenly kingdom of God where Jesus has prepared dwellings for them (see 14:2–3). The means of salvation is given in the third section. The shepherd lays down his life for the sheep. This act, which brings salvation, is both the command of the Father and the free act of Jesus (10:17–18).

Other Literary Features of This Image

This passage is a good example of many of the themes and literary features of John's Gospel. First, Jesus begins his discourse in chapter 10 with the statement, "Very truly, I tell you." This phrase, which in Greek is "Amen, Amen," is unique to John and is used to introduce important sayings of Jesus. Second, the narrator tells us that Jesus' audience did not understand the figure of speech of the shepherd. Their misunderstanding prompts Jesus to expand the image in a different direction. Third, this passage is a good example of an "I AM" saying with an object—the gate and the good shepherd. The context of the "I AM" saying in John's Gospel makes the gate and the shepherd more than simple metaphors. As the gate and as the good shepherd, Jesus acts as God (the I AM) acts. Finally, the discourse concludes with Jesus saying that no one takes his life from him. Instead, he has the power to lay down his life and the power to take it up again. This is a strong statement of high Christology. In the Synoptic Gospels, and Mark especially, Jesus is the victim of the plotting of the Pharisees, the betrayal of Judas, and the desertion of his disciples. Even if his death is the will of God and the source of salvation in the Synoptic Gospels, his death is still not seen as his own act of laying down his life. More than the other gospels, John's language places the emphasis on Jesus' action in union with the will of the Father.

World in front of the Text

Other Sheep

Toward the end of the Good Shepherd Discourse, Jesus says, "I have other sheep that do not belong to this fold. I must bring them also, and they will listen to my voice. So there will be one flock, one shepherd" (10:16). This passing remark, although not that central to the discourse, can be important in its implications for us today. In the world behind the text, the other sheep almost certainly refer to Samaritans and Gentiles who are not of the Jewish flock and whom Jesus must also lead. In a world in front of the text, we can see that Jesus opens the doors to the care and salvation of those beyond the flock that he shepherds. Jesus says there will be one flock and one shepherd. Contemporary Christians might be challenged to see that Jesus is the shepherd of other flocks than ours and that under the one shepherd we are all one flock. Slowly Christians are learning that we must first see ourselves as one flock, and then we must see that we are joined in an even larger flock with Jews, Muslims, Hindus, Buddhists, and all who seek God.

Learning Achievements

After studying this chapter, students should be able to:

- Define the synoptic problem and describe the two-source hypothesis.

- Outline the three stages of gospel development.

- Describe the Markan themes of Messianic Secret and Failure of Disciples.

- Discuss the Matthean themes of New Law, Anti-Pharisee sentiment, and Delay of Parousia.

- Do redaction criticism on a text from Matthew, whose source is Mark.

- Discuss the high Christology in John and define the "I AM" sayings.

Recommended Reading

Allen, O. Wesley. *Reading the Synoptic Gospels: Basic Methods for Interpreting Matthew, Mark, and Luke*. St. Louis: Chalice Press, 2000.

Brown, Raymond. *The Community of the Beloved Disciple*. New York: Paulist, 1979.

Brown, Raymond, and John Meier. *Antioch and Rome*. New York, Paulist, 2004.

Fitzmyer, Joseph. *A Christological Catechism: New Testament Answers*. New York: Paulist, 1993.

Kingsbury, Jack Dean, ed. *Gospel Interpretation: Narrative-Critical & Social-Scientific Approaches*. Harrisburg, Pa.: Trinity Press, 1997.

Malina, Bruce, and Richard Rohrbaugh. *Social-Science Commentary on the Synoptic Gospels*. Minneapolis: Fortress, 1992.

Nickle, Keith. *The Synoptic Gospels: An Introduction*, rev. ed. Louisville, Ky.: Westminster John Knox, 2001.

Powell, Mark Allen. *The Gospels*. Minneapolis: Fortress, 1998.

Schneiders, Sandra. *Written That You May Believe*. New York: Crossroad, 1999.

Chapter 9
LETTERS OF PAUL

Introduction

World behind the Text

Biography of Paul

Doing a biography of Paul is difficult because of the lack of sources. We have at least seven letters that Paul himself wrote, but they contain very little personal information. Much of the biographical information we have about Paul comes from the Acts of the Apostles (written by the author of the Gospel of Luke). It is generally agreed that even though some of Luke's information is accurate, his account of the life of Paul is exaggerated and modified to fit his theological purposes. The following account of the life of Paul is not based on certain facts but is a best guess based on a critical reading of Paul's letters and the Acts of the Apostles.

Paul was born in Tarsus, a predominantly Greek city in eastern Asia Minor with close ties to Rome. Tarsus was arguably the preeminent city of higher learning in the eastern Roman Empire, having eclipsed even Alexandria. The city had a large Jewish population. Paul was born to Jewish parents and given the Hebrew name Saul and the Greek name Paul. Luke tells us that Paul was a Roman citizen by birth, which would mean that his father was a Roman citizen, an important and rather rare title given to friends of the empire. Some have postulated that Paul's father was a tent maker (Paul's occupation) who had been particularly helpful during the campaigns of Pompey. Paul himself tells us that he is a Hebrew from among Hebrews (Phil 3:5), which means that his family would have been traditional Jews, reading the scriptures in the original Hebrew. Hellenistic Jews (Jews living in Greek cities outside of Palestine) would normally have read the scriptures in

Figure 4. Mediterranean World of Paul's Missionary Journeys

Greek (the Septuagint). We do not know the precise date of Paul's birth. However, his letters and Acts indicate that his conversion experience on the road to Damascus took place soon after the death of Jesus and when Paul was a young man. If we date the conversion to about 33 C.E., we can guess that he was born sometime around 10 C.E.

Paul tells us only that he was of the party of the Pharisees. This means that he would have held not only to the written law but also to the oral law handed down among the Pharisees, would have believed in the resurrection of the dead, and would have looked for the coming of a messiah at the end of the world. Although he was an educated man, from what Paul tells us, he was neither imposing nor articulate. He was not a great orator or a shining personality. His letters however are powerful, revealing his education in both the Hebrew scriptures and in Greek rhetoric. In his letters he is persistent, fearless, demanding, and single-minded. His letters also indicate that he must have come across to his new converts as deeply convinced and convincing about the great event that had taken place in Jesus Christ. Acts tells us that Paul performed several miraculous healings. Paul himself indicates that he had prophetic and visionary gifts.

The root of Paul's theology is his experience of the risen Jesus. Luke, in Acts, describes in some detail Paul's journey to Damascus, the bright light that blinds him, and his hearing the voice of Jesus Christ. Paul tells us only that the risen Christ appeared to him (1 Cor 15:8). Previous to his experience of the risen Christ, Paul had been convinced that Jesus was cursed by God (in Gal 3 Paul cites Deut 21:23 that anyone hung on a tree is under God's curse). The appearance of the risen Christ meant that Jesus Christ was raised to glory by God and was God's chosen one. Paul trusts his experience and comes to the conclusion that the law is wrong. This also leads Paul to the conclusion that being right with God is a free gift from God and is not a reward for obedience to the law. Paul's own experience confirms this. He was opposing God's chosen one, and God still freely granted him the grace of seeing the risen Christ. This experience and the resulting interpretation is what leads Paul to conclude that Gentiles and Jews are equally invited by God to be God's people and are made right with God in the same manner—by a free gift.

Because of Paul's discussions of sexuality, marriage, and relations between husbands and wives, the question of Paul's marital status has frequently been discussed. All Paul tells us is that he is unmarried at the time he wrote the letter to the Corinthians. Was he ever married? Was he divorced or widowed? There is not enough evidence in the letters to give us an answer, and Acts does not address the issue. It is likely that Paul died as a martyr in Rome about 66–67 C.E.

The Jewish Background for Paul

It was common in the past to separate the Jewish world of the first century from the Hellenistic world and find in Paul an original and unique blending of the two cultures. Now we know that Judaism in the first century was not as separate from the surrounding culture as we had thought. Even Palestinian Judaism was well aware of Hellenistic culture, ideas, literature, and rhetoric. Jews were living throughout the Roman Empire in large numbers, were recognized and respected members of these communities, and even pursued a policy of proselytizing. The Jews in Alexandria, Egypt, constituted nearly one-half of the entire population. Some have suggested that in the eastern half of the Roman Empire nearly one fifth of the population was Jewish. Even if these numbers are inflated, it is clear that Jews were not a tiny reclusive minority in the Roman Empire, confined mostly to Palestine. When Paul traveled to the cities of Asia Minor and then to Greece he would have found a synagogue in almost every city. He also would have found many Gentiles who were knowledgeable about Judaism, its laws, and scriptures. Even the general citizenry of a larger Greek city would have been familiar with some of the ideas and stories of Judaism. We have the writings of a number of Jews living in the Greek Diaspora, the most famous being Philo of Alexandria. His writings indicate a well-accepted practice of reinterpreting Judaism in the language and concepts of Hellenistic culture and philosophy. Hellenistic Judaism described God in terms of the Greek ideas of perfection, impassibility, and knowledge. Old Testament Wisdom was equated with the Logos of Stoic philosophy.

Apocalyptic expectation was an aspect of Judaism important for Paul's thinking. Among many of the Palestinian groups of Judaism (Pharisees, Essenes, and others) there was the expectation of God's coming intervention into history. These Jews expected that God would send an anointed figure (the Messiah) to come and make things right at the end of time. This figure could be either a military figure who would correct the political situation or a priestly figure who would correct the religious situation or both. This expectation of a new world-order often included the resurrection of the dead.

The Hellenistic Background for Paul

The religion and philosophy of Hellenism was in flux during the first century C.E. The preceding centuries saw a decline in the traditional religions and social institutions of Greece and Rome. A spirit of skepticism characterized this age. Although there was no real atheism at this time in history, there was a lack of confidence in the old myths about the gods. With the extended reach of the empire and the disintegration of local institutions, rituals, and even gods, people were looking for something new and different that would speak to their present situation.

The religious landscape for non-Jews in the empire was eclectic and even incorporated many foreign (non-Greek or Roman) ideas and gods. First, there were the three major camps of philosophy: Stoics, Cynics, and Neo-Pythagoreans. Stoicism seems to have sprung out of the collapse of the Hellenistic ideals that followed on the death of Alexander the Great. With this collapse, the question was raised: why do the gods not repay evildoers with punishment and the righteous with the blessings they deserve? The **Stoics'** answer was to reject the old gods who acted out of their own self-interest. For the Stoics, there were no individual personal gods, but only an impersonal divine principle of reason in the world. This principle was known as the *logos* (word). If bad things happened to a just person, there was a reason for that to have happened. The Stoic was to remain unperturbed by any misfortunes, knowing that the right thing was always happening.

The **Cynics** were fanatical moral teachers, who believed that most people spent their lives accumulating wealth and status and living a life of pretense. They attempted to simplify their lives to the essentials and by word and deed to convince people to live a natural life. They were known for not bathing, wearing old rags, eating only fruits and vegetables, and performing "natural" functions (urination, defecation, and copulation) in public. The name *cynic* (meaning "dog") was used for them because of their seemingly uncivilized behavior. They were disdained by many as repulsive and as hucksters who would preach for money, but were also admired by many who were moved by their moral purity, their convictions, and their authentic lifestyles.

The **Neo-Pythagoreans** focused on the divine element within each person. The soul of each person was immortal and was the true self. Neo-Pythagoreanism sought to return to the divine source of human life. The body was a lower nature and must be subordinated to this spiritual ascent. Celibacy, silence, and vegetarianism were only some of the ways the Neo-Pythagoreans used to strip away the lower nature and ascend to the divine.

There were also a number of **mystery religions** that attracted many adherents. The Eleusinian mysteries were based on the myth of Hades/Pluto's kidnap of Kore/Persephone. Persephone's mother, Demeter the goddess of fertility, mourned her absence, and the earth ceased to produce. Eventually Zeus intervened and Persephone spent eight months of every year on earth bringing fertility and four months in the underworld when the earth lay dormant (the four months of summer when it is too hot and dry for the grain). This mystery celebrated the dying and rising of the goddess. The form that this mystery took in the Roman Empire of the first century was not so much concerned with agricultural renewal as with the renewal of life after death. Cicero tells how this mystery allowed its adherents to live with joy and die with hope. One feature of this mystery was its highly individualistic nature; it was concerned with a person's own personal future life.

The Isis–Osiris mystery, imported from Egypt, was based on the myth of Osiris who was killed by his jealous brother, Seth, chopped into pieces, and thrown into the Nile. Osiris's consort, Isis, found all of the pieces of his body and reassembled them. She breathed life into the corpse and consummated their marriage. From their union came Horus who was the pharaoh of Egypt. Osiris returned to the netherworld to be lord of both the netherworld and the Nile, presiding over life after death and the cycles of agricultural fertility in Egypt. In the Greco-Roman version, the mystery focused on Isis as the dominant figure. It was her power that brought life to the dead. Again, the attraction of this mystery was that it promised the victory of life over death.

Perhaps the most influential mystery at this time was the Dionysiac mystery. Dionysus had a human mother but Zeus for a father. When his mother died looking on Zeus, Dionysus (who was still in the womb) was rescued by Zeus and inserted into Zeus's own thigh to complete his gestation. Because of this, Dionysus was said to have been born twice, but it was his second birth that made him divine. Dionysus offered freedom from everyday drudgery. He was both the god of wine and debauchery and the god of culture and refinement. His followers were born again in divine possession and revelry. Festivals of drinking wine were accompanied by bloody sacrifices. In eating the bloody flesh and drinking the wine, the adherents received the god within. The primary emphasis of this mystery was the struggle between life and death, and the transcendence of death through the fullest participation in life.

Another cult that was important in the first-century Greco-Roman world was the **healing cult of Asclepius.** Asclepius was the son of Apollo and a mortal woman. He died as a human but returned to earth as a god to bring healing to humans. He mainly served the poor and disadvantaged and was known for compassion. The centers of his cult were healing centers, reminiscent of modern-day spas for holistic medicine. Religious centers for physical healing were common in Greco-Roman culture.

The final religious view that we will discuss could have been placed with the discussion of Judaism, with the philosophical schools, or even with the mystery religions. **Gnosticism** was a hybrid of many things. Gnosticism, in the form that we have come to know it, developed out of Jewish–Christian beliefs. According to the Gnostics, Yahweh was an evil God or demigod who created the earth. Therefore, all material things were evil and mortal. The true God, however, was Spirit and the source of true spiritual life. This God sent his Son into the world to reveal true spirit. This Son, the Logos, came from God and returned to God. The believer was enlightened by the revelation of the Logos and began to live a truly spiritual life transcending matter. The rejection of material things could take either the form of asceticism or promiscuity. Either way, the enlightened ones were untouched by the material world because they had been raised up to God in the spirit. Scholars debate whether there was any form of Jewish or pagan Gnosticism before Christianity. Certainly the Gnosticism that is found in the Gnostic texts discovered in Egypt and known from the anti-Gnostic writings of the church fathers is derived from Christian imagery and ideas. At the time of Paul's letters, Gnosticism has not yet formed into the belief system that we find a century later, although certain forms of Jewish-Christian beliefs at that time may properly be called proto-Gnostic.

In all, we can see that there was a stirring of religious ideas in the first century. There was dissatisfaction with the old gods of mythology, an eagerness to accept foreign ideas and myths, and a desire for transcendence over death and the tribulations of the material world. We can see in many of the philosophies and religions similarities to the message that Paul will preach—life after death, second birth, incorporation into the god, healings, sacred meals, and rejection of the values and powers of this world. These similarities will be both a help and a hindrance to the Gentiles' acceptance of the authentic gospel of Jesus Christ.

Paul's Journeys and Communities

Paul's first missionary journey began from the city of Antioch, where he was sent out as a missionary into Asia Minor. On his first trip he was probably the companion of Barnabas. After an argument with Peter, Barnabas, and the Antioch community over eating freely with Gentiles, Paul set out on his own. Paul made at least three missionary journeys on his own. In his first solo journey, he traveled to the northern parts of Asia Minor, to Galatia. In the second, he traveled to Greece. In the third, he retraced his steps.

Paul's usual mode of operation was to go to the synagogue in the city (if there was one) and preach about the Jewish messiah Jesus. He would also teach and preach from his stall in the marketplace where he made tents. Usually he was more successful with the God-Fearers (Gentiles who had not become Jews but were attracted to Judaism and attended the synagogue) than with the Jews. Paul would collect a group of followers who would listen to him teach and who would meet at the home of one of the followers for the Lord's Supper and for teaching. The communities that he formed were made up of merchants, artisans, laborers, and slaves. There were sometimes a few members with some wealth, but mostly it was the poorer members of society who were attracted to Paul's message. Women seem to have been more numerous than men in the early communities and were coworkers with Paul and leaders of the churches. The communities that we know about were in important cities. Paul went to the cities that were the hubs of travel and commerce with the idea that from that central location his communities would be able to spread the good news to the surrounding areas. He could minister to large areas through the one central community. His letters would be distributed from there, and news from the smaller communities would be brought to the central community.

Paul's Letters

Paul wrote his letters only to the communities that he himself had formed. The one exception to this was the letter to the Romans (Paul was planning to visit them and hoped to make them a center for his missionary activity to the west), and Paul went to great pains to give reasons why he should write to them even though they were not a community that he had founded. It is certain that Paul wrote more letters than the ones we have (1 Corinthians mentions a previous letter). Of the thirteen letters in the New Testament that are attributed to Paul (these letters state in the opening greeting that the letter is from Paul), scholars are certain of only seven as having been written by Paul himself. It is generally agreed that Paul did not write the three Pastoral Epistles (1 Timothy, 2 Timothy, and Titus). They were written by a later interpreter of Paul. The letters of Colossians, Ephesians, and 2 Thessalonians are disputed, with the letter to the Colossians often being included among the authentic letters of Paul. The letter to the Hebrews was attributed to Paul by the later church (during the discussions about the canon) but does not have Paul as the addressee in the letter itself and today is universally rejected as having been written by Paul.

In recent decades, scholars have come to a better understanding of Paul's authorship of the letters. First, it is clear from several of the letters that Paul himself did not write out the letters, but dictated them to a scribe and then signed them. (In 1 Cor 16:21 Paul says that he is writing this greeting "with my own hand.") Second, the amount of freedom that the scribe had in composition is a matter of debate. Some scholars think that Paul gave the outline of his message and even the examples and images, but the scribe was free to compose in the language and style in which he was trained. Others believe that Paul dictated the letters word for word.

There is also a problem with the integrity of Paul's letters in the form that we have them. Several of the letters (most notably 2 Corinthians and Philippians) seem to be composites of two or more letters. In the process of the dissemination and preservation of Paul's letters, parts of letters were distributed separately or were added to other letters. It also seems that at times, later editors or copiers of the letters have added material to Paul's letters.

There have been many attempts to resolve contradictions in Paul's letters by suggesting that a certain verse is not from Paul himself but is a later addition (an interpolation). Paul's comment that women should be silent in the churches (1 Cor 14:34) is one example; his comment that the Jews were the ones who killed Jesus and who are being overtaken by the wrath of God (1 Thess 2:15–16) is another example. The danger in maintaining that these verses are later interpolations is that any saying in Paul's letters that is difficult to understand or accept or seems to contradict another saying of Paul's is relegated to a later editor. In this way, the reader does not need to grapple with the text in understanding Paul. This is most often a cop-out. However, there are times when it is necessary to admit that there probably were some later alterations to the texts of Paul's letters.

> Textual criticism and narrative criticism allow us to make judgments about the original shape and content of a particular letter.

World of the Text

The Letter Form

The form of Paul's letters is not a genre unique to him, but is like any personal letter written in the Hellenistic world in the first century C.E. The **Salutation** of the letter contains the name of the sender, the name of the recipient(s), and a greeting. It is not unusual for the salutation to give some attribute or designation to the sender and recipient, such as: "Claudius, your loyal nephew, to Titus, my doting uncle." In the case of Paul's letters, the designations given to the sender usually refer to Paul's claim to be an apostle and his having been commissioned by God. The designations given to the recipients usually make some allusion to what will be the issue addressed in the letter. Because the Corinthians are not living up to their calling to separate themselves from the iniquity of the world, Paul addresses them as "the church of God that is in Corinth...called to be saints." Paul changes the word used for the greeting from the more normal "greetings" to "grace to you and peace from God our Father and our Lord Jesus Christ."

The next element in Paul's letters is the **Thanksgiving.** In an ordinary letter, there would often be a blessing of the recipient at this point. In Paul's letters, there is a thanksgiving to God for what good has been happening in the community. The Galatians are the only recipients not given a thanksgiving, probably because Paul was so upset with how they were rejecting the great gift God had given to them. The third element in a letter is the **Main Body.** This section of the letter makes the request or states the purpose of the sender. In Paul's letters, the main body can be divided into a doctrinal section and a hortatory section. The doctrinal section is usually made up of a number of different points in which Paul responds to questions from the communities or to things he has heard about their problems. Exhortations to good behavior (the hortatory section) close out the main body of the letter. The final element of the letters is the **Closing.** The closing usually includes greetings to friends and family members of the receiver (in Paul's letters he usually sends greetings to the members of the church that he knows personally) and concludes with a benediction.

Pauline Letter Form

Salutation

   Sender

   Recipient

   Grace

Thanksgiving

Main Body

   Doctrinal Section

   Hortatory Section

Closing

   Greetings

   Benediction

Paul's Rhetoric

The letters of Paul are part of a conversation with his communities and are written because of some problem in the community that Paul feels compelled to address. The letters are written to convince the community of Paul's point of view (sometimes against great resistance). As instruments to convince an audience the letters are rhetorical devices. Paul's letters, more than any other of the books of the New Testament, use the rhetorical techniques of classical Greek oratory to convince the readers. Some of these techniques include: diatribe, lists of virtues and vices, mockery, self-deprecation, and personal examples. One of the most interesting and often used techniques is **diatribe,** in which Paul engages in a discussion with an imaginary opponent or student. In this technique, the position and words of the dialogue partner are given first, followed by Paul's answer. A good example is found in Rom 9:19–20: "You will say to me then, 'Why then does he still find fault? For who can resist his will?' But who indeed are you, a human being, to argue with God?"

Although these techniques of rhetoric are taken from Hellenistic culture and oratory, Paul is also adept at using methods of argumentation from Jewish rabbinic circles. The way Paul argues using scripture and scriptural examples is consistent with his Pharisaic training. Paul uses persons from the Old Testament as models for understanding the significance of Christ (typology). He also develops Old Testament stories in an inventive and interpretive fashion (what we called midrashic interpretation in the chapter on the gospels). Paul also makes frequent use of the rabbinic technique of arguing from lesser to greater. In Romans 5:15 Paul argues that "if the many died through the one man's trespass, much more surely have the grace of God and the free gift in the grace of the one man, Jesus Christ, abounded for the many."

The Theology of Paul's Letters

It is difficult to develop a "theology of Paul" because Paul was writing his letters to a particular community about a particular problem and not writing any kind of treatise on theology. Recently scholars have given a great deal of attention to this issue and suggested that although Paul is addressing very specific and time-conditioned problems in the letters, he also grounds his reactions and arguments in his own deep-seated convictions that can be read beneath the surface of the letters. In the process of dealing with specific issues, Paul is forced to think out the implications of his beliefs and so develop a sort of "theology." In discussing a theology of Paul, scholars distinguish between the contingency and the coherence in Paul's letters. The problem in the community and Paul's answer to that problem are expressions of the contingency. The problems are particular to the life of that community and to that culture, and Paul's own experiences and place in the culture condition his responses. However, using methodologies of close readings, and understanding how rhetoric and argumentation reveal convictions, scholars have made great strides in getting behind the surface level issues that Paul's letters are addressing to the deeper convictions that he held and that ground his responses to the specific problems. These deeper convictions form the coherence of Paul's letters. Therefore, scholars today who seek to develop a theology of Paul will focus on his deep convictions that underlie his more immediate responses to the problems of his communities.

World in front of the Text

Paul's Reputation and Influence

Of the twenty-three books of the New Testament thirteen are written by or attributed to Paul, and nearly two-thirds of the Acts of the Apostles are devoted to Paul. During his lifetime Paul was controversial and not universally respected, but in the early church his reputation grew. Although it is not accurate to say that Paul is the real founder of Christianity, his influence on the development of Christianity is enormous and second only to that of Jesus. As early as 100 C.E. the letters of Paul were being referred to as authoritative by the church fathers, although it is Augustine of Hippo (354–430) who raises Paul to the level of Christianity's preeminent theologian by his use of Paul's letters.

The influence and controversial nature of Paul grew again with the Protestant Reformation. Luther turned to Paul's discussion of righteousness by faith alone (and not through the works of the law) to critique the practices of the Roman church. From that time on, Paul has been at the center of the arguments between Catholics and Protestants.

Paul and Women

Until quite recently Paul has been considered no friend of women. His words about marriage, women speaking in the churches, women's hairdos, and sexual relations have led people to accuse Paul of being a misogynist, although this is where modern scholarship has been most helpful. First we must make a distinction between the authentic letters of Paul and later letters attributed to him (many of the problematic texts come from the later letters). Second, the distinction between coherence and contingency is important. It is absurd to think that a Christian in the twenty-first century should try to follow Paul's advice on women's hairstyles. This is the ultimate of contingency. Whatever the problem was for the Corinthian community in 50 C.E., it was specific to that time and culture. What we should try to understand, however, is what were Paul's deep convictions that grounded his specific advice. In Galatians, Paul says that in Christ there is neither man nor woman (3:28). This comes closer to giving us Paul's deep convictions, although it too is just one saying and cannot be used alone to argue for an unadulterated egalitarianism in Paul.

By separating the contingent advice of Paul from his coherent beliefs, scholars have been better able to appreciate the liberated and liberating genius of Paul.

Romans

INTRODUCTION

World behind the Text

The Church at Rome

We are not sure when the Roman church was founded or by whom. Tradition has held that the church was dually founded by both Peter and Paul, but it is fairly certain that neither of these two figures was actually the first to bring the gospel message to Rome. (We are, however, fairly certain that Paul was martyred there, and it is quite possible that Peter also was.) Because there were frequent travelers, pilgrims, merchants, and public officials who traveled all over the Roman Empire, it is not surprising that the message about Christ reached Rome, the center of the empire, at a very early date, perhaps as early as 40 C.E. The Christian community at Rome was originally predominantly Jewish, but in 49 C.E., Claudius expelled Jews from Rome. It is likely that many of the Jewish Christians in Rome were targeted or felt it expedient to leave Rome. When Nero became emperor and the Jews returned to Rome, the returning Jewish Christians found that the Christian community in Rome had grown considerably and was now predominantly Gentile. This was the background for an important issue addressed by Paul in his letter to Rome. Paul spoke at length about the issue of the relationship of Jews to Gentiles in the new age of Christ. Paul addressed the painful problem of why God's chosen people, the Jews, had not, on the whole, accepted Jesus as the Messiah they had longed for. Paul also addressed the problem of the "weak" and the "strong," an issue that seemed to relate to Jewish concerns for food associated with idols.

Is the Letter to the Romans?

There is one important textual problem with Paul's letter to the Romans. Some ancient manuscripts end the letter after chapter 14, several end it after chapter 15, and others end it after chapter 16. Chapter 16 contains a list of greetings to over thirty

Christians whom Paul knows. Many doubt whether Paul could have known that many people in Rome, a community that he had never visited. These scholars suggest that chapter 16 was a greeting added to the letter when Paul decided to send the letter also to the community at Ephesus. The reason scholars suggest the community of Ephesus as the intended recipients of the greetings, is that we know from Paul's letters and from Acts that Prisca and Aquila were settled, for a time at least, in Ephesus. Given the amount of traveling that was done by urban people at that time, and given that some of the members Paul greets in chapter 16 may have been Jewish Christians who had only recently returned to Rome, it is not impossible that Paul did know this many people in the Roman community.

Why Paul Wrote to the Romans

The letter to the Romans is the only letter that Paul wrote to a community that he did not found. It was written from Corinth as Paul was about to leave for Jerusalem to deliver the money that had been collected from the Gentile churches for the "poor" of Jerusalem (about 58 C.E.). One of the major issues that confront students of the letter is the reason that the letter was written. Why would Paul write to a community that he had not founded? Scholarly opinion runs along two lines. One group of scholars suggest that a religious crisis in the community was the reason for his writing Romans. Paul is concerned about the problems between Jews and Gentiles in the community, and feels that as the apostle to the Gentiles he has a right and duty to offer his advice. Other scholars maintain that Paul is not writing because of some crisis in the community; in fact, he does not know much about the situation of the community. Paul is writing because he wants to introduce himself and his version of the gospel to the Romans so that he can establish a base there for his missionary work to the west (especially to Spain). He writes to this community to impress on them that his gospel is not off the wall and unique to him, and that he is very much a missionary of the whole church—Jews and Gentiles alike. His concern is to get the Roman Christians on his side and instill in them a desire to help him continue his work by providing a base community and financial support. The second theory is the stronger of the two reasons for Paul writing this letter, but it may be that both reasons played a part.

World of the Text

Outline of Romans

Romans is the longest and most carefully written of Paul's letters. It is also perhaps one of the best examples of Paul's use of rhetoric. He makes extensive use of diatribe and biblical examples. Like most of Paul's letters, its body can be divided into two parts: a doctrinal section and a hortatory section. In the doctrinal section Paul addresses the issue of how one becomes righteous with God. The doctrinal section of Romans is the culmination of Paul's thinking about what has taken place in the Christ event. After the usual Salutation and Thanksgiving (1:1–15), Paul states the thesis of his whole letter. The gospel is the power of God for salvation (1:16–17). Paul then develops this thesis negatively, showing that on their own all humans have become enemies of God by their sinfulness (1:18—3:20). Paul then restates the theme of the letter (3:21—26) before proceeding to develop the theme in a positive way (3:27—8:39). In chapters 9—11 Paul deals with the difficult issue of why the Jews have not accepted the gospel, and what God's plan for them is now. The hortatory section of the letter begins in chapter 12. First, Paul reminds the Romans of the importance of love and respect in the community and then advises them on how to live in the empire in a way that is both faithful to their calling as Christians and obedient to the secular authorities (12:1—13:14). In the next two chapters, Paul deals with the issue of eating meat that is sacrificed to idols, an action that some considered of no relevance whatsoever and others viewed as idolatry (14:1—15:13). Finally, Paul concludes with his travel plans and greetings to the community (15:14—16:27).

Outline of Romans

Salutation

Thanksgiving

Body

    Doctrinal Section

        Negative Development of Thesis

        Positive Development of Thesis

        Jews and Gentiles in God's Plan

    Hortatory Section

        Christians in the World

        The Weak and the Strong

Closing

    Travel Plans

    Greetings

    Benediction

Message of Romans

The primary theme of Romans is God's power for the salvation of all people. In Romans Paul presents a grand vision of God's plan to bring all humans to union with God. The plan begins with the call of Abraham who will be the father of a nation (the Jews) who will be God's instrument in bringing salvation to the whole world. As part of this plan, the Jews will reject the Messiah and so open the doors for the Gentiles to accept the Messiah. Once the Gentiles are drawn into the family of God, the Jews will recognize God's revelation of salvation in Christ and so return to the family of God. In the end, God, in Jesus Christ, will draw all humans into one family to live the new life in God's Spirit. However, one must remember that all this, for Paul, takes place in the context of Judaism. It is a plan for the people Israel who will ultimately include the whole human race. Paul never thinks of this plan of God as involving the formation of a new religion supplanting Judaism.

World in front of the Text

Creating One Family of God

After Vatican II there has been a great renewal of Paul's vision that God has a plan to save all humanity. Like Paul, the Catholic Church has renewed its conviction that God's plan of salvation was first revealed to the Israelites, especially in the prophets. God's plan was to create a holy people out of whom would come the Messiah as fulfillment of the promises God had made to his people and as fulfillment of the laws God had given to his people to guide their lives. It was also part of God's plan that the Jews as a whole would not accept Jesus as Messiah right away. (A remnant of the Jews did accept Jesus as Messiah and were the foundation of a new understanding of the people of God.) For modern Christians, this is not understood in a mechanistic way. We do not envision God as deliberately preventing the Jews from accepting Jesus to make God's plan work. Rather, we understand the insight of Paul to be that in spite of what seems to be a failure of God's plan (God's first chosen people, the Israelites, have not accepted the Messiah of God and therefore seem excluded from God's plan), we can trust that God will be faithful to God's promises to Abraham and will join this group to the new people of God that now includes Gentiles who have been joined to Israel by their faith in Jesus Christ.

What is happening now in the church is a process of discovering God's plan being worked out in history. The church, under the leadership of Pope John Paul II, is doing the work of God by drawing the two communities (the people of God according to the covenant with Abraham and Moses and the people of God according to the covenant in Jesus Christ) into greater dialogue and closer relationship with each other. The church no longer works under the assumption that by some great miracle we will wake up one morning and all Jews will have converted to Christianity. Rather, the church, trusting in the power and plan of God, works to bring about greater harmony and understanding between all of God's people and respects God's right to work in many and varied ways to bring about the unity of one family.

ROMANS 3:21–26

World behind the Text

The Righteousness of God and the Faith of Christ

One of the most annoying but also rewarding aspects of Paul's grammar is his use of the genitive case. The genitive in Greek is comparable to the possessive in English. In English, the possessive can have either an objective or a subjective meaning. In Greek the genitive is even more complex with possible meanings, but we will concern ourselves with just the subjective and objective. As an example, we can speak of "the love of God." If the genitive (God is in the genitive case in Greek) is objective, then the phrase makes God the object of love. "The love of God" means someone's love for God. If the genitive is subjective, then the phrase makes God the subject of the act of loving or the one who possesses the love. "The love of God" then means God's love for someone or the love that is inherent in God's person. In Romans 3:21–26, two genitive phrases concern us: "righteousness of God" and "faith of Jesus Christ."

The righteousness of God can have many possible meanings, and it is important for us to try to discover what Paul intended by this phrase to understand the meaning of our text. First, if Paul was using the genitive as an objective genitive, the righteousness is something that God gives to humans. The righteousness of God is a thing (object) that is given to human beings. This kind of genitive is also called a genitive of origin. Romans 3:22 seems to imply that the righteousness of God is something that the believer acquires through "faith of Christ." The righteousness of God as an objective genitive or genitive of origin was the interpretation chosen by Luther and many other interpreters of the past. Righteousness was a human attribute. God made or declared humans righteous. If righteousness of God is a subjective genitive, the righteousness is a quality that God possesses. If righteousness is a quality that God possesses, what would it mean to say that God is righteous? Certainly, God is not capable of being unrighteous. Scholars tend to see the righteousness of God in three ways: God is faithful, God is fair, and God is just. In 4:13–24 Paul will explain that God made a promise to Abraham and to his seed, which has been fulfilled in the one person Jesus Christ. So, he proves that God is faithful to his promise. Second, in 3:22–23 Paul argues that the righteousness of God is for all who believe, without distinction. Because all have sinned and are separated from God, all are equally justified freely by grace. The point is that God is fair. There is no distinction between Jews who have the Law and Gentiles who do not have the Law. God treats all fairly, because all are justified in the same way. Finally, in 3:25 Paul says that Jesus was a sacrifice of atonement to show God's righteousness because of the divine forbearance of sins previously committed. Paul maintains that God was patient and did not punish human sin as he ought in the past. In fact, it seemed as if God was not just because he let people get away with sins. Paul argues that this forbearance on the part of God was actually to prove his righteousness in the present time because now in Christ those sins are forgiven and Sin itself is being destroyed. So God is seen as just: meaning that he deals with and gets rid of sin. Today it is more common among scholars to interpret the righteousness of God as being a subjective genitive: the gospel of Jesus Christ proves that God is faithful, fair, and just.

The "faith of Jesus Christ" has traditionally been translated as "faith in Jesus Christ." This would be to understand the phrase as an objective genitive. Christ is the object of faith, although more and more scholars believe that it makes better sense in the context of Paul's arguments (this phrase occurs numerous times in Paul) to translate the phrase as a subjective or possessive genitive. It is through the faith that Christ has that believers are justified. In the text we are studying it would seem to be redundant for Paul to speak of "the righteousness of God through faith in Jesus Christ for all who believe" (3:22). It makes more sense if Paul is saying, "the righteousness of God through the faithfulness of Jesus Christ for all of us who believe (in Christ)." The "faith of Christ" thus means

Jesus' faithfulness to the will and plan of God exemplified in his accepting death on a cross. It is this faithful act of Jesus that allows us to be justified. A second argument that is made is that if it were our faith in Christ that brought our justification, then it would again be a human work not unlike the doing of the law.

A careful analysis of Greek grammar can tell us much about the meaning of a text. The reader of an English Bible should recognize that many of the nuances of Paul's Greek will be lost in a translation.

Images for the Christ Event

In 3:24 Paul says that all are justified through "redemption" in Christ Jesus, and in v. 25 Paul calls Jesus a "sacrifice of atonement" put forward by God. It is important to understand the Paul uses a wide variety of images to describe what God has done for us in Christ. We are ransomed, saved, adopted, redeemed. To appreciate what Paul is saying in this text, we need to examine the images he uses. The word *redemption* comes from the context of slavery in the ancient world. In the ancient world, slavery was not the same social structure as it was later developed in the sixteenth to nineteenth centuries. Slaves were not considered subhuman or racially destined for slavery. Slavery was an economic or political calamity only. A person might go into debt to such a degree that the only possibility open to them was to sell themselves (or a member of their family) into slavery, or a person captured in war could be held in slavery. In almost all of these cases, slavery was a temporary situation. The relatives of the person in slavery or the slaves themselves could pay the price that would buy them out of slavery. The term that Paul uses here can have the strict meaning of the price that one pays to buy a person out of slavery, or it can have the more general metaphorical meaning of the act of freeing or liberating a person. The term was used in the Septuagint to refer to the liberation of the Hebrews from slavery in Egypt. The reason this discussion is important is that some have interpreted Jesus' death as a real price that was paid to God (or the Devil) to liberate humans from the slavery to sin. It is better to understand that Paul uses this word metaphorically.

The precise meaning of the word that is translated as "sacrifice of atonement" in v. 25 has been debated almost ever since the letter was written. The first problem is that even the English word *atonement* makes little sense to most modern readers. The Greek word in our text is *hilasterion*, and in its related verbal form, it was used in ancient Greek with the meaning to appease. It was an act meant to rectify a situation when one party had wronged another. In the Septuagint this Greek word was used to translate the Hebrew word for atonement, as in the Day of Atonement. In the Psalms the Hebrew word that refers to atonement is also used to mean cover over something, to forgive it, or not count it. In the Septuagint the Greek word *hilasterion* is used to translate this meaning. In Exodus 25 the covering over the ark is called the *hilasterion*. Given this background, the argument has continued unabated over how to understand Jesus' death. Was it meant to appease God in God's wrath against sinners? Was Jesus' blood a sacrifice that brought about atonement? Was Jesus' death an act of God's covering over and forgiving our sins? Given that Paul's argument continues in vv. 25–26 by referring to "the forgiveness of sins previously committed, through the forbearance of God," it can be argued that Paul means Jesus as a *hilasterion* in the sense of a covering over of sins; however, the interpretation of Jesus' blood as a sacrifice that brings atonement is the meaning chosen by many modern interpreters.

World of the Text

The Now Time

In 1:18—3:20, Paul has argued that all are under the power of sin and enemies of God, not only Gentiles who do not know God, but also Jews who know God and have the utterances of God. In 3:11–18 Paul quotes a series of lines from the Psalms to the effect that no one is just or does good, but all are worthless and sinful. That is the situation before Christ. Verse 21 introduces the "now time." God has done something that has changed the whole situation of the world. Paul has shown that even with the best of intentions humans could not change this situation of enmity between God and humans. So now, God has acted to change the situation. What God has done is reveal God's righteousness. This is then explained in the four ways that correspond to the possible meanings of this genitive phrase (see the discussion of the righteousness of God above). First, the righteousness of God was testified to by the law and the prophets (v. 21). This points to the faithfulness of God. God made promises, and they are now being fulfilled. Second, the righteousness of God is for all who believe (v. 22). This points to the meaning that righteousness is something given to human beings. Third, the righteousness is given to all by the same means because all have sinned and are justified freely by God's grace (vv. 23–24). This implies that God is fair. Fourth, God proves God's righteousness by using a sacrifice of atonement for sins previously committed, showing that God does not let sins slide but in the end deals with all in justice (v. 25–26a). Paul concludes this section in v. 26b by returning to the second point—righteousness as something given to humans. The righteousness of God as an attribute of God cannot be separated from the righteousness that God gives to believers in justifying them. Because God is faithful to his promise to form a people of God, it is necessary for God to justify believers to be that people. Because the promise was made to Abraham who believed, justification that creates a people of God must also be of those who believe. Because God is fair and justifies all equally, justification must be by faith and not by the law. Because God is just and must deal with all sin, the faithful act of Jesus that brings justification to believers also destroys all sins that were committed in the past. Paul has thus shown that what God has done in Jesus Christ fulfills all the requirements of how God ought to act (the righteousness of God).

Faith and the Law

A diatribe that confirms the analysis above follows our text. If God really is righteous and justifies sinners in this way, it raises serious questions. Paul's imaginary dialogue companion asks what a human can take credit for if this is how God works, and Paul answers that there is nothing a human can take credit for. This raises the question of whether Paul's description of how God works to justify Jew and Gentile through faith does not nullify the law. This of course is the main accusation made against Paul: that he encouraged breaking the law and declared the law no longer valid. Here Paul claims that justification by faith does not annul the law but supports it. According to Paul, justification by faith proves the righteousness of God and justifies humans. The law was a statement of God's justice and a description of living a just life. God, through justification by faith, has brought about the goal of the law. The law is fulfilled in this new plan of salvation.

> The rhetorical technique of the diatribe allows Paul to raise objections to his preceding argument and then answer those objections. By examining the objections in the diatribe, we can discover what Paul considered essential to his argument.

World in front of the Text

Luther, Imputed Righteousness, and Covering Our Sins

This text has been at the center of debate throughout the centuries, but especially during the time of the Reformation. As we discussed earlier, one issue is whether God's righteousness is something that God possesses or is something that is given to humans. If it is something given to humans, does God declare humans righteous by a legal verdict or does God make believers righteous in fact? Connected with this is how one translates and understands the *hilasterion*. Luther translated the *hilasterion* as a covering over of sins. He claimed that God declares believers righteous although, in fact, we are sinners. In so doing God covers over our sins and disregards them in Christ. Luther's image to describe a person was a pile of manure. God's grace in Christ was like snow that covered over the pile of manure but did not change the pile itself. The Roman Catholic position is that in Christ, the believer not only has his/her sins forgiven, but is in fact transformed into a new and righteous person by the grace of God in Christ. The believer becomes righteous and can do righteous acts.

Paul's God-Centered Theology

Often the discussions of justification, faith, and God's plan of salvation are either Christ-centered or human-centered. So much of modern religion is even "me" centered. How can I be righteous? How can I get to heaven? How can I be happy and fulfilled? How can I become spiritually enlightened and fully integrated? Paul's argument reminds us that our salvation is ultimately about God. God's love created the universe. God's patience puts up with sinful humanity. God's justice destroyed the power of sin. God's fairness made this available to all. God's incredible wisdom brought all this about in a simple act of love. We should be overjoyed, amazed, and in awe of what God has done for us in Jesus Christ. Although this plan of salvation is for our benefit and was accomplished through Jesus Christ, it is God's plan and God who has done the work. That is why in numerous places in his letters Paul will simply break into praise and benediction of God for being so incredibly wise and loving (e.g., 6:17; 7:25).

1 Thessalonians

INTRODUCTION

World behind the Text

Thessalonica

Thessalonica, named after the half sister of Alexander the Great, is in Macedonia on the Thermatic Gulf of the Aegean Sea. Founded by Cassander, the husband of Thessalonike, in 316 B.C.E., the city was always an important port city. When the Romans constructed the Via Egnatia from the Adriatic Sea, across the Greek peninsula to the Aegean (with Thessalonica being the first Aegean port on the road) and on to Asia Minor, the city became even more prominent. Records show that Thessalonica had very close relations with Rome, belonging to Rome's direct rule and paying its taxes to Rome and not to the governor of the region. There was a very strong cult of the emperor in the city, with both Julius and Augustus Caesar being worshiped as gods.

This very close relationship between Rome and Thessalonica meant that the local population of Greeks who lived in Thessalonica was composed primarily of artisans and laborers, whereas the wealthy elites were Roman. Workers labored twelve hours a day and seven days a week to make a living. It was to the local working class that Paul's message was directed. Paul probably got a job as a tent maker in the city and worked in a shop in the market. It would have been typical for Paul to begin preaching about Jesus in the synagogue meetings but also in the shop where he worked. There would have been a hunger among the workers for Paul's message of a lowly peasant (a man known for his healings and his compassion for the poor and outcasts) who was executed by the state but raised by God. In fact, there was a local mystery cult that celebrated Cabirus, a young man murdered by his two brothers, who was expected to return from the dead and aid the powerless. Before the arrival of the Romans, this cult was very important among the working classes. By the time of Paul, however, this cult had been taken over by the Romans and transformed into an official cult that supported the ruling elite. The local laborers were without a hero and protector, without hope for liberation and a better future. Paul's message of Jesus would have fallen on very receptive ears.

Historical and archaeological studies provide us with a picture of the community to which Paul's letter was directed.

Paul's Mission to Thessalonica

Paul probably arrived in Thessalonica from Philippi in about 48 C.E. He was heading west, but probably spent several months and maybe even a full year in Thessalonica founding the church there. The letter to the Thessalonians was written by Paul some months after he had left the city and moved on to Athens and then to Corinth. Paul was forced to leave the city because of political pressure (it is not clear whether this pressure originated from Jewish or Gentile opponents). It would be a good guess that the ruling elite considered his preaching about an executed peasant hero who was going to return and bring freedom and liberation to his followers as too dangerous. After Paul arrived in Athens, he sent Timothy back to Thessalonica to find out how his young church was holding up. The journey from Athens to Thessalonica (approximately 360 miles) would take about three weeks each way. Paul wrote to the Thessalonians from Corinth after Timothy returned to him with a report. Paul's first letter to the Thessalonians, therefore, may have been written as soon as three months after he left them. It is clear from the letter that he missed them and was anxious about their welfare.

World of the Text

Structure of 1 Thessalonians

Although some have argued that the first letter of Paul to the Thessalonians is actually a composite of two different letters (they see two or more separate Thanksgivings in the letter), for our purposes we will study it as one letter. The Salutation, Thanksgiving, and Closing are fairly standard in this letter. The Body of the letter is made up of two sections.

In the first section of the Body (2:1—3:13) Paul defends his ministry. He begins by recalling his mission among the Thessalonians and how they responded to him; then he continues with the visit of Timothy. Paul may be reacting to some sort of opposition to or complaint about him. It is not clear whether those accusing him are outsiders or insiders. It may be that the Thessalonians are not pleased that he has left them nor convinced that he has been completely straightforward with them about the persecutions they will suffer. It is also possible that there is no specific complaint but that Paul is merely reminding the Thessalonians of the kind of life that he lived among them as a way to encourage them to live a similarly authentic life.

The second section of the Body of the letter (4:1—5:25) consists of ethical exhortations and instructions on how to live out their faith. The ethical exhortations consist of a reminder of what Paul taught them previously and exhortations to keep themselves sanctified, to love one another, and to refrain from idleness. The instructions have to do with the Second Coming of Jesus. Paul tells them that the dead will not miss the Second Coming and reminds them that Christ's coming will be like a thief in the night.

World in front of the Text

Suffering with Christ

An important theme in Paul's letter to the Thessalonians is the suffering that both he and they endure for the gospel. Paul argues that they are imitators of him and of Jesus in the fact that they receive the word of God in affliction as well as with joy and the Holy Spirit (1:6). He tells them that they were destined (by God) for this and that he warned them in advance. We cannot expect to experience the world in the same way as Paul or have the world react to us in the same way that it did to Christians in the first century. However, Paul's letter to the Christians at Thessalonica should give modern first-world Christians pause when they consider how little they suffer because of their faith. The question that should challenge modern Christians is: has the world become so much more tolerant or accepting of the gospel message of Jesus, or have Christians become so assimilated into the world that we do not preach the true gospel that would bring down affliction and persecution on us? There are no simple answers to these questions, but they need to be asked and courageously grappled with if we are to be true to the gospel and to our brother Paul.

1 THESSALONIANS 4:13–18

World behind the Text

Apocalyptic Expectation

As we noted earlier, an important aspect of Paul's preaching to his new converts was the return of Jesus at the end of the age. Paul understood that God had intervened in history with the resurrection of Jesus and that this marked the inauguration of the end time when all the dead would be raised. The Christians at Thessalonica came to expect that Christ would return in their lifetime and that being there for his return to share in his triumph was part of their reward for faithfulness. So when members of the community died (in Greek Paul speaks of those "who have fallen asleep," a common euphemism for death) before the return of Christ, it caused a problem for the community. It seemed to some that these faithful Christians were going to miss the joyous victory of Christ.

A Word of the Lord

Paul tells the Thessalonians that what he has to tell them is "the word of the Lord." Does he mean that he is quoting a saying of the earthly Jesus, or does he mean that he has received a prophetic word of the Lord about this particular situation? A further problem has to do with which part of this teaching Paul understands as "the word of the Lord." Is the word of the Lord simply the statement that those left alive will not precede those who have died, or is the word of the Lord the entire image of the Second Coming? If we take the word to refer to the whole image, Paul could mean that he is quoting a known saying of the historical Jesus. The image of the return of Jesus is found in the Synoptic Gospels. In Mark 13:26 (and parallels) Jesus quotes Daniel 7:13 (about the Son of man coming in the clouds) in reference to himself. Therefore, Paul could be simply saying that the return of Christ from heaven was predicted by Jesus. But would it have been necessary to inform or remind the Thessalonians that Jesus spoke of his Second Coming? However, if "the word of the Lord" refers only to the statement that those who are left alive at the Second Coming will not precede those who have died (which is the real answer to the Thessalonians' problem), then it seems that it must be a prophetic message received by Paul from the risen Jesus. There is no saying like this in any of the gospels. Paul seems intent to answer the Thessalonians' concerns by telling them of "the word of the Lord" that they do not know about. Therefore, it is best to understand "the word of the Lord" as a prophetic revelation given to Paul that refers only to the fact that the living will not precede the dead at the Second Coming.

The Parousia

To counteract their disillusionment and fear, Paul uses an image drawn from the cult of the emperor. When the emperor returned from a battle or a state visit he would assemble his entourage some miles from the city, and the people of the city would come out to welcome him home. The people would process with the emperor back into the city with trumpets, banners, singing, and dancing. The emperor would symbolically reassert his authority and rule over the city. This event was called a "parousia." Paul uses both the term and the image to describe Christ's return to reclaim his authority over the world. Because Christ was in heaven at the Father's right hand, his return would be vertical and not horizontal. Paul therefore pictures Christians going up into the air to meet Christ and march with him down to the earth to assert his authority. As this parousia required a raising up into the sky for all, it was no problem for the dead Christians first to be raised up from the dead to join all the rest of the Christians who then together would be raised up into the sky to meet Christ.

World of the Text

Those Who Have Died Have a Central Place in the Parousia

The text begins with a statement of the problem as Paul sees it: the Christians are unaware of what will happen to those who die and are therefore grieving. Paul makes the comment that the Christians are acting like pagans who have no hope (4:13). Then Paul gives his argument in the form of an "if-then" clause. Paul tells them that if they believe that God raised Jesus (which is the most central belief of every Christian) then they should also believe that God will raise all Christians who die. Paul's main point is that there should be no difference between believing that God's power raised Jesus from the dead and believing that God's power will also raise all Christians from the dead. Paul uses the same argument in his letter to the Corinthians (1 Cor 15:12–19). Then Paul goes on to give an example of what this will be like (1 Thess 4:15–17). The image has a concentric structure to it that gives precedence to those who have died. Paul begins by saying that (a) we who are alive until the coming of the Lord will not precede (b) those who have fallen asleep. For (c) the Lord will come down from heaven with archangel and trumpet and (b') the dead in Christ will rise first and then (a') we who are left will be caught up with them to meet the Lord in the air. The reader can see that Paul presents the image in such a way that the center is the coming of the Lord from heaven accompanied by apocalyptic signs (angel and trumpet). On both sides of the central figure of Christ are those who have died who are given precedence in being raised from the dead first. Finally, those who are alive until the end will join in being raised up to heaven to meet the Lord and march back with him down to earth. In its literary structure, this text shows the disillusioned and fearful Thessalonian community that those who die will in no way miss the blessings of the Second Coming of Christ.

> The literary structure of the image of Christ's return helps make the point that those who have died will not miss out but will be at the center of the action.

World in front of the Text

The Rapture

The word Paul uses to describe the raising up of both the living and the dead into the air to be with Christ (to march back down to earth) is *harpaxo*. The word means to be carried off or caught up and refers to the power of God that will transport all to be with Christ to march into the world. In his Latin translation of the New Testament, St. Jerome translates this word into Latin as *rapiemur*. Influenced by the Book of Revelation, some interpreted this passage in 1 Thessalonians in such a way that being caught up into heaven was understood as a final liberation or salvation. The "rapture" (from the Latin word *rapiemur*) referred to the time when Christians (both the living and the dead) would be snatched up into heaven to be with Christ and thus be delivered from the terrible plagues inflicted on those on earth by the wrath of God. It should be clear from our study of

1 Thessalonians 4 that this interpretation is a significant depar-
ture from what Paul intended. Paul himself does not understand
being "caught up" as being delivered from the evil world and its
final death throes. Paul sees being "caught up" as being joined
to the heavenly procession that will come down to earth to celebrate the rule of God in Christ. There is nothing in this text,
or even most other texts of Paul, that speaks of any terrible punishments or plagues that the world is to suffer (such as those in
the Book of Revelation). The "rapture" is the creation of a community in front of the text that has a negative view of the world
and sees the only hope for Christ's reign in the destruction of the
world and its inhabitants. This is not the view of Paul or of most
Christian traditions.

The challenge for modern Christians is how to take seriously the apocalyptic expectation of Paul. Some wish to rush to
a full-blown catastrophic apocalypse with wars between angels
and devils and numerous plagues and cosmic destruction.
Others see no value whatsoever in this kind of language and
believe it to be a demented worldview. The challenge for a serious reader of Paul is to find the deeper truth in Paul's assurance
that the power of God is able to bring about not only the resurrection of Christ, but also the resurrection of dead Christians,
and the resurrection of the world. The challenge of
1 Thessalonians 4 is: How can we become readers who are convinced by Paul's arguments to trust in a God who brings life out
of death when we live in a world that "grieves" (has no hope for
a truly liberated and loving future with God)?

Learning Achievements

After studying this chapter, students should be able to:

- Summarize the life of Paul of Tarsus.

- Describe the cultural and religious situation of the Roman Empire.

- Explain the form of Paul's letters and some features of Greek rhetoric, especially diatribe.

- Discuss the apocalyptic expectation of Paul and early Christians.

- Explain why Paul wrote the letter to the Romans.

- Define the meanings of "righteousness of God" and "faith of Christ."

- Explain Paul's argument for the resurrection of Christians.

- Explain where Paul gets the image of parousia and the new meaning Paul gives to it.

Recommended Reading

Bassler, Jouette, ed. *Pauline Theology*. vol. 1. Minneapolis: Fortress, 1991.

Johnson, Luke Timothy. *Reading Romans: A Literary and Theological Commentary*. New York: Crossroad, 1997.

Murphy-O'Connor, Jerome. *Paul: A Critical Life*. New York: Oxford University Press, 1996.

Roetzel, Calvin. *The Letters of Paul: Conversations in Context*. Louisville, Ky.: Westminster John Knox, 1998.

Wright, N. T. *What Saint Paul Really Said: Was Paul of Tarsus the Real Founder of Christianity?* Grand Rapids, Mich.: Eerdmans, 1997.

Chapter 10
LATER NEW TESTAMENT WRITINGS

Introduction

World behind the Text

The writings in this section, often called the "Catholic Letters," reflect the "churches the apostles left behind," to use a phrase from Raymond Brown. These writings (Hebrews, James, 1 Peter, 2 Peter, 1 John, 2 John, 3 John, Jude, and Revelation) reflect the generation after the epistles and gospels. The three letters of John, although probably not written by the author of the Gospel of John, are clearly in that tradition and written for communities that used the Gospel of John. The Book of Revelation is considered part of the Johannine School of writings because of shared images and themes. 1 Peter has many connections to the Pauline letters, but also seems indebted to 1 John and James. 2 Peter presents itself as the second letter of Peter but is much later than 1 Peter and not consistent with it in theme or style. The letter of James is not a real letter but is a piece of moral exhortation. It is dependent on the synoptic sayings of Jesus, but cannot be placed in the school of any one gospel. The letter to the Hebrews comes out of a very distinct tradition in the early church, but it too is related to the letters of Paul and the synoptic gospels.

World of the Text

The only real connection between any of these documents is among the three letters of John, all of which come out of the Johannine community. Whether they all have the same author is another question. Otherwise, there is no unity to this collection of writings. Unlike the other six sections of the Bible we have studied so far, these are an unrelated and heterogeneous group of writings. Hebrews is first in this collection because it was associated with the Pauline letters that come before it. Revelation is placed at the end because it was understood as a prediction of the end time and because it was the last of the books to be accepted into the canon.

World in front of the Text

As a whole, how might these documents speak to readers today? Perhaps what they offer to us is some alternative voices in the New Testament. It is not the case that the gospels and letters of Paul are all of one mind, but these later works offer even more variety and offer a glimpse of the development of the early church. They even provide a commentary on the previous works. Commentators have long maintained that 1 John serves as an orthodox interpretation of the Gospel of John, which permitted that gospel's inclusion into the canon. These books can help us see the challenges faced by the early church and see the various solutions offered.

1 Peter

INTRODUCTION

World behind the Text

Peter, an Author?

There are numerous problems with maintaining that the apostle Peter is the author of this letter. First, the Greek of the letter is some of the best in the New Testament. Although Peter may not have been illiterate, it is unlikely that he could have been able to write like this. Second, there is nothing in the letter that would indicate that its author had spent any time in the company of Jesus, much less being such a close associate as Simon Peter was. Third, the author of the letter seems to be familiar with some of Paul's letters, especially the later Pauline letter of Ephesians. Fourth, the letter claims to be written from Babylon (1 Pet 5:13) and is addressed to five provinces in Asia Minor. Almost certainly, the reference to Babylon is a code name for Rome. This symbolic use of Babylon for Rome was not used until after the fall of Jerusalem to Rome in 70 C.E. (Jerusalem having fallen to Babylon in 586 B.C.E.). This would put the letter after the accepted date for the martyrdom of Peter. Rome as the place of origin might explain the use of Peter as a pseudonym. It is likely that Peter spent some time in Rome and probably was martyred there. Even though the letter is probably written sometime after 70 C.E., it is not as late as others of the later writings. The structure of the community that is presumed by the letter does not seem as developed and hierarchical as the later letters of 1 Timothy, Titus, and James.

Institutionalization of the Church

One of the features of the later documents of the New Testament is that they chronicle the institutionalization of the church. The earliest communities seem to have had very little structure, and what leadership roles there were, were charismatic. In the later Pauline letters to the Ephesians, Timothy, and Titus, the letters of John, and the letters of Peter, we see a developing church structure. Bishops are overseers and administrators of the larger community of a city or province. The bishops are in charge of appointing elders (presbyters) and deacons who are responsible for the running of the life of the local churches. There would seem to be a group of elders appointed for each city. In the early Pauline communities, there was a broader distribution of authority, in teachers, apostles, prophets, healers, and deacons (see especially 1 Cor 12:28; Rom 12:6–8). The community of 1 Peter is in the transitional stage between the structure of a community at the time of Paul and a later community such as that reflected in 1 Timothy or Titus. Elders/presbyters lead the community, but it is not clear that they are a select group appointed by a bishop. Rather the elders/presbyters in the community of 1 Peter are made up of all those who have been Christians for a substantial amount of time and who have gained wisdom and maturity in Christ. They are contrasted with the younger members of the community (5:5).

Strangers and Aliens

The author of 1 Peter refers to the members of the five communities as exiles, strangers, and aliens. Is this description to be taken literally to mean that the majority of the community were outsiders and transients whose place of origin was not in Asia Minor? Or is to be understood metaphorically as referring to the fact that Christians have a true home with God and are in exile now on earth? There is some metaphorical language in 1 Peter that refers to the inheritance kept for the believer in heaven (1:4). However, it is likely that the author is referring to the real situation of the community as socially, economically, and politically marginalized, irrespective of whether they were originally from the area. Given that one whole section of the text is directed to slaves, it might be the case that a sizable number of the community were in fact aliens (slaves were frequently, but not necessarily, from another country). Whether one was an alien or not, conversion to Christianity from paganism caused severe social disruption. Christian converts might no longer be able to work for the patron under whom they had previously served (because of requirements to partake in idolatrous worship and meals). They might no longer be able to practice the craft by which they had previously made their living (most craft guilds were intimately connected with the worship of gods or goddesses and again required idolatrous worship and meals).

The Christian community identified itself as a family, with members being brothers and sisters to each other, and teachers being mother or father to new members. The Christian community provided an alternative family to the convert because conversion often meant being ostracized from one's family. So even if many of the members of the communities of Asia Minor to which 1 Peter is addressed were natives of the communities in which they lived, they would still have experienced themselves as strangers and aliens. They would have been exiles sojourning in a foreign country, not sojourning in the material world waiting for heaven, but sojourning among unbelievers in a world that was powered by idolatry, while at the same time belonging to a new family with a new Lord.

285

Persecution of Early Christianity

There are many references in 1 Peter to the suffering and persecution endured by the recipients. They seem to have been suffering financially, socially, and even physically for their faith, even though there was not a widespread and officially sanctioned persecution of Christians until about 250 C.E. At the time of 1 Peter (roughly, 90 C.E.), Christians were considered disturbers of the peace and antisocial. They kept separate from other members of the cities and towns in which they lived. The evidence we have from the period shows that Christians were not persecuted for being Christians *per se*. It was not illegal to worship a new God. Christians were persecuted for their refusal to show reverence and worship for the gods of the empire, their refusal to take part in military service, their refusal to take part in meals and festivals that involved worship of gods, and their setting themselves apart from the rest of the people. They were accused of being haters of humanity, of being involved in sexual orgies (that were considered incestuous because they called each other brother and sister), and even of cannibalism. They were an easy target for litigation and punishment when anything went wrong. Natural disasters were often attributed to the fact that they had given offense to the gods.

World of the Text

Some scholars question the unity of 1 Peter because 4:11 seems to be a concluding doxology. These commentators suggest that 4:12—5:13 was written later by another author when the situation of persecution became worse. However, most feel that 4:11 merely ends a section of the letter and is not meant to be the conclusion of the letter. The situation of persecution described in 4:12–19 is probably not different from the situation described in the rest of the letter.

The Body can be divided into 2 main parts: 1:3—4:11 is a more liturgical exhortation on living in the community, and 4:12—5:11 contains specific advice on particular issues. The first part can also be divided into two sections: 1:3—2:10 contains the theological background for what the author will have to say, and 2:11—

4:11 contains the exhortation that flows from the beliefs. The first part includes a number of references to baptism and so may have been a baptismal sermon or training manual.

Outline of 1 Peter

Salutation 1:1–2

Body 1:3—5:11

    Part I—Baptismal Exhortation 1:3—4:11

    A—Theological Background 1:3—2:10

    B—Exhortation on Living in the World 2:11—4:11

    Part II—Advice on Persecution and Internal Order
        4:12—5:11

Closing 5:12–13

Household Code

The exhortation on living in the world (Part I, section B) is a *household code*, a form of teaching common in Hellenistic literature and in the New Testament. A household code gives advice on how the main relationships in a household should work: master, slave; parent, child; husband, wife. Often the relationship of the household to the larger community (the local government or the empire) is also included. In chapter 2, vv. 13–17 advise Christians to be good subjects to the emperor and governors, and vv. 18–25 advise Christians who are slaves on how to act toward their masters. In chapter 3, vv. 1–7 advise Christian wives how to deal with their (probably pagan) husbands and Christian husbands how to treat their wives. Verses 8–12 are about the relations of all members in the community. It is also possible to understand 5:1–7 as imitating the household code by giving advice to presbyters (parents) and to younger members (children) within the family context of the Christian community. In using the Hellenistic household code as part of Christian exhortation, 1 Peter shows itself as most similar to Ephesians (to which it shows many other similarities) and Colossians. Even in Paul's authentic letters (e.g., Corinthians), pieces of household codes are used.

World in front of the Text

"Family Values"

Taken out of context, the advice we find in the household codes of the New Testament, especially here in 1 Peter, can seem reactionary and having very little to offer us today. The statement, "Wives, in the same way, accept the authority of your husbands," does not fit very well in the twenty-first century. However, it is possible to look at the household code in 1 Peter in a different light and see that it has much to say to us today. 1 Peter gives us a picture of what it meant to make the choice to become a follower of Jesus Christ in the late first century C.E. in Asia Minor (and probably in most of the Roman Empire). Becoming a follower of Christ had major economic, social, political, and familial consequences. One's whole life was changed. It was likely that one became estranged from one's family, lost one's job and friends, and could no longer belong to the clubs and social organizations one formerly did. In almost all ways, the new Christian became a "man without a country." In exchange for that, the new Christian became a member of a new family that was structured in a totally different way than the surrounding society. This new family was much more egalitarian and was based on service and love. Members sought the good of the other and did not seek to gain honor at the expense of an opponent, as they had done in the outside world.

Christians today should read 1 Peter and wonder why modern Christians live not in a Christian family but in the world. For most Christians today, nothing changes in their lives because they are Christian. They have the same jobs and friends. They are not estranged from family. They belong to the same clubs and go to the same bars and restaurants. It is true that worship of gods is not a part of the festivities at the country club or at meetings of the labor union. Nor do restaurants serve meat that is sacrificed to idols. Nonetheless we should ask ourselves whether the surrounding society is completely acceptable to Christ's vision of the kingdom. Are our "families" and our "family values" determined by the surrounding culture or by the life and message of Christ?

A question to ask is how does the social dislocation of being a Christian as described in 1 Peter translate into our world today?

---

1 PETER 3:13–22

World behind the Text

Persecution in Asia Minor

1 Peter 3:14 speaks of suffering for doing what is right. In 3:17 it says that it is better to suffer for doing good than for doing evil. The author has in mind the suffering that the members of the community endure because of the accusations being made against Christians for being antisocial and blasphemous or for engaging in orgies and cannibalism. To suffer for doing what is right meant to suffer because one kept oneself apart from idolatry and the debauchery that accompanied idolatry (see 4:3). The author was exhorting the members of the community to be ready to give an explanation for their hope instead of denying that they were Christians. This is not because being a Christian was against the law but because it was associated in the popular imagination with lawlessness and antisocial behavior.

Noah and the Flood

The author of 1 Peter uses the story of the flood as part of his argument. In Genesis 7:21–23, the Yahwist writer tells how all living beings, including all humans, were wiped out by the flood. Only Noah, his wife, and his three sons and their wives (eight in all) were saved. The author of 1 Peter interprets the drowning of all humans on earth as a kind of baptism, but not a baptism that cleansed the people (3:19–20). Their baptism was rather a cry for help. The flood, for the author of 1 Peter, is unfinished business. The drowning of humans was a cry for help that is now answered by Christ. It was the first half of a baptism—being dunked under water. In Christ, the second half of their baptism—being raised out of the water—will occur.

> Notice how the author of 1 Peter does not interpret the story of the flood in its literal or obvious sense. He uses the hermeneutical lens of baptism to argue that the drowning of these humans was not final punishment but was the first part of a baptism to raise them to eternal life. This allows him to conclude that the flood was not final punishment but the beginning of salvation.

Baptism

In 3:21 the author speaks of the prefigured baptism that saves the Christian. The author notes that baptism (probably by immersion) is not meant to be a removal of dirt from the body but is an appeal to God for a clear conscience through the resurrection of Jesus Christ. This is similar to Paul's understanding of baptism as expressed in Romans 6. Baptism is a matter of being freed from sin (clear conscience) by the death/resurrection of Jesus Christ. The author sees that the baptism of the Christian in being submerged in water and dying to sin and being resurrected to a clear conscience in Christ is prefigured in the lives of those who were drowned in the flood at the time of Noah. It seems that the author is saying that Christ, coming to life in the Spirit, could also preach to the spirits of those drowned at the time of Noah and imprisoned in the underworld. These have died, but Christ can bring their spirits to life because he is now living in the Spirit. The fate of the contemporaries of Noah prefigures the baptism of Christians who are drowned and die in the flesh but are raised to new life by Christ in the Spirit.

World of the Text

Part of the Household of God

The text we are studying comes at the end of what is called the household code. The household code is introduced in 2:13 with a discussion of the way members of the community should be in relationship with the rulers of the empire. The next three sections deal with relations of master and slave (2:18–25), husband and wife (3:1–7), and member to member in the community (3:8–12). Our text returns to the issue of the way the Christian must relate to the outside community.

Structure and Meaning of the Text

The text has two parts: 3:13–17 is about the persecution and suffering a Christian endures and the kind of attitude the Christian should have toward that suffering, and 3:18–22 describes Jesus' suffering on behalf of all and how baptism is a sharing in his death/resurrection that brings about a clear conscience. The connection between the two parts is not entirely clear, but the author may be arguing that the Christian's suffering can positively affect his or her persecutors just as Jesus' death and resurrection affected all. In 4:4 the author says that outsiders will be surprised at the way Christians act. 1 Peter 4:6 implies that "the dead" (probably those drowned in the flood) will receive salvation ("live in the spirit as God does"). In 2:12 the author advises, "Conduct yourselves honorably among the Gentiles, so that, though they malign you as evildoers, they may see your honorable deeds and glorify God when he comes to judge." The fact that our text juxtaposes the persecution of Christians and the salvific death of Jesus leads to the conclusion that the suffering of persecuted Christians is in some way salvific for their persecutors. Just as God was patient with those who sinned and were drowned at the time of Noah by later sending Christ in the Spirit to preach to their spirits and so bring them to salvation, so also God will be patient with those in the present who accuse Christians of being evildoers and who persecute them. God will use the patient suffering and good works of the Christian to eventually bring about the salvation of the persecutors. It is the juxtaposition of the exhortation to persevere in persecution with the image of baptism for those of Noah's time and the meaning of baptism for the Christian that allows the author to make this amazing point about Christian suffering.

> The reader must pay careful attention to the juxtaposition of images and other textual clues to appreciate the point that the author is making.

World in front of the Text

God's Patience beyond Death

The death of the people in Noah's time is seen as a prefigured baptism and is attributed to the patience of God. Christ in the Spirit goes even to the dead spirits to preach the good news. This might challenge us to see the power of God on a wider and deeper plane. Our thinking tends to be very time bound. We think that during our life we get one chance to get it right. This text challenges our thinking. Time and space do not limit the power of God to reveal the good news and raise people to new life.

The Power of Nonviolent Resistance

Another important insight in this text is that those who suffer for doing what is right, by reacting to hatred and persecution with gentleness and reverence, do what Christ did in dying for sinners. The nonviolent response of Christians will put their oppressors to shame. This is not another way of taking vengeance on them, but a way of making them recognize where true goodness lies, even if that recognition does not come until the day when God comes to judge. Enduring persecution is an act of preaching the gospel that has power to transform the persecutors.

Revelation

INTRODUCTION

World behind the Text

Author and Date

In the greeting of the letter to the seven churches in Asia at the beginning of the Book of Revelation, the author identifies himself as John. Traditionally John, the author of Revelation, was equated with the author of the Gospel of John who was believed to be John the son of Zebedee, one of the twelve apostles of Jesus. It is now clear that the author of Revelation is not the same person as the author of the Gospel of John. Because there is no attempt by the author of Revelation to equate himself with John the son of Zebedee, with the Beloved Disciple, or with the author of the Gospel of John, scholars believe that the author is using his own name and not a pseudonym. A person by the name of John, who appears to be well known to the churches of Asia, is the author of this letter/revelation.

The author tells us that he found himself "on the island called Patmos because of the word of God and the testimony of Jesus" (1:9). It was commonly thought that Patmos (which is in the Aegean Sea between Greece and Asia Minor) must have been used as a prison and John had been imprisoned there because of his witness to Jesus. However, scholars now find this explanation doubtful. There is no evidence of imprisonment on Patmos, or anywhere else, as a form of punishment. Prisons were used only to hold prisoners until their trials. After the trial the prisoner was released, fined, exiled, or executed. Imprisonment was not a form of punishment in the Roman Empire. So, why is John on the island of Patmos? We do not know. John may have gone to Patmos on a missionary trip or he may have gone there to escape persecution on the mainland. The churches to which Revelation is written are all in the western part of Asia Minor near the Aegean.

There is very little to go on in trying to date this work. Irenaeus says that it was written during the time of the emperor Domitian (81–96 C.E.). In the book itself, the author speaks of Babylon when referring to Rome. The connection between Rome and Babylon was made because Rome destroyed Jerusalem and the Temple in 70 C.E. just as Babylon had done in 586 B.C.E. It is therefore fairly certain that the book was written after the fall of Jerusalem in 70 C.E. Scholars speculate that the date for Revelation is about 90–95 C.E., during the last years of Domitian's reign.

Background and Purpose: Persecution or Threat of Assimilation

Even though Eusebius claims that Christians were persecuted during the final years of the reign of Domitian, there is no evidence to suggest a widespread, state-sanctioned persecution of Christians during that period. During Nero's reign, Christians were blamed for the burning of Rome and persecuted (64 C.E.). Since that time, Christians suffered only localized persecution and social ostracization. The descriptions of Domitian in certain Roman writings of the period, which portray him as a cruel and tyrannical megalomaniac who demanded that he be hailed as "lord and god," were thought to indicate that a severe and widespread persecution of Christians was likely. However, these writings are from the reign of the next emperor and are intent to show that the old age of the Flavian emperors (Domitian being the last) is at an end and the new age of the Antonine emperors (beginning with Trajan) has begun. These writers had reason to paint Domitian as negatively as possible. Writings from the actual reign of Domitian do not indicate that he was extraordinary in his cruelty nor that he demanded the use of the titles "lord" and "god." For these reasons, most modern scholars do not believe that the Book of Revelation was written in response to a crisis of severe persecution of the Christian communities. Instead, they believe that John was trying to make a powerful argument for the way Christians should relate to the Roman Empire. Only forty or so years earlier Paul wrote to communities in the same geographical area. His advice was to respect and obey Roman power (Rom 13:1–7) and not to worry about eating meat sacrificed to idols unless it caused the weaker Christians to be scandalized (1 Cor 10:25–30). John of Revelation, however, saw an unbridgeable rift between the ethos of the Roman Empire and that of the Christian community. There could be no accommodation to this world ruled by Satan. For John, the power and wealth of the empire was proving to be a greater stumbling block and opponent to the gospel than was envisioned by Paul and other early Christians. John explicitly attacked members of the communities to which he was writing who practiced and taught accommodation with the empire (Rev 2:14–15, 20–23). John was concerned not because the community was suffering severe persecution and martyrdom (only Antipas is mentioned as a martyr in 2:13) but because the community had become lax (2:4; 3:1–4, 15–19). So although there may not have been a severe persecution of Christians during the time of the writing of Revelation, the author of Revelation considered the situation a crisis. Christians were under attack by the empire, even if the weapons were not swords.

World of the Text

The Genre of Apocalypse

The word *revelation* is the English translation of the Greek word *apocalypsis*, the word the author uses to describe his work. The word is now used to refer to all the Jewish and Christian texts from this period (200 B.C.E. to 200 C.E.), which share certain characteristics. (Included in these writings are 1 Enoch, Daniel 7–12, Jubilees, 4 Ezra, 2 Baruch, and the Isaiah Apocalypse.) Scholars have developed a working definition of the genre of apocalypse based on the characteristics of these works. An *apocalypse* is a revelation about a future time and a new order that is given to a human seer through the mediation of an angel interpreter.

Revelation is classed as an apocalypse because it is the account of a revelation received by the seer in a heavenly vision. The material of the revelation could not be known by humans other than by this special revelation. The revelation includes a vision of the throne of God and God's attending angels and is symbolic in describing the action of God. Symbolic meanings for animals and numbers occur throughout the book. Also, the revelation has to do with the direct intervention of God in history. Often in apocalypses, there are descriptions of great natural and supernatural disasters.

Without a doubt, the Book of Revelation should be read as an example of the genre of apocalypse, but many characteristics of this book set it apart from the rest of the genre. First, most apocalypses are pseudonymous, claiming to be written by a famous person of the past and making use of "prophecy after the fact."

Some great hero of the past is given a revelation of the events that will happen in the future (the future for the past hero is the past and present for the real author). This hero writes it down, and the reader in the real author's own time finds that in fact all of these events have happened just as it was revealed. Thus, the reader trusts that the message of the book that points ahead to a still unfulfilled future will also come true. In contrast to this apocalyptic technique, the author of Revelation is a well-known prophet of the community who uses his own name and his own prophetic charism to support the claims he is making on the community. He does not give a review of history purporting to be telling the future. In this area, at least, Revelation has more in common with prophecy than with apocalypticism.

Second, no other apocalypse uses the Old Testament the way Revelation does. In the four hundred verses of Revelation, there are approximately five hundred twenty allusions to the Old Testament, but no direct quotations of scripture. Revelation presents the Christ event as the fulfillment of all of Old Testament prophecy. No other apocalypse so thoroughly understands itself as the fulfillment of scripture.

Third, Revelation is more concerned with what has happened in Christ than with some future intervention of God. Other apocalypses try to predict a future intervention of God and give a review of history leading up to that intervention. Revelation describes the intervention as having taken place already. The Lamb who was slain has received the kingdom of God. In many ways, the Book of Revelation turns apocalyptic imagery on its head. For the author of Revelation, the intervention of God has already taken place and in a way that was unexpected.

Finally, the most distinct feature of the Book of Revelation, in terms of genre, is that it begins with an open letter to seven specific churches. This letter does not seem to be fictional or general, but a concrete and real letter. John is familiar with the life and struggles of these communities. Whereas the historical situation at the time of the writing of other apocalypses is often hidden in the metaphorical language of those revelations, in the letter to the seven churches in the Book of Revelation we are given a glimpse of the real situation of the communities of late first-century Asia

Minor. Although the letter serves as an introduction to the book, the genre of the book as a whole is still more of an apocalypse than it is a letter.

Structure of Revelation

The most notable feature of the Book of Revelation is its collections of sevens. There are the seven churches, the seven seals, the seven trumpets, and the seven bowls. It is possible to outline the book as a series of these groupings of seven.

Prologue 1:1–8
I. The Seven Churches 1:9—3:22
II. The Seven Seals 4:1—8:1
III. The Seven Trumpets 8:2—11:19
IV. The Seven Bowls 12:1—22:5
Epilogue 22:6–21

One problem with such an outline is that its parts are not comparable in size. The section on the seven bowls constitutes ten chapters, whereas the other sections constitute only three or four chapters. The outline also does not account for all the complexity of the text, given that there are many other elements of the vision that do not fit into the groupings of seven. A number of scholars add two, three, or four unnumbered series of seven visions to these four groupings, although this is doubtful because the author does not indicate this. However, this outline based on groupings of seven does allow us to see the repetition inherent in Revelation. Some have seen the separate groups of seven as describing the same event and reality in different ways. This is the theory of **recapitulation.** Others see the separate groups as describing successive historical events. Recapitulation is the more dominant theory for understanding the Book of Revelation.

Another repeated element that has been used to define the structure of the book is the scroll. As part of the inaugural vision in 5:1, the seer sees a scroll in the hand of God. There is a search for one worthy to open the scroll. Eventually, it is revealed that the Lamb who was slain is worthy to open the scroll. Then begins the opening of the seven seals on the scroll.

After the blowing of the seven trumpets, the seer in 10:2 sees an angel descend from heaven with a small scroll (already opened) in his hand. The seer is told to eat the scroll and is commanded to prophesy again about many peoples and nations. Finally, in 20:12 another scroll is opened that is described as the book of life. It is possible to see Revelation as structured around these three scrolls. Chapters 4—9 represent the mysteries of the past (Old Testament) that have been revealed and fulfilled only in the death/resurrection of Jesus, whereas chapters 10—20 represent the new things that are happening as God brings about the kingdom of God. This includes the defeat of God's enemies, the dragon, and the beasts. Finally, chapters 20—22 describe the coming situation of the kingdom of God realized.

A third way to define the structure of Revelation is by topic. The first section of Revelation has to do with a description of God and Christ and the heavenly realm. The second section describes the dragon, the beasts, Babylon, and the fallen earthly realm. The third section returns (mostly) to a description of the future rule of God after the victory over the dragon and the beasts. The earthly realm is now united with the heavenly realm. We can see that this is quite similar to the structure suggested by the scrolls.

World in front of the Text

Dispensationalism and Millennialism

It should be noted that in the Eastern churches, Greek Orthodox and Syrian, the Book of Revelation is not considered canonical. In the Roman church the book has always been the subject of speculation and criticism. Numerous early church fathers believed that it should not be included in the canon. Controversy over the book has not lessened today. In our own time the book has been interpreted as a symbolically coded description of the events of history, usually with the focus on present events. This mode of interpretation is called *dispensationalism*, because it sees God working in seven different ages (dispensations). The present time is the seventh dispensation.

The events symbolically portrayed in the book refer to contemporary events.

There is also a tendency to read the book with a focus on the one thousand–year reign of Christ mentioned in 20:1–10. This mode of interpretation is called *millennialism*. There are premillenarianists and postmillenarianists depending on whether this one thousand–year reign begins with the Second Coming of Christ or ends with it. Millenarianist interpretations are faulty on three counts. First, they make the one thousand–year reign of Christ mentioned in 20:1–10 the main focus of the book, and it definitely is not. The one thousand–year reign is symbolic of the beginning of Christ's reign that will be enjoyed first by his followers before being extended to the entire world, although the focus of the book is on the victory of Christ and the defeat of human empire.

Second, millenarianists interpret the symbolism in the Book of Revelation as referring to a specific person or event, usually in the interpreter's own time. The symbolism of Revelation at a primary level does refer to persons or events of the author's own time, but is meant to be multivalent—referring to many possible persons and events. So, Babylon refers first to Rome but also to any and all human empires. A millenarianist interpretation would want to equate Babylon with one particular nation in the present time. Millenarianist interpretations seek to make the one thousand–year reign of Christ a literally dated one thousand years, which is not the intent of the author.

Third, these interpretations are always ideological and serve to promote not the victory of Christ but the political agenda of the interpreters. The symbolism of Revelation is so rich that almost any person or nation could be identified as the dragon, beast, or Babylon. The particular interpretation is chosen because the interpreter wants to make a particular identification and not because the symbolism points unequivocally to that identification.

REVELATION 14:14–20

World behind the Text

Angels in Apocalyptic Literature

Angels are common in apocalyptic literature. We find that after the Babylonian Exile, the Jews developed a much more extensive angelology, probably from Persian influence. In apocalyptic literature, there are two parallel worlds: the heavenly realm and the earthly realm. Often in apocalyptic literature, the same conflict between God's people and her enemies is staged in heaven as a conflict between the angels of God's people and the angels of the foreign nation (see Daniel 10). In the Book of Revelation, angels represent the divine will and presence and are on the side of God's people. However, the angels serve the function of destruction and cataclysm but only as it represents the will of God in judgment. The opposing forces in the heavenly realm are represented by the dragon and the beasts, and perhaps by some of the stars of heaven.

The Danielic Son of Man

Verse 14 describes the appearance of one like the Son of man on a white cloud, an image taken from the Book of Daniel. In Daniel 7 the Son of man is a messianic/angelic figure who comes before the throne of God at the end of time and receives dominion over the whole world. In Daniel this figure represents the holy nation of Israel. In Revelation 5 we are introduced to a similar picture of the royal court of God and the handing over of dominion to the Messianic figure, but in Revelation 5 the figure is the Lamb that was slaughtered and not one like the Son of man. At the beginning of chapter 14 we again have the Lamb surrounded by 144,000 followers. Only then are we introduced to the one like the Son of man. It would seem that John wishes us to make the connection between the Lamb and the Son of man, but also to recognize that he has reinterpreted the traditional understanding of one like the Son of man in terms of the Lamb that was slaughtered. This will be important for our interpretation of the passage.

The author uses traditional apocalyptic images, such as the Son of man, but reinvents them in new and surprising ways. The victorious warrior Son of man of Daniel becomes in Revelation the Lamb that was slaughtered.

The Wrath of God

The "wrath of God" in Revelation 14 seems out of step with the rest of the New Testament and so needs careful interpretation. It will be helpful for us to see how Paul uses the term *wrath (orge)* because it is possible that Revelation has a similar view. For Paul the wrath of God is much more a consequence of sin than an angry action that God takes in punishing with violence. In Romans 1:18, Paul says that "the wrath of God is revealed from heaven against all ungodliness and wickedness of those who by their wickedness suppress the truth." He goes on to describe, however, not actions of God in violently punishing people, but instead the sinful behavior of humans that leaves them in a situation of degradation. Paul says that "God gave them up in the lusts of their hearts to impurity, to the degrading of their bodies among themselves" (1:24). Or again Paul says that "God gave them up to a debased mind and to things that should not be done" (1:28). For Paul the wrath of God is what sinners (all humans) deserve at the final judgment and is already apparent in the degraded situation in which humans live. For Paul, however, God has priceless kindness, forbearance, and patience in the face of the wrath that humans are storing up for themselves (Rom 2:4–5). In the end God's wrath will be a victory over Sin, but will be the salvation of the sinner by forbearance and forgiveness (Rom 3:25–26). The wrath of God in Revelation can been seen in a similar way. Those who worship the beast (those who accept the idolatry, violence, and oppression of the empire) will drink the wine of God's wrath (14:9–10). When the ripe grapes are harvested and put into the great winepress of God's wrath, blood pours out to the height of a horse's bridle. It does not make sense that the wine of God's wrath that the idolaters drink is their own blood. In fact, in 14:10 it also says they will be tormented in burning sulfur before the holy angels and before the Lamb. The winepress is trodden outside the city (14:20). It seems more likely that the wine of wrath that the idolaters drink is the blood of the Lamb and of all the holy martyrs. This blood, which will overwhelm them and is the wrath of God, is the result of their own violence and degradation but is also a situation that can allow for their salvation.

World of the Text

Christ's Harvest

After seeing the Lamb on Mount Zion surrounded by his 144,000 followers, the seer notices another angel. In the following narrative the seer will see six angels and a figure like the Son of man. The first three angels make announcements about God, the fall of Babylon, and God's judgment. The image for the judgment of God is the wine of his wrath and burning sulfur. Then the figure like the Son of man appears and is given a sickle to reap the harvest. The fourth angel tells the Son of man figure to use his sickle to harvest the earth. The fifth angel also has a sickle and is instructed by the sixth angel (who is said to be in charge of the fire) to harvest the grapes of the earth.

We can see a clear correspondence between the two parts. In the first half (vv. 6–13) there is a statement of the positive judgment for those who fear God (v. 7) and a statement of the negative judgment in the destruction of Babylon (v. 8). The third angel describes the negative judgment in terms of drinking the wine of wrath and in suffering burning sulfur (v. 10). The positive judgment is described in terms of a promise of blessing in death and rest from labor (v. 13). In the second part (vv. 14–20) we have the fourth angel instructing the harvest of the earth, which is probably a positive judgment of harvesting the followers of Jesus (vv. 15–16). The fifth and sixth angels then represent the negative judgment in the wine of God's wrath and in fire (vv. 17–20).

Here it is important to see the correspondence between the two parts so that this jarring text is not misinterpreted. Many, even among scholars, assume that the blood that pours out in vv. 19–20 is the blood of the evil ones who are being killed by the wrath of God. Given the correspondence with the first part, however, it is more likely that the blood that pours out represents the death of Jesus and his followers that will be the judgment on the forces of the empire. In the first part, the enemies of God will drink the wine of God's wrath as a punishment. The blood that they have shed will be the punishment of God against them. In the second part, the blood rises to the height of a horse's bridle making it impossible for the horse to continue. It is possible that the blood of Jesus and his followers is pictured as impeding the horses of the empire in the same way that the Reed Sea flowing back against the Egyptians impeded their pursuit of the Hebrews. That this is meant to be the blood of Jesus is confirmed by the statement that the winepress was trodden outside the city, a clear reference to the death of Jesus outside the city (see Matt 21:39; John 19:17; Heb 13:12).

Son of Man

A second and related problem in this text is making sense of the overlapping imagery in Revelation. It is not always possible to have a clear view of what the author is doing. In 1:13, the seer has a vision of one like the Son of man, wearing a robe with a golden sash. In his right hand he holds seven stars. A two-edged sword comes out of his mouth and his face shines like the sun. In 5:6 the Lamb that was slaughtered is described as having seven horns and seven eyes (he is also called the Lion of Judah and the Root of David—royal, messianic titles). In 6:2 there is a rider on a white horse who has a bow. He is given a crown and rides forth victorious. In 14:14 there is one like the Son of man with a golden crown on his head and a sharp sickle in his hand. Finally in 19:11–16 there is a rider on a white horse whose robe is dipped in blood. His eyes are flames of fire; on his head are many diadems; and out of his mouth comes a sharp sword. He is called the Word of God, and it is said that he himself will tread the winepress of the fury of the wrath of God. Are all these the same figure, and are they all Christ? Very often, the rider in 6:2 is considered a symbol of the Parthian invasion of the Roman Empire and not a symbol of Christ. What is the purpose of the variation in images? Is the figure in our chapter just another angel, or is he Christ, the Lamb and Son of man? Does treading out the wine mean killing all God's enemies or does it mean dying and shedding one's own blood? Is the cloak of the rider in chapter 19 stained with his own or others' blood? In chapter 5, the Lamb that was slaughtered is said to have ransomed for God with his blood those from every tribe and language, people, and nation. Does the same figure ransom all nations with his blood and trod out the blood of some in a fit of rage? Or has the author of Revelation subverted the Old Testament images of God's wrath and final judgment, and the Old Testament and Jewish expectations of a nationalistic military messiah?

World in front of the Text

Violence

The violence in the Book of Revelation is one of the most confusing and disturbing features of this very difficult book. Because of it the book has been described as bloodthirsty and pagan. John the seer gives us a picture of the Lamb (a very passive figure) who was slaughtered and who is the one to share the throne of God, but he also has figures on horseback with swords and sickles. Which one is more central? Is Christ a suffering and nonviolent Messiah, or is he a vindictive and victorious warrior? The images of Christ as warrior leading his troops to destroy all those opposed to him has been used to defend some of the most shameful periods of Christian history—the Crusades, the Inquisition, the conquest of the Western Hemisphere. Is the book of two minds about Christ, or have we not been able to read it correctly because of our addiction to violence? There is increasing recognition that violence is one of the most deeply rooted sins of humankind, and it is violence that the Lamb of God has come to destroy—not by more violence but by a rejection of violence that brings the violent face to face with their own violence. The author of Revelation transforms the victorious military messiah into the nonviolent Lamb that was slaughtered. The destruction of God's enemies is accomplished through the self-defeating excesses of the enemies themselves as they confront the nonviolent resistors of the empire. The message is that violence, greed, oppression, and debauchery themselves destroy those caught in their web.

Learning Achievements

After studying this chapter, students should be able to:

• Describe the historical context of late first-century Christianity, including the persecution and ostracization that were suffered.

• Define a Hellenistic household code and describe how it was used in early Christian exhortation.

• Define the genre of Apocalypse.

• Outline the structure of the Book of Revelation with its repetition of seven and its three scrolls. The student should know what recapitulation means with reference to Revelation.

• Discuss the images for Christ used in Revelation, especially the Son of man and the Lamb.

Recommended Reading

Brown, Raymond. *The Churches the Apostles Left Behind*. New York: Paulist, 1984.

Elliot, John. *A Home for the Homeless: A Sociological Exegesis of 1 Peter: Its Situation and Strategy*. Philadelphia: Fortress, 1981.

Harrington, Wilfred J. *Revelation*. Sacra Pagina 16. Collegeville, Minn.: Liturgical Press, 1993.

Howard-Brook, Wes, and Anthony Gwyther. *Unveiling Empire: Reading Revelation Then and Now*. Maryknoll, N.Y.: Orbis, 1999.

Richard, Pablo. *Apocalypse: A People's Commentary on the Book of Revelation*. Maryknoll, N.Y.: Orbis, 1994.

GLOSSARY

aphorism. A short concise statement that makes a connection between two things to reveal some truth about life.

apocalypse/apocalyptic. A genre of Jewish and Christian writing that features a revelation about the heavenly realm or the future, usually mediated through an angelic interpreter.

Apocrypha. Books of the Old Testament that are sometimes included in Protestant Bibles but that, for Protestants, are not part of the canon. These include: Judith, Tobit, Wisdom, Sirach, Baruch, and 1 and 2 Maccabees. Catholics include these books in the canon and refer to them as Deuterocanonical.

apodictic law. Law that states a general principle or prohibition.

archetype. A character or event that represents all persons or events. It is usually a major element of a myth.

Baal. The Canaanite god of thunder and rain who ruled over the other gods in heaven. He was killed by Mot, the god of the underworld, and brought back to life by his sister, Anat. Each year during the summer months, he was a captive of the underworld (during the dry season). When the fall rains began, he returned to his throne in the heavens.

Babylonian Exile. The deportation to Babylon of a large number of Israelites from Judah after Judah was conquered by King Nebuchadnezzar in 586 B.C.E.

Beloved Disciple. A disciple of Jesus in the Gospel of John who is never named but who has a special place at Jesus' side and who may be the source of the traditions behind the Gospel of John.

Booths. The Jewish fall festival during the grape harvest that celebrated the time of wandering in the desert (during the Exodus), when the people lived in tents or booths.

canon. The collection of books in the Bible that is considered inspired and normative. The canon of the Hebrew Bible or of the Protestant Old Testament differs from the canon of the Old Testament for the Roman Catholic Church because the Roman Church includes books in the canon as inspired and normative that are not in the canon of the Hebrew Bible or the Protestant Old Testament.

casuistic (case) law. A law that is very specific in identifying a particular crime and its specific punishment.

covenant. The law in the Pentateuch was understood as part of a legal agreement made between God and Israel. God made a covenant with the people that bound them to keep the law. For God's part, God was to protect the people and make them prosperous. Early Christians came to believe that in Jesus Christ, God had made a new agreement (now with all peoples of the world) that was based on the death and resurrection of Jesus.

Dead Sea Scrolls. Parchment scrolls found in caves in the cliffs surrounding the Dead Sea. They were probably hidden in the caves just prior to the Roman victory in the Jewish war (70 C.E.). The scrolls contain many books of the Bible as well as sectarian writings of the Essenes.

Deuteronomic principle. Based on the theology of the Book of Deuteronomy and the Deuteronomistic History, the principle states that if you are faithful to the covenant you will be blessed and if you break the covenant you will be cursed.

Deuteronomistic History. The historical books from Joshua to 2 Kings, which are written according to the same theological and ideological principles found in the Book of Deuteronomy. This history is based on the principle that when Israel obeyed the covenant it prospered and when it disobeyed the covenant it suffered.

Diaspora. The situation of the Jews being dispersed in countries other than Judea after the Exile in Babylonia.

documentary hypothesis. The theory that the Pentateuch is composed of material from four sources: the Yahwist, the Elohist, the Deuteronomist, and the Priestly.

El/Elohim. The Hebrew word for God, used by the Israelites to refer to Yahweh and also by the Canaanites to refer to the father god of their pantheon.

Enuma Elish. An ancient writing from Babylonia that tells the story of the creation of humans through the murder of the goddess of chaos, Tiamat, by the ruler of the heavens, Marduk.

eschatology. The study of the end times.

Essenes. An apocalyptic sect of Judaism at the time of Jesus. They wrote the Dead Sea Scrolls and lived in a monastery at Qumran. They expected a future cataclysmic intervention of God to destroy all those not faithful to the covenant.

Eusebius. An early Christian writer who wrote the *Ecclesiastical History*.

Exodus. When the Hebrew slaves left Egypt by crossing the Reed Sea into the Sinai wilderness.

Gilgamesh epic. An ancient Babylonian writing that tells the story of the hero Gilgamesh. One of Gilgamesh's adventures takes him to meet Utnapishtim, who was the only human to survive the ancient flood. This section of the epic is the Babylonian version of Noah and the flood.

Gnosticism. A philosophy/religion that began in the second century C.E. It was a mix of Christianity and Greek philosophies. The goal of Gnosticism was for its adherents to be raised above the material world by spiritual enlightenment.

gospel. A genre unique to the New Testament. The word means "good news," and was used first to describe the message about what God did for humanity in Jesus Christ. Mark used the word to describe his narrative of Jesus' life and work.

Hanukkah. The Feast of Lights or Feast of Dedication, celebrated in early winter. It commemorates the rededication of the Temple by the Maccabees in 164 B.C.E.

Hasmoneans. The Jewish dynasty that came from the Maccabees. They ruled in Judea for approximately one hundred years.

Hellenism. Greek culture, language, and learning that Alexander the Great and his successors sought to spread throughout the world.

hermeneutics. An interpretation of a biblical text that seeks to make the text relevant to the present. This kind of interpretation uses a contemporary "lens" with which to transform the text. Feminism, Marxism, and Liberation Theology are all lenses that are often used.

inerrancy. The principle that the Bible does not contain errors. For Catholics, this principle is not applied to every fact or statement. Rather, Catholics hold that the Bible as a whole, when interpreted in light of tradition and in communion with the church, does not contain error.

Josephus. The Jewish general who was captured by the Romans in the Jewish war and went on to write a history of the Jewish wars.

logos. Greek for "word." For the Stoics it was the rational principle that created and ordered the universe. Hellenistic Jews equated the Logos with Lady Wisdom of the Old Testament.

Maccabees. The Jewish family who led the revolt against Antiochus IV (the Syrian overlord) in 168 B.C.E. The eldest brother, Judas, was called Maccabeus, meaning "the hammer."

Marduk. The patron god of Babylon. He was the god of sky and storm who defeated Tiamat, the goddess of chaos, to give order to the cosmos and to create humans. For this feat, he was given dominion over all the other gods.

Mesopotamia. The region surrounding the Euphrates and Tigris rivers. The word literally means "between the rivers."

messiah. The title given to the anointed king. It means "anointed" and could refer to any person (king, general, or priest) who was specially chosen by God for a task. After the Exile, the term came to mean the anointed king or priest who would come at the end of time to bring God's kingdom to completion.

messianic secret. A theme in the Gospel of Mark. It refers to Jesus' penchant for telling demons, those he healed, and his disciples not to reveal who he is.

mystery religions. Hellenistic religions associated with a deity who had overcome death or defeat. Devotees were initiated in a secret ceremony that allowed them to share in the immortality of the deity. Among them are the religions of Isis and Osiris, Demeter, Dionysus, and Mithra.

myth. A literary genre in narrative form that reveals a universal truth. Myths are foundational or archetypal for a culture or religion.

Papias. Christian author who is quoted by Eusebius as identifying the authors of the four gospels.

parable. A metaphorical form of speech about everyday life that, by exaggeration or plot twist, forces its hearers to consider the story at a deeper level.

parousia. The Second Coming of Christ. It was a word used for the glorious return of the Roman emperor after a battle or state visit. Paul uses the word to describe Christ's return from heaven.

Passover. The Jewish festival in the early spring that commemorates the angel of death passing over the houses of the Hebrews and the Hebrews passing through the waters to escape from Egypt.

Pentateuch. The Greek name given to the first five books of the Bible.

Pentecost. The Festival of Weeks, the Jewish festival at the end of the grain harvest that celebrated the giving of the Law on Mount Sinai. It was seven weeks (or fifty days) after Passover and so was called Pentecost in Greek. The early Christians made it a feast celebrating Christ's gift of the Holy Spirit to his followers.

Pharisees. A sect of Judaism at the time of Jesus who were the teachers of the law. After the destruction of the Temple by the Romans in 70 C.E., the Pharisees became the leaders of Judaism.

Philistines. A group of people who settled along the southern Mediterranean coast of Canaan about the same time that the Hebrews moved into the hill country of the same region. The Philistines were concentrated in five major city-states along the coast, but during the time of the Judges were a constant threat to the Hebrews in the hill country. Palestine, as the name for the whole region, is taken from the name Philistines.

Philo of Alexandria. A Jewish writer who lived in Alexandria at the time of Jesus. His writing sought to interpret Judaism in the categories and language of Hellenistic philosophy.

Phoenicians. A group of people who settled along the Mediterranean coast north of Palestine, in what would today be Lebanon. Their major cities were Tyre and Sidon. Their relationship with Israel was mostly amicable.

preexistence. Refers to the Son of God existing before taking flesh. In John's Gospel, the Logos (Son of God) existed with God in heaven before becoming human.

presbyter. The word means "elder" and was used to designate the leaders of the Christian communities.

proselyte. A person who was in the process of converting to Judaism.

pseudipigrapha. The word means false writing and refers to those extrabiblical books that claim to be authored by some great hero of the past (Moses, Elijah, Enoch) but were in fact written much later.

Q. The hypothetical document, containing sayings of Jesus, that scholars believe was used by Matthew and Luke as a source for writing their gospels.

Qumran. The place on the shore of the Dead Sea where the Dead Sea Scrolls were found. The site also contains archaeological remains of what appears to be a monastery for the Jewish sect known as the Essenes.

rabbi. The title, which means "my master," given to teachers in Judaism.

Sabbath. The seventh day of the week, the day on which God rested from creation and on which Jews rest from all labor.

Sadducees. A sect of Judaism composed mainly of the aristocracy and Temple priesthood. They did not accept the new ideas of an oral law on a par with the written law of Moses or resurrection from the dead.

Samaritans. The residents of the central area of Palestine around the city of Samaria. They were the descendants of Jews who did not go into exile in Babylonia. They accepted a different version of the Law of Moses and developed different traditions and theology, for which they were considered heretics by the Jews returning from exile. At the time of Jesus, there was considerable enmity between Samaritans and Jews.

Sanhedrin. The ruling assembly of the Jews at the time of Jesus. It was composed of the high priest, other priests, and important members of the Sadducee and Pharisee parties. The Roman governor allowed the Sanhedrin to govern internal Jewish affairs that did not affect Roman rule.

Satan. The prosecuting attorney in the heavenly court of God. The word means "adversary," although this figure was not originally the adversary of God. In later Judaism, Satan was combined with Beelzebub, the devil, and other demonic figures. Through the influence of Zoroastrianism, Judaism developed an evil figure who was God's opposite and adversary.

Semitic. The name for a specific language type. Hebrew, Aramaic, Arabic, and Syriac are all Semitic languages. A Semite is a person who speaks one of these languages.

Septuagint. The Greek translation of the Hebrew Bible made for Ptolemy in about 250 B.C.E. It gets its name from the legend that seventy-two Jewish elders (six from each tribe) each translated it simultaneously and each made the exact same translation.

Sinai. The peninsula east of Egypt in which the Hebrews wandered after leaving Egypt during the Exodus. On a mountain in this peninsula, Moses received the law from God.

Son of man. A title originally denoting a human. In Ezekiel and other prophetic books, angelic and divine beings were described as "like a son of man," meaning that they were in human form. Eventually, a specific heavenly figure called "One like a Son of Man" came to be expected at the end time.

stoicism. A Greek philosophical school that held that life was not governed by the gods but by a rational principle called the Logos. Everything that happened had a purpose, even if a mere mortal could not understand that purpose. The correct attitude toward life was patient acceptance of the way things were because that is the way they were supposed to be.

synagogue. Originally the word meant the gathering together of Jews for prayer and study. By the time of Jesus, the word referred to the building used for this purpose. There was only one Temple for worship and sacrifice, but most cities in which Jews resided contained a building set aside for prayer and study.

Synoptic Gospels. The first three gospels in the New Testament (Matthew, Mark, and Luke), called this because they are so similar.

Synoptic problem. The question of how the three Synoptic Gospels came to be so similar. The problem has to do with which gospels were copied and which gospel served as the source. The main theory is that Mark was written first and was used as the main source for Matthew and Luke. Matthew and Luke also share another source known as Q.

TaNaK. The acronym for Torah (Law), Nebiim (Prophets), and Ketubim (Writings), the three divisions of the Jewish scriptures.

textual criticism. The study of which reading in the surviving texts of the Bible represents the original text.

Torah. The Hebrew word for teaching. It is the word used to describe God's commands to the Hebrews given at Mount Sinai. It is commonly translated as "law."

Yahweh. The sacred and individual name of the God of Israel revealed to Moses in Exodus. The name was probably derived from the verb "to be" and is often translated as "I AM." The Old

Testament uses the name frequently, but later Judaism, out of reverence for God's personal name, did not say the name. Instead of the sacred name they would say "Lord."

zealots. A group of Jewish revolutionaries who surfaced during the Jewish war against Rome. They modeled themselves after Phineas, who was commended by God for his zeal in killing a Hebrew man and his Moabite wife in Numbers 25.

Zion. The symbolic name for Jerusalem. Most often referred to as Mount Zion. It is the center of the universe, the highest place on earth, and God's footstool.